VICTORIA'S ENEMIES

Other published titles by Donald Featherstone

WARGAMES
NAVAL WARGAMES
AIR WARGAMES
ADVANCED WARGAMES
WARGAMES CAMPAIGNS
BATTLES WITH MODEL SOLDIERS
WARGAMES THROUGH THE AGES
   Vol. 1 3000 BC–AD 1500
   Vol. 2 1420–1783
   Vol. 3 1792–1859
   Vol. 4 1861–1945
POITIERS 1356 – BATTLES FOR WARGAMERS
BATTLE NOTES FOR WARGAMERS
SOLO WARGAMING
TANK BATTLES IN MINIATURE: THE WESTERN DESERT CAMPAIGN
TANK BATTLES IN MINIATURE: THE MEDITERRANEAN THEATRE
SKIRMISH WARGAMES
WARGAMING THE ANCIENT AND MEDIEVAL PERIODS
WARGAMING THE PIKE AND SHOT PERIOD
THE WARGAMES HANDBOOK OF THE AMERICAN REVOLUTION
WARGAMING AIRBORNE OPERATIONS
BATTLES WITH MODEL TANKS (with Keith Robinson)
TACKLE MODEL SOLDIERS THIS WAY
HANDBOOK FOR MODEL SOLDIER COLLECTORS
MILITARY MODELLING
BETTER MILITARY MODELLING
ALL FOR A SHILLING A DAY
MACDONALD OF THE 42nd
CAPTAIN CAREY'S BLUNDER
AT THEM WITH THE BAYONET!
COLONIAL SMALL WARS 1837–1901
CONFLICT IN HAMPSHIRE
THE BOWMEN OF ENGLAND
WEAPONS AND EQUIPMENT OF THE VICTORIAN SOLDIER
FEATHERSTONE'S COMPLETE WARGAMING

VICTORIA'S ENEMIES

An A–Z of British Colonial Warfare

Donald Featherstone

BLANDFORD

First published in the UK 1989 by **Blandford Press,**
An imprint of Cassell,
Artillery House, Artillery Row, London SW1P 1RT

Distributed in the United States by
Sterling Publishing Co., Inc.,
2 Park Avenue, New York, NY 10016

Distributed in Australia by
Capricorn Link (Australia) Pty Ltd,
PO Box 665, Lane Cove, NSW 2066

British Library Cataloguing in Publication Data
Featherstone, Donald, *1918–*
   Victoria's enemies: an A – Z of British colonial
   warfare.
   1. Military operations, 1837–1901 by British
   military forces
   I. Title
   355.4'0941

ISBN 0 7137 2081 6

The author wishes to thank *The Illustrated London
News* for the use of their engravings.

Typeset by Graphicraft Typesetters Ltd, Hong Kong

Printed and bound in Great Britain by
Courier International Ltd, Tiptree, Essex

Contents

CONTENTS

Foreword

In a lifetime of reading military history – official, factual and fictional – a marked feature has invariably been detailed descriptions of 'our side' (playing away) – the British soldier, his weapons and uniform, his leaders and tactics – and a corresponding absence of all those facts about the enemy he was fighting. There are few enough books providing, under *one* cover, accounts of ALL the 400-odd battles and 60 or so campaigns that brought pride and sadness to Queen Victoria during the 64 years of her reign, but none at all considering those conflicts from the enemy's point of view! This book seeks to remedy that by emphasising the two sides of colonialism and empire-building, while showing that the actual combatants were but nameless pawns in a far wider game.

Writing it has been an enlightening experience, warmed by admiration for the stark courage displayed without exception by all Victoria's Enemies, and by our ancestors – British soldiers – thrust into conflict with this conglomerate of peoples in four of the world's five continents. It has also been chastening, revealing what mankind has painfully discovered over the centuries – that courage alone will not prevail in the face of military technology. History can teach many lessons, perhaps this is one that should be more heeded today.

The criteria for the illustrations are that each should depict one of the 'Enemy'; every drawing, woodcut, and photograph is contemporary and, in their day, these were the sole means whereby our great-grandfathers learned of these wars. Poring over them, agonising over the sufferings of the hitherto despised British soldier during the Russian winter in front of Sebastopol, he was saddened by the massacre at Isandlhwana, and no doubt seethed at defeats by despised Boer farmers in South Africa. None are more stirring or suitable than the graphic drawings done on the battlefield by intrepid Victorian artists and reproduced as woodcuts in the pages of the Illustrated London News, that unique journal still flourishing today, which has given permission for their reproduction. Acknowledgements, where known, are given for other illustrations although many have been acquired from unknown sources over a period of at least a quarter of a century – in anticipation of writing just such a book as this!

My much amended manuscript has been brilliantly deciphered and typed by Amanda Kilby, whose imperturbability, I am happy to note, has on occasions been shaken by those brave men whose courage and fine qualities I am proud to chronicle.

Donald Featherstone

A British cavalry patrol in uniforms of the Boer War, 1881.

Introduction – British Military Campaigns, 1837–1901

Queen Victoria came to the throne of Great Britain on 20 June 1837, in one of those rare periods during her reign when her soldiers were not fighting on foreign soil; however, within three months Sir John Colbourne's force was busily quelling rebellious Canadians. The Queen gave her name to an era of 64 years when the wide spread of British rule brought Western-style civilisation to an increasingly growing Empire. Chauvinism and nostalgia indicate it to be a great and glorious period of British history, when hardly a year passed without the Army being engaged in some far-flung corner of all five continents, fighting more than 400 pitched battles in over 60 campaigns. Occasionally the emotions of the British public were aroused by news of a hard-pressed garrison being relieved; otherwise there was precious little stimulation in the bare details of small-scale and hard-fought affrays against fierce native foes and harsh tropical climates. Casualties were often relatively light because the soldier was better armed and disciplined, but, up against a primitive and barbarous enemy unafraid of death, losses could be unpleasantly heavy.

In this 64-year period, the British soldier encountered many diverse foes of innumerable nations, countries, tribes and sects. Among them were: Abyssinians; Afghans; Afridis; Arabs; Ashantis; Australians; Baluchis; Bengalis; Boers; Bunerwals; Burmese; Canadians; Chamalwals; Chamkannis; Chinese; Chitralis; Dervishes; Egyptians; Fingoes; Gaikas; Galekas; Ghazis; Hadendowahs; Hassanzais; Hottentots; Hunzas; Indians; Isazais; Japanese; Jawaki Afridis; Kaffirs; Khudu-kels; Kodakhel Baezais; Kostwals; Lushais; Madda Khels; Mahrattas; Mahsud Wazirs; Malays; Mangals; Maoris; Mashonas; Masais; Matabeles; Mohmands; Orakzais; Pathans; Peraks; Persians; Punjabis; Russians; Sepoys; Shinwarris; Shiranis; Sikhs; Somalis; Sudanese; Tibetans; Utman Khels; Wazaris; Zaimukhts; Zakha Khel Afridis and Zulus. The wars and campaigns in which this multiplicity of foes were engaged began, and ended, anomalously in an era noted for successful wars against native opponents, against Europeans – the rebellious Canadians in 1837, and at the time of the old Queen's death on 22 January 1901, the Boer leader De Wet was concentrating his forces for a fresh invasion of Cape Colony.

There were few barren years and Victorian wars were always in season, taking place in the most diverse corners of the world.

In all these years the only European opponents faced by the British Regular Army were the Russians in the Crimea in 1854/5; rebellious Australian gold-miners and Canadian half-breeds; South African Boers in 1881 (when they inflicted the sole defeat in a war of the entire period) and in 1898–1902, when the costly lessons learned in defeating them revolutionised the training of the British Army in the decade that followed. Commanded by excellent natural leaders, gifted with unusual mobility and exceptional cunning, the daring and well-armed Boers were a highly formidable enemy on their own familiar terrain. The years 1879 and 1880 saw two of the greatest military disasters of the Victorian era, although this was a three-year period when in a single quarter of the African continent British troops came successively into conflict with the astonishingly different methods of fighting of Kaffirs, Zulus and Boers, while at the same time the Regular Army were heavily committed on the North-West Frontier of India and in Afghanistan.

In January 1879 at Isandlhwana, Zulu impis overran and massacred more than 1,300 British and Native soldiers, the 24th Regiment being wiped out – save for a single company who defended Rorke's Drift the next day against 4,000 Zulu warriors. Eleven Victoria Crosses were won in this action, a perfect illustration of how superior numbers of courageous native opponents could be defeated by the power of modern firearms in the hands of trained and well-led troops. This, of course, is really the story of the colonial conquests of any Western nation. Cetewayo's Zulus were a well-organised and disciplined army capable of carrying out battlefield

1837	Canada			
1838	Aden	Afghanistan		
1840	China	The Levant		
1841	Afghanistan	China		
1842	Afghanistan			
1843	Gwalior	Sind		
1845	The Punjab	South Africa		
1846	The Punjab	South Africa		
1847	South Africa			
1848	North-West Frontier of India	Punjab	South Africa	
1849	North-West Frontier of India	Punjab	South Africa	
1850	North-West Frontier of India			
1851	South Africa			
1852	Burma	NW Frontier	Crimea (Russia)	
1855	Crimea			
1856	Crimea	Persia		
1857	Crimea	Oudh & Bengal	Persia	
1858	Oudh & Bengal	Central India		
1859	Oudh & Benghal	China		
1860	China			
1861	New Zealand	Sikkim (India)		
1862	New Zealand			
1863	New Zealand	Ambela (NW Frontier)		
1864	New Zealand	Bhutan	Japan	NW Frontier
1865	Bhutan			
1866/7	NW Frontier			
1868	Abyssinia			
1870	Canada			
1871	Lushai (India)			
1874	Ashanti			
1875	Perak (Malay)			
1876	Perak (Malay)			
1877	NW Frontier	South Africa		
1878	Afghanistan	NW Frontier	Malta	
1879	Afghanistan	NW Frontier	Natal	South Africa Zululand
1880	NW Frontier			
1881	NW Frontier	Transvaal (South Africa)		
1882	Egypt			
1884	Burma	NW Frontier	Sudan	
1885	Burma	Sudan		
1888	NW Frontier	Sikkim (India)	Tibet	
1890	NW Frontier	Somaliland		
1891	NW Frontier	Hunza (India)	Manipur (India)	Burma
1892	NW Frontier	Chilas (India)		
1894	Waziristan (India)			
1895	Chitral (India)			
1896	Mashonaland	Egypt	Mombasa	Zanzibar
1897	Benin	Tirah	Egypt (Sudan)	NW Frontier (Malakand & Tochi)
1898	Buner (India)	Juberland	Niger	South Africa (Transvaal)
1899	South Africa (Transvaal)			
1900	South Africa (Transvaal)	Ashanti	China	
1901	South Africa (Transvaal)	China		

manoeuvres with order and precision, efficiently employing primitive but effective weapons. The massacre at Isandlhwana was directly attributable to a total misconception of Zulu tactics; the reverses of the two Boer Wars were, in part, because of a lack of cavalry, the one essential arm for this type of warfare.

A year later on 27 July 1880 at Maiwand, an Afghan army of about 12,000 infantry and cavalry – some Regulars and hillmen – with 30 guns heavily defeated General Burrows' Force of 2,300 (66th Regt, Bombay Grenadiers and Jacob's Rifles) and six guns, inflicting 1,302 casualties and capturing all their guns. Within six months there came another shattering disaster in 1881 when a collection of sharpshooting Boer farmers triumphed over British forces at Laing's Nek – on the last occasion when the Colours were carried into action – at Ingogo River, and Majuba Hill, where General Sir George Colley, the British Commander, was killed. This was the only war lost during the entire 64 years of the Queen's reign and prior to it there had been nearly 40 years of unbroken success since 1842, when a British force was virtually wiped out in the retreat from Kabul – although there had been many occasions and numerous close-run battles when victory had been desperately snatched from the jaws of defeat.

Hindsight indicates that right was not always on the side of the British; while the politicians plotted, the soldier obeyed orders and played the role of unsung hero in an unpublished quarrel. Drilled into blind obedience by harsh discipline and lacking knowledge of cause or reason, he displayed courage, endurance and humour under appalling conditions, fighting and dying well amid harsh terrain in fierce and bloody campaigns where the difference between outright success and stalemate was annihilation, when capture invariably meant a slow and agonising death.

It is both wrong and unjust to credit success in these Victorian 'small wars' to the Martini-Henry rifle, the Gatling and the screw-gun. Victory was gained through the unremitting observance of regimental honour, tradition, spirit, and high standards of duty combining to produce first-class morale and comradeship. From commanding officer to lowly drummer-boy, every man in the regiment sought opportunities to win distinction and reputation, encouraged by the Victoria Cross being awarded for acts of outstanding

gallantry and sheer cold-blooded courage, often with little military value beyond the raising of morale. Among officers a reputation for personal courage led to promotion, so they regarded campaigns against native foes as a dangerous sport providing a most satisfactory solution to the eternal quest for adventure and danger. They pursued transfers to small colonial forces commanded by Regular Army officers, aware that the surviving officers of victorious expeditions won both public acclaim and substantial awards. The men in the ranks got nothing – even looting was either forbidden or on a strictly regulated basis.

Doubtless innumerable soldiers died knowing little or nothing of their enemy, except their own ribald version of his native name. And that foe undoubtedly knew even less about this white-faced invader armed with fearsome death-dealing weapons – perhaps the apparent shortcomings of both British soldier and native opponent can be cancelled out by the noble virtue of courage. For it was rarely that natives revealed cowardice or ignoble qualities, almost invariably displaying exceptional courage and dignity despite incredibly high casualties, far greater than it was within their power to inflict. This aroused respect among the Regular soldiers who admired many of their foes, such as the Dervishes of the Sudan who attempted to overwhelm British formations by fearless impetuous rushes that forced the revival of old Orders of Battle to cope with their recklessness, courage and tactical unsophistication. Ten battalions of British infantry were sent to New Zealand to break the power of the brave and chivalrous Maoris, whose code of war made them capable of slaughtering wounded prisoners and sometimes even eating them, but also saw them plunge through the fire of both sides to save the life of a fallen foe. Recognising his noble side while overlooking his inherent savagery, he was held in high respect by the British soldier.

Victorian small wars were expeditions and campaigns undertaken by the Queen's disciplined soldiers and their native allies against savages and semi-civilised races, frequently developing into campaigns of conquest or annexation that added vast countries and territories to the British Crown, as in the Zulu War of 1879. Sometimes they were mounted to suppress rebellion or lawlessness in the annexed territories or, as in the Abyssinian Campaign of 1868, to avenge a wrong or wipe out an insult by sending a puni-

tive force to chastise or overthrow a dangerous or troublesome enemy. Or they were wars of expediency fought for political reasons, as in the case of the two Afghan Wars and the Egyptian War of 1882.

These ends were achieved by soldiers scorned by the British public, who revelled in the colourful accounts of the war correspondents that completely obscured the human purchasing price when hastily formed expeditions, invariably unsuitably equipped, were sent to take on superior numbers of warrior-races fighting in their own country. In red coats or dusty khaki, men from every British shire and country marched in slow-moving columns, where elephants jostled camels and bullocks plodded with donkeys and yaks, to a background clatter and jingle of the mule-carried mountain guns. Sometimes parties of boisterous straw-hatted sailors and Marines were landed from men-of-war, and under dashing leaders such as Lord Charles Beresford, dragged Gatling and Gardner guns through the sand of the Sudan and, treating camels like boats, caulked their huge sores with pitch. Typical yet unique, each campaign was made notable by the men who fought them – the British Regular soldier, grumblingly obeying orders and doing his duty against militant tribesmen on the rugged North-West Frontier of India; subduing stubborn Boers, brave Maoris, wily Afghans or fierce and fanatical Dervishes; or battling against the organised military formations of Sikhs, Zulus, Russians and rebellious Indian Sepoys. None of this great variety of opponents fought in the same fashion and rarely was there any prior knowledge of their strength, weapons, fighting ability or methods of warfare.

Primitive conditions and the enemy's peculiar style of fighting caused the conduct of Victorian colonial wars to diverge widely from the conditions and principles of regular warfare, where each side was well aware of what to expect from the enemy, and both sides were governed by common rules. In these small wars all manner of opponents were met and none fought in the same fashion, their methods of fighting varying to such an extent that each presented new features which, if not foreseen, brought difficulty and

even grievous misfortune to the Regular troops. Terrain played a big part, when an enemy not particularly noted for courage and poorly armed – such as the Kaffirs in South Africa between 1838 and 1852 – proved most difficult to subdue through utilising the natural advantages of their familiar bush and jungle. Operations on the North-West Frontier of India produced all the problems of fighting guerrilla warfare, when well-armed and fanatical tribesmen took full advantage of a harsh terrain well suited to their style of fighting. Natives did not always utilise familiar terrain or fight in their accustomed style; in 1874 the Ashantis never flinched from risking a general engagement if they felt it gave them a better chance of victory.

Often sickness caused greater losses than did battle, as most campaigns degenerated into struggles against Nature rather than hostile armies, when unaccustomed climatic conditions affected the health of the troops while lack of communications prevented evacuation of the sick and wounded besides limiting supplies. In these small wars organised Regular forces were at an undoubted strategical disadvantage despite their backing of the resources of science, wealth, manpower and navies, their strength representing virtual weakness because the arms and equipment that ensured tactical superiority and eventual success required long non-combatant 'tails' tied to bases and lines of communication.

In minor campaigns against native foes material success was of far greater importance than the moral effect of beating them – this was recognised by Lord Wolseley, who said:

'In planning a war against an uncivilised nation who has perhaps no capital city, your first object should be the capture of whatever he prizes most, and the destruction or deprivation of which will probably bring the war most rapidly to a conclusion. When the enemy could not be touched in his patriotism or his honour, he was touched through his pocket by carrying off his flocks and destroying his crops.'

So these operations sometimes necessarily included depredations and havoc unsanctioned by the laws of regular warfare. It was known to be useless merely to drive a native enemy off the field without causing him very heavy casualties – having accepted combat the natives had to be made to feel the real effects of battle against disciplined armies, hence the vast disparity in losses at most actions. For example, at Omdur-

British infantry dressed as they fought the Crimean War.

A British infantryman in Marching-Order,
Boer War, 1898–1902.

man in 1898, the Khalifa's army was wiped out, losing 11,000 killed, 16,000 wounded and 4,000 prisoners out of a total strength of about 40,000 men; Kitchener's losses were 48 killed and 382 wounded. The one great principle observed by Regular troops during these small wars was to hit the uncivilised enemy very hard by bold initiative and resolute action on the battlefield.

In mitigation, perhaps the Regular forces had brutality, prejudice and ruthlessness thrust upon them by the imperative need to survive through sheer domination of the enemy under conditions of being grossly outnumbered, often physically inferior, affected detrimentally by alien climate and terrain, inadequately equipped for the prevailing conditions, and occasionally led by bad commanders. Sometimes it was engendered by British indignation and revulsion at the opponent's natural barbarity and savagery, such as the Zulus' ritual disembowelling of dead foes, countered by those occasions when the British were cruel and remorseless. Nevertheless, like those before and after him, the Victorian soldier took no pleasure in killing and often suffered through his trusting readiness to accept treacherous signs of surrender; he did not hate his enemies and was always ready to acknowledge the courage of a native foe, rarely bearing malice even when that enemy through intent or ignorance might have transgressed all his own established concepts of what was fair in war.

It cannot be denied that British soldiers slaughtered innocent natives in India during the Mutiny of 1857, largely because of the common belief that all men with brown faces were accessories to the massacres that aroused such fury within his simple heart. Every soldier knew of helpless comrades lying in the lagging litters at the rear of the column, prostrate with wounds or sunstroke, whose throats were cut by mutinous Sepoys surging upon the undefended procession. Meeting those soldiers in battle they gave no quarter nor expected any, but after the first furies of fighting had died away, there was no wanton slaughtering.

Not all the enemy encountered in Victorian colonial wars were savage or irregular warriors; some wars were against an enemy trained and organised as regular troops by instructors with knowledge and experience of European methods, so that subsequent operations resembled the conventional warfare of the time. It occurred in the Punjab in 1845–6 and in 1849 when, after some of the fiercest-fought battles in British colonial history, the British regiments of the East India Company – inauspiciously supported by native troops – defeated the martial Sikhs. The 1857 Mutiny in India found British Regulars and loyal native units faced by field armies in superior numbers, composed of experienced and competent Sepoys trained along British lines. In the Crimea the British and their French allies were opposed by a trained and well-armed European army which, had it not been commanded in an even more inefficient manner than the Allies, could have resulted, in that harsh climate, in a major disaster. In 1882 Arabi Pasha led a well-armed, trained and disciplined Egyptian army to defeat by Wolseley at Tel-el-Kebir and Kassassin; the disastrous defeat at Maiwand in 1880 was at the hands of a trained Regular Afghanistan army, armed with high-quality artillery and aided by Russian gunnery instructors.

If and when such organised resistance was overcome it was often necessary to suppress guerrilla warfare, with the inevitable aftermath of stern and savage reprisals in a manner familiar today – the subtle difference between a rebel and a nationalist defending his homeland often defies definition.

Although organised on the Zulu system, the Matabele did not have such a high degree of efficiency and not being such great warriors were nowhere near as formidable as Cetewayo's Impis. The Sudanese and the Afghan Ghazi lacked Zulu discipline but fought with bravery and a recklessness requiring a return to old-style tactics of tight battle formations. All these races fought in a totally different fashion to such other native opponents as the Chinese, the Ashantis and the hillmen of the North-West Frontier, but all usually managed to put up a very stern resistance.

What has been written so far could well be criticised as a saga of pacification and punishment in four continents, and held up as rabid anti-colonial propaganda. But when considering colonialism it should be remembered that in the nineteenth century the British successfully organised and maintained military and policy formations from the people of regions recently conquered in Africa, India, Asia, Borneo, and the West Indies – and in every case it worked with harmony and loyalty. Entering their country as an invader, the British soldier invariably became a respected friend through his innate gift of

making himself intelligible to all peoples, nations and languages. Indeed, it was an age when as a matter of routine, small forces under energetic commanders pacified frontiers, quelled rebellions and administered vast tracts of territory. Queen Victoria, deeply conscious of her position as Queen–Empress, held high-minded concepts of Empire and a faith in Britain's Imperial destiny that was shared by that remarkable assortment of strong-minded generals who, throughout her reign, were blessed with the ability and fortune invariably to be in the right place at the right time. Echoing from campaign to campaign, war to war, and country to country, their names became household words – there was Hugh Gough in China and the Punjab; Harry Smith in India and South Africa; Havelock in Persia and India; Colin Campbell in the Punjab, the Crimea and the Indian Mutiny; the Napiers; Neville Chamberlain; Redvers Buller in Natal, the Sudan and South Africa; Sale; Nott; Hodson; Lumsden; the Lawrences; Nicholson; Outram; Hugh Rose; Stuart; Earle; Lowe; Bindon Blood; Baden-Powell and a host of others perhaps not so fortunate as to find fortuitous wars in which to shine.

From the safety and comfort of their familiar surroundings, the British public found the assorted collection of kings, princes, chiefs, religious and military commanders who led each successive foreign foe to be more humorous than frightening. Their ludicrous names were lampooned and reviled in newspaper and song-sheet – the Sikh leaders Lal and Tej Sing; Kaffir chieftains Kreli and Sandilli; Canadian half-breed Louis Riel; Kings Theodore of Abyssinia and Thibaw of Burma; Afghanistan's Dost Muhammed, Yacoub Khan and Ayoub Khan (he who wiped out Burrows' force at Maiwand in 1880); Cetewayo the Zulu king – another enemy who humbled a British army – was received in Britain by the Queen after his capture. But only revulsion and vengeful anger were aroused by Indian Mutiny leaders Nana Sahib and the Ranee of Jhansi, while Gordon's death at Khartoum made public enemies of the Mahdi, Osman Digna and the Khalifa. In the mid-1850s the Russian Tsar and Prince Menschikoff came in for their share of characteristic British scurrility, although the peak was reached as the century turned, in public contempt and scorn for Boer leaders Cronje, De Wet, Kruger, Smuts and others.

It is not possible to write of Victorian colonial

wars without encountering General Frederick Roberts and the ubiquitous Sir Garnet Wolseley, both the very epitome of the brave Victorian commander triumphant on a host of foreign fields against an astonishing variety of opponents. Perhaps Wolseley summed up the Victorian ethos best in a letter to his wife in 1880 – 'I am a Jingo in the best acceptation of that sobriquet...to see England great is my highest aspiration, and to lead in contributing to that greatness is my only real ambition.'

Like the rest of the colourful characters of the Victorian era, he had no hesitation about Imperialism!

1   The Abyssinians

When, in the middle of the nineteenth century, the British Foreign Office ignored a letter to Queen Victoria sent by the despotic Emperor Theodore of Abyssinia, he indicated his displeasure by imprisoning the British Consul and numerous other Europeans. Deciding that honour and prestige outranked expenditure, in 1867 Britain mounted a massive rescue campaign commanded by competent General Sir Robert Napier. By any standards such an undertaking was a major effort, for that day and age it was an extraordinary feat involving some 13,000 British and Indian soldiers, plus a host of servants and workmen handling more than 36,000 draft animals. Mules by the thousand were bought in Asia Minor, Italy and Spain; camels purchased in Arabia and Egypt; transport trains, including artillery elephants organised in India, and a complete railway – locomotives, rolling-stock and lines – sent from Bombay. About 300 ships of varying sizes were required to transport the force.

An imposing figure, 6 feet 8 inches tall, endowed with a naturally dignified bearing, the ruler of Abyssinia was seemingly every inch a sovereign and, although only the son of a minor nobleman, he had single-mindedly carved his way into a position of authority over the assortment of petty feudal states and princedoms that made up the country in the mid-nineteenth century. By 1855 he was powerful enough to have himself crowned Emperor Theodore III, King of Ethiopia, and The Chosen of God. Seeing himself as a Champion of Christianity, his ambition was to conquer his Muslim neighbours and lead an expedition to free Jerusalem from the Turks, but first he had to drag his kingdom out of the Middle Ages and transform it into a modern power. To provide the essential nineteenth-century weapons, Theodore's agents purchased firearms throughout Europe and he encouraged European engineers, artisans and skilled mechanics to come and set up cannon foundries to cast guns, and to establish powder-mills. Such attempts at the necessary modernisation of his backward country caused bitter civil conflict; eventually the numerous revolts, allied to the loss of a moderating influence when his wife died, transformed him into a half-mad and highly unstable tyrant, from whose hands it was deemed essential to extract the luckless European prisoners.

The full-scale military expedition mounted by Britain took nine months from the day the troops first set foot in Africa, to reach the mountain-fortress of Magdala, release the prisoners, retrace footsteps to the coast, and evacuate. Sailing from India, Napier's expedition landed at Annesley Bay and built a camp; early in December 1867 the Advance Guard moved up onto the plateau 7,000 feet above the sea, and the remainder of the force followed during January. It was not done without difficulty as they were desperately short of baggage animals because many of the mules died almost as soon as being but ashore,

Emperor Theodore of Abyssinia.

17

largely from neglect and lack of water. No opposition was encountered during the long approach march; Theodore made no attempt to harass Napier, and the only problems arose from difficulties of obtaining forage and provisions in a thinly populated country, and the steady deterioration of the baggage animals.

At least a month before Napier moved inland he had heard that Theodore was slowly wending his way to Magdala with some 8,000 warriors, 6 large guns and 14 wagons of ammunition, all being incredibly manhandled over a road being laboriously built across an almost trackless waste traversed by mountains and cut by vast and deep ravines. Dwindling rapidly through desertions, Theodore's force was all that remained of his large army; about half were armed with reasonably modern small arms, mostly double-barrelled percussion guns of European manufacture; the rest had ancient flintlocks and matchlocks, all possessed a sword, spear and shield. His mechanics and artisans were with him, together with thousands of refugees and hundreds of hapless captives. However, if he could inflict even a slight reverse on the invaders, Theodore knew his reputation for invincibility would

Theodore's troops drag a giant mortar known as 'Theodorus' after the Emperor, up to Magdala.

be restored and men would flock to his standard. Once at Magdala, it was an army that could not be underestimated as it consisted of the hard core, the men who had hauled the heavy guns over the roads they had built through the wilderness; the weaker elements had died or deserted. Firmly ensconced in the near-impregnable fortress, well supplied with guns and ammunition, they could cause innumerable casualties in a storm or siege.

Guns were a cherished symbol of power to Abyssinians and Theodore loved artillery for its own sake, but his train, formed of guns of enormous weight and size, was his greatest encumbrance – however, he would never abandon these sole remaining symbols of his strength. During this herculean and painfully slow march – averaging less than two miles a day – much of his former military greatness returned as he urged and coerced his soldiers into moving great boulders, building causeways across rivers and ravines, and constructing roads up and down sheer precipices. The vast Jedda Ravine with precipitous sides and a vertical depth of over 3,000 feet took two months to cross; steep gradients were blasted, dug and graded; guns lowered to the bottom and wagons inched down with hundreds of men on ropes to prevent them plunging to the bottom. Then it all had to be done again to get them out on the other side. It was an epic saga of supreme human effort by a few thousand naked and half-starving men, driven on by their mad king. Finally, the guns – including the great 5-ton brass mortar called Theodorus – were on the plateau of Islamgi just below the main fortress of Magdala. Later, he had seven of them, including Theodorus, manhandled to Fala and sited to cover the approaches from the North.

The Emperor stationed himself on the highest point of his fortress, watching through a telescope the inexorable advance of the British expedition. He was a competent commander with a fairly wide – if theoretical – idea of the capabilities of the modern European soldier; he had heard so much about these disciplined armies that he was eager to see one in action, despite it being against himself. He realised they would be very different from Abyssinian armies, usually formed for a particular campaign of forces from the various provinces of the country and often in a state of mutual hostility; there were no formal units or regiments, the men of a district were commanded by their chief and the combined forces of a province were led by a Ras (Abyssinian prince). Lacking an Order of March, in battle they adopted a loose form of order relative to their commander's assigned position; at close quarters it was usual to charge in undisciplined masses at the nearest enemy. Always aggressive and very courageous, some men were armed with European percussion muskets or rifles; everyone carried a double-edged knife with a 6- to 8-inch blade, and a short, single-edged cutting sword, carried in a leather scabbard thrust through a linen belt, usually on the right side. Chief's swords were usually long, curved and double-edged. Spears had an iron blade shaped like a laurel leaf and were more than 6 feet in length; shields, made from buffalo or rhinocerous hide, were circular and convex, 20 to 24 inches in diameter; those of chiefs had a silver boss. As with most tribesmen, Abyssinian soldiers did not wear uniform but were clad in a shamma (an upper covering of white cotton) and a pair of kneelength white cotton pantaloons,

held up by a long linen cummerbund. Chiefs' shammas were often edged with scarlet; and during the 1868 war it was noted that some of the mounted chiefs and a number of footmen were dressed entirely in scarlet robes. Theodore himself is said to have worn loose white silk jodhpurs and a gold-embroidered red robe.

The Abyssinian Army at the time of King Menelik's victory over the Italians at Adowa on 1 March 1896 were uniformed as follows:

Regular Abyssinian Soldier. French de Gras rifle, webbed or leather cartridge belt, sword and oryx hide shield also usually carried. Trousers and shirt made from white or off-white cotton cloth. A *shamma*, or loose-woven robe, was often worn over these, and the loins were bound with the *makannat*, or waist sash. Many men wore hats, black or grey soft-felt 'wideawakes' were most popular.

Abyssinian Officer. Head-dress decorated with lion's mane. Lion- or leopard-skin shirt, usually covered with long black silk cape, the *kabba*. Oryx-hide shield, decorated with brass, tin or silver. Richly ornamented curved sword, a revolver and one or two knives were usually worn in the *makannat*. Leather sandals, or *chamma*, were worn only when operating in low or thorny country.

Irregular Abyssinian Spearman. Leopard skin worn over white cotton trousers. Lightweight throwing spear and oval oryx hide shield.

Despite the difference of nearly 30 years, it is quite likely that there is little difference in these uniforms and those worn by Theodore's troops in 1868.

When the British force reached the Dalanta Plateau on 7th April, some eight miles from Magdala, they were only about 4,000 strong, having left detachments *en route* to guard the line of communications. The area to be advanced over, possibly against enemy opposition, was an impressive sight – descending some 4,000 feet down to the Bachelo River, the ground rose beyond in a succession of billows with the steep crags of Magdala rearing above a 'saddle' formed between two steep peaks, flat-topped Fala to the right, and Selassi a few hundred feet higher to the left. Native encampments and gun positions could be made out through the glasses, and the only ascent was by a zigzag road cut in the face

Abyssinian warriors, 1868.

of Fala. From the Bachelo River a steep ravine ran upwards through the hills almost directly towards Magdala, carrying the road Theodore's soldiers had laboriously built for the transport of his guns. At daybreak on 10th April, the Advance Guard began to descend the road into the ravine, before striking off to the right over the hills leading onto the Arogi Plateau opposite the enemy guns sited on Fala – then a misunderstanding sent the baggage train and guns alone and unprotected up the ravine in full view of the enemy above.

Up on the plateau Theodore saw the long line of baggage mules emerge from the mouth of the defile and guessed they were the baggage train, whose capture would stiffen the morale of his troops by giving them a chance to loot. He decided to paralyse the British with his irresistible artillery, sending his soldiers into the attack under cover of his cannonade. The guns had been loaded and laid by his European artisans who may well have been reluctant to do anything to harm the approaching British, so they put in maximum powder-charges and let others fire them. One heavy 60-pounder burst on first firing, doing considerable damage to those around it;

but the Emperor's initial fury was overcome by the excitement of hearing his guns booming away, knowing that nothing could withstand them. It did not seem to the British to be a particularly effective bombardment, but the Abyssinians had considerable technical problems in laying guns of such a variety of weights and calibres, at a target so far below and at extreme range. The cannonade was enlivened by the peculiar whirring noise of chain-shot (two halves of a cannon-ball linked together with a short length of chain, intended to sever ship's rigging in naval battles) perhaps part of a bargain-lot bought from an enterprising European arms salesman!

Theodore gave orders to his favourite general, old Fitaurari Gabri, resplendent in embroidered scarlet cloak, who rode over to the troops squatting a few yards back from the edge of the Fala Saddle; rising on his order, they roared and whooped as he waved them forward towards the oncoming British. Sun glinting on swords and spears, the great horde poured over the edge, erupting into view and swarming from rock to rock down the steep hillside; the mules and sure-footed Galla ponies of the chieftains negotiating the almost precipitous drop with the same ease as the footmen. Reaching the bottom, the host halted momentarily to extend its front then came on at a steady trot, seven men deep on a front of three-quarters of a mile. At the time it was said that this Abyssinian advance was as pretty a sight as has ever been presented in modern warfare, with galloping chiefs in scarlet, footmen in white or scarlet, and innumerable flags waving above them. It was a glorious but wild attack that was to destroy half the army and shatter the morale of those left, without the slightest advantage to Theodore's cause.

Now began a wild race for the baggage train, British infantry scrambling breathlessly up a steep slope to the crest of a low hill overlooking the plateau, while Punjab Pioneers and the Naval Rocket Brigade rushed left to a small crest. Less than a minute after reaching it, the well-drilled rocket team had their projectors unloaded from the mules and the first rocket whooshed out over the plain, followed by a stream of erratic missiles whistling and hissing one after the other. The onrushing Abyssinians momentarily halted, then their chiefs urged them on and they came plunging rapidly forward until less than 100 yards from the low hill towards which the infantry were laboriously toiling. In the nick of time the line of skirmishers breasted the crest and set foot on the plateau, to open a rapid fire with their new Snider rifles – it was the first time that these breech-loaders had been in action and the unending hail of fire had a devastating effect upon the Abyssinians, causing them to recoil before slowly and reluctantly retreating. Increasing numbers of British and Indian infantry arrived on the plateau, to advance rapidly and drive the enemy before them, many to the right into a ravine where the rockets continued to force them further away from Magdala. Then Penn's steel guns unlimbered alongside the Punjabis and began firing over open sights to further scatter and disorganise the Abyssinians, until they were finally dispersed by a series of bayonet charges.

In a few minutes the remnants of the force that had so confidently poured down into the valley were fleeing up the opposite side of the ravine under heavy fire from front and flanks. The courage of the poorly armed Abyssinians impressed the British soldiers, who observed that they had not thrown away their weapons as they re-

Punjab Pioneers charge the Abyssinians at Arogi.

treated, nor had they gone back in rout, but reluctantly and with dignity. Throughout the action Theodore's guns on Fala maintained a constant but erratic fire, the majority of their shells passing high over the heads of the troops and bursting behind them. When the Naval Brigade ran out of targets they turned their rocket-tubes against these guns; one hissing missile narrowly missed Theodore himself, causing him to raise his studded shield in alarm, exclaiming: 'What a terrible weapon! Who can fight against it?' Bullets, shells, rockets and bayonets exacted a heavy toll and by seven in the evening no less than 700 lay dead under the torrential rain now falling; among them was their leader General Fitaurari Gabi, and there were 1,200 wounded. British losses were 20 men wounded, two of them subsequently dying. It was a grim demonstration of the superiority of well-armed, trained and disciplined troops over less sophisticated masses. Theodore's attack at Arogi was unworthy of his not inconsiderable powers of command, but it seemed his men – ignorant of what they were up against – were eager to go. With hindsight, had he abandoned his fixed defences and dispersed into his own familiar terrain to set about harassing the column and its long line of communications, then his hardy tribesmen fighting a guerrilla war deep in their own territory might well have brought about a very different and less successful end to the expedition.

During the two days that followed, Abyssinian chiefs came in and promised to surrender their arms and disperse their men; in the hope of securing better terms, Theodore released some of his captives before changing his mind and addressing his troops on Islamgi, telling them he intended to die fighting in Magdala but any man not wishing to stay with him could go. Probably to his surprise the army virtually disbanded itself, leaving him with but a handful of chiefs and followers.

Inflamed by the discovery of the gashed and mutilated bodies of 350 slaughtered prisoners lying in a pile on the plateau a hundred feet below the British camp, Napier and his commanders planned their attack. Next day, with guns and rockets firing overhead, infantry and Engineers went forward towards the gate of the fortress, under fire from riflemen behind a high wall; then it was realised that the explosives to blow the gate had not been taken forward! Providentially a spot was found where a broken wall allowed men to scramble through; running along narrow streets and alleys they burst upon the defenders and scattered them, then opened the gate for the rest of the party. Progressing through the town in the face of minimal resistance, they came upon the body of King Theodore, who had shot himself. All resistance ceased, the town was taken over and more than a hundred chained prisoners were released. After three days rest, Napier put the place to the torch and the army began their long march back to the coast, to crown one of the most remarkable expeditions of the nineteenth century. Mounted with no thought of annexation, the expedition did not add one square mile to the British Empire. Loss of life was miraculously slight and the financial cost was an enormous £8,600,000, but as Disraeli said: 'Money is not to be considered in such matters.'

2   The Afghans

Afghanistan reveals striking varieties of terrain, climate and people – to the north are the cold harsh mountainous strongholds of the Hindu Kush and Kafiristan, where live Uzberg, Turkic, Hazaran and Mongolian peoples; then there are the bleak and stony passes of the British North-West Frontier Province with its variety of untamed hillmen; to the south and east the blistering Baluchi Desert – with Baluchis in the southeast, Kohistanis and Pathans in the east; and the fertile valleys and plateaux leading westward to fabled Herat. Most prominent in the turbulent events of the nineteenth century were the Afghans proper and the largest tribe, the Ghilzyes. In mid-eighteenth century, the military genius of Ahmed Shah had welded the Afghan Empire out of a host of petty city-states, with boundaries extending to and including Sind, Baluchistan, Kashmir and Peshawar. By the early nineteenth century his descendants had lost much of it and the Empire began to disintegrate as the Royal Family's clan, the Suddozyes, feuded with the Barukzyes until Futteh Khan of that clan was virtual ruler of the country with the surviving Suddozyes, Prince Suja and his blinded brother Shah Zemaun, under protection of the British Raj at Ludhiana. When Futteh Khan was murdered in the early 1800s, his brother Dost Mahomed, after much internecine strife, became Amir of Afghanistan in 1826, to rule firmly and wisely in Kabul.

In 1838 Lord Auckland, Governor-General of India, wishing to set up Afghanistan as a barrier against Russian aspirations in India, approached Dost Mahomed for an alliance. But the Afghan ruler's demands for aid against the neighbouring Sikhs could not be met as Auckland preferred the friendship of the aged Ranjit Singh and his powerful Sikh army, so hope of an alliance faded. Instead, the British government decided to replace the vigorous and masterful Dost Mahomed by a puppet-king, Shah Suja, claimant to the Afghan throne, sending an army into Afghanistan to enforce their wishes. Subsequently, quite unaware of what lay ahead, a Bengal division commanded by Sir Willoughby Cotton assembled at the Sikh city of Ferozepore, under the critical eye of Ranjit Singh, while Sir John Keane marched another division from Bombay – they were to meet in the Indus Delta, then march another 400 miles, much of it through harsh terrain and fearful rocky mountain passes.

This wild and forbidding country was inhabited by a nation of tough and militant mountain men of mixed races, half of them Pathans – the true Afghans, said to be of Israelite origin through the Ten Lost Tribes deported from Palestine by the Assyrians. The rest were Hazaras of Tartar origin, Parsiwans of Arab descent, and Kuzzilbashis whose ancestors had been mercenaries from Persia; plus others of fair complexion and blue eyes who proudly claimed descent from the soldiers of Alexander the Great who passed through on his way to invade India.

Dost Mahomed.

23

Afghanistan was not a wealthy country and its inhabitants made their living as farmers, shepherds or soldiers, despising the life of the tradesman; unfortunately this did not produce sufficient revenue to pay a large army. In the halcyon days of Ahmed Shah it was said he could have put 200,000 men in the field if he could have paid them, for the Afghan was a natural soldier, an intelligent marksman who had an innate instinct for taking advantage of cover, concealing himself behind rocks and stones and only revealing his presence when opening fire. Using the rocks as aiming-rests, he seldom missed his target or wasted a single shot; taking deliberate aim he appeared to pick off officers in particular. In a country too mountainous for wheeled traffic and lacking a navigable river, most Afghans were good horsemen and the strongest arm was usually their cavalry. A favourite tactic was to take up men behind them on their horses, dropping them fresh for combat at the spot where they were required to fire or fight from. Afghans would stand against firing but could not endure the sight of cold steel, running at the sight of the bayonet. Perhaps this was economy of effort, for when charges against them were wasted on thin air, the Afghans returned to their former positions and resumed their deadly sniping. For more than a century, English soldiers learned that, against the Afghans, no rules of military science could be abandoned with impunity. They showed no cowardice in standing against artillery when they had none themselves, and never scrupled to use their long knives – an enemy who fell into their hands need expect no mercy; they did not greatly value human life and displayed towards foes a ferocity equal to anything found in the Old Testament; expert practitioners in the art of dismemberment, both men and women worked industriously and delicately upon the squirming bodies of prisoners.

Afghans wore their Moslem religion lightly, yet on occasions could work up fanatical enthusiasm for the Faith, causing deadly feuds between rival sects of Sunni and Shia. Despite religious rules that forbade alcohol, they produced their own wine and enjoyed drinking it, a cynical and carefree attitude that, over the years, appealed to the British soldier who saw them as being cheerful and lively while admitting that '...they can sneak, lie, cheat and practise any other of the smaller virtues to attain an object...' yet '...side by side with other Asiatic nations, their truthfulness and honesty were conspicuous...'. It was a country wracked with interminable feuds and vendettas, regularly torn by bloody raids and forays by feudal chieftains and their devoted and loyal followers. Yet, through all this turbulence the one passion transcending all others was their love of independence and accompanying violent hatred of outside interference – a national characteristic more recently discovered by the Russians and, 150 years ago, by the British – with disastrous consequences.

THE FIRST AFGHAN WAR

Cotton's force marched out from Ferozeshah on 10 December 1838, in five columns following each other at a day's interval, with supplies and stores coming last. The troops, carrying packs instead of loading them onto baggage animals they hired themselves, were encumbered by about 60,000 camp followers and half that number of camels. Marching steadily, they reached Baluchistan by March and were persistently attacked by wild mountaineers, swooping down upon them to cut down camp followers, carry off cattle and camels, and attack ambulance-wagons. Later, General Nott said: 'The Baluchi is a very different fellow to the Afghan, he is obstinately brave and undoubtedly the best swordsman in the world...'.

By great exertion and with heavy loss of transport animals and baggage, the column got through the 60-mile-long Bolan Pass; harassed by tribesmen, men and animals dragged themselves along in great distress with the thermometer at over 100°F. After marching just over 1,000 miles in 137 days and on half rations for the past 28 days, on 26th April the Bengal Division marched into Kandahar. On 5th May Keane's Bombay Division marched in, similarly, suffering from the great heat, inadequate nourishment and sickness. After resting for a month or so, the army moved on against Kabul and Dost Mohamed, leaving General Sir William Nott to hold Kandahar; General Keane decided against taking the four 18-pounder siege-guns. Probably thankful during the arduous 200-mile, month-long march to Ghazni, the sole enemy stronghold on the route to Kabul, on arrival it

Afghan riflemen in rifle pit.

24

was realised with dismay that the strongly occupied fortress's massive walls and gates were untouchable by their light artillery; parapets were about 70 feet high and a wet-ditch made mining them out of the question. With only three days' food remaining, Ghazni had to be taken at once or the army would perish. A method was devised that was to be used by the British in reducing many of the numerous mud forts dotting Afghanistan, explained by Captain Mackenzie of the 41st Regiment:

'An Afghan fort, consists of a square with a tower at each corner, the walls being built of huge masses of mud, some six or eight feet thick at the base and perhaps two or three at the top, the main building varying in height from twenty to forty feet, and all being pierced with numerous loopholes for wall-pieces and matchlocks. In general, they have only one strong gate, and our mode of taking them is very simple. If a few rounds from a great gun do not do the office of a key, two covering parties keep up a rattling covering fire on the walls while an officer rushes forward with a bag of powder, which he nails to the gate, fires by means of a slow match, and gets out of the way as fast as possible. The gate being shattered, the storming party enters and slays the garrison, if pugnaciously given.'

So Keane decided to blow in the Kabul gate and carry the fortress by surprise, but before that the British had their first encounter with a foe to be a thorn in their flesh for many years to come – fighting under the green banner of Islam the Ghazis were terrifying fanatics, fearless and dedicated to the belief that the path to Paradise was gained by either slaying the infidel in battle or dying in the attempt. They swooped down on Shah Suja's camp, supported by guns firing from the fortress, to be repelled by cavalry and British infantry under James Outram, a name to become familiar in later years. After the action, Shah Suja bloodily dispatched 50 Ghazi prisoners. At first light next day, the gate was blown, the advance party mastered the defenders until the storming column came up to gain both city and citadel and Ghazni, impregnable by native tradition, had fallen at the cost of only 17 killed and 165 wounded. This achievement should not be minimised because the British had been accustomed to walk into Indian fortresses as a matter of course for more than a century and a half – only Bhurtpore had defeated them.

Dost Mahomed sent an emissary to Ghazni on 28th July tendering his submission to Shah Suja, but his conditions were rejected; no more favourable terms than dignified captivity in India would be granted. They marched out on the 30th July for Kabul, halting on the 3rd August to allow the rear to close up and received news that Dost Mahomed, his troops melting away, had fled from Kabul and headed westward over the mountains. On 6 August 1839, the army encamped three miles west of Kabul and on the 7th Shah Suja made his formal entry into the city before a vast but undemonstrative and unenthusiastic crowd. The British troops, after a weary march of 1,500 miles, had reached their goal at last and could assume with some justification that the object of their enterprise had been attained.

Steps were taken to punish chiefs who had supported Dost Mahomed; on 7th September Outram marched from Kabul with a mixed force of the Shah's troops and a field battery against refractory Ghilzai chiefs between Ghazni and Kandahar. Successfully concluded, Outram later joined General Willshire and the Bombay Division (about 1,000 men), ordered during their homeward march to the Indus to deal with the second and more important culprit, Mehrab Khan of Kalat.

On 13th November they came in sight of Kalat to find Mehrab Khan's Baluchi infantry crowded on three hills to the north-west of the fortress, sheltered by three redoubts and supported by five guns in position behind the breastworks. Although outnumbered two to one, Willshire prepared to storm Kalat in broad daylight; his assaulting columns advanced steadily while the little 6-pounder guns opened a very accurate fire of shrapnel at 700 yards on the enemy, who attempted to withdraw inside the citadel, dragging their guns with them. The attackers rushed the Kandahar gate at the northern angle, and the Baluchis abandoned their guns to secure the gate. The storming columns dashed in against fierce resistance; simultaneously, another force entered the fort by a southern gate; the citadel was assaulted and Mehrab Khan was slain. The enemy then surrendered on condition that their lives were spared. It was a smart little affair, a more brilliant success than Ghazni, costing 31 killed and 107 wounded.

Dost Mahomed was not the man to submit tamely to the loss of his throne and sought allies to fight the invaders in Kabul – rugged Uzbegs from the grim country of the Hindu Kush, to be defeated by a far smaller force of native infantry and Afghan cavalry under Colonel Dennie; then Kohistanis rallied to him and defeated Sale in the Purwandurrah Valley in November 1840. It was here that five British officers, deserted by their native cavalry, charged a large enemy cavalry body, so impressing Dost Mahomed with their valour that he immediately surrendered in person to the British; having won his little battle he could now give himself up with honour untarnished.

Things were so quiet for the next two years that wives and families joined soldier-husbands in Kabul, taking part in sports and social events in the almost defenceless cantonment. But the storm was gathering and powerful tribes, subsidies stopped, were in revolt, led by Akbar Khan, son of Dost Mahomed. In October Sale's 13th Regiment lost heavily when attacked by tribesmen. Then the mob murdered Sir Alexander Burnes, running riot to plunder, burn and slay; and outlying detachments were attacked. On 13 November 1841, a strong column of cavalry and infantry with two guns went out to clear enemy from the Behmaru Hills, a few hundred yards from the north-west corner of the cantonment. The 44th Regiment, in column, charged by Afghan cavalry waited until the horsemen were within ten yards or so and fired a volley; when the smoke cleared it was seen that not a man or a horse had been hit, and the 44th – not surprisingly having no faith in their weapons – broke and fled. It seems that the Afghans, artillery apart, were better armed than the British and Sepoy infantry, whose smoothbore flintlock muskets were mostly old, often missed fire and had such worn barrels that they possessed no accuracy. The Afghan jezail, with its long-rifled barrel, outranged the British musket and was far more accurate. Some were so heavy they were fired from rests and could throw bullets nearly half a mile.

When Behmaru was attacked again, thousands of horsemen and infantry surged out of the city, posting themselves on a hill separated by a narrow gorge from Shelton's force, opening a telling fire with their jezails. Incredibly, Shelton put his men on a ridge inaccessible to horsemen into two close-packed squares as though to repel cavalry – within the killing range of perhaps the best marksmen in the world, who mowed them down in safety. Inevitably the squares broke up and the

AKBAR KHAN.

whole force fled in disorderly rout, pursued by Afghan cavalry who could have done far more damage had they not been restrained by their commander, Osman Khan, generally considered to be '...the most moderate and sensible man of the insurgent party...'. Lady Sale, who suffered as much as anyone at their hands, paid a generous tribute to the Afghans:

'I often hear the Afghans designated as cowards: they are a fine, manly-looking set, and I can only suppose it arises from the British idea among civilized people that assassination is a cowardly act. The Afghans never scruple to use their long knives for that purpose, ergo they are cowards; but they show no cowardice in standing as they do against guns without using any themselves, and in escalading and taking forts which we cannot retake. To our deep humiliation we found that instead of being stalwart and devoted clansmen, the troops who had chased the British banner from the field chiefly consisted of tradesmen and artizans from Caubul.'

With their spirit for resistance at low ebb and feeling there was little alternative after the murder of Sir William Macnaghten, the British Envoy, it was agreed to accept degrading Afghan demands to abandon Kabul and withdraw. In

The battle against Sale at Jellalabad, 1842.

the most appalling winter conditions a column of British and native troops, large numbers of women and children and a huge mob of camp followers set out through the snow on 6 January 1842. The unwieldy column was attacked at once, Afghans closing in to plunder, hack and slay, charging horses right into the heart of the barely-moving mass. Tribesmen came from all parts – Kohistanis, Ghilzyes and a host of others – to destroy and loot, for the sake of God and the Prophet, the unenlightened infidels; even small Afghan children slashed and hacked among the fallen. By the 20th, apart from those taken by Akbar Khan as 'hostages', the route was marked by the bodies of the entire column, save for 20 officers and 45 British soldiers of the 44th Regiment. Unable to struggle forward any longer, they took up a defensive position on a hillock at Gandamak and fought off increasing hordes of surrounding enemy, fighting with sword and bayonet when ammunition had gone, until finally overwhelmed. Only one man escaped to ride a solitary figure into Jellalabad – Surgeon Brydon was the sole survivor of the British Army which

had quit Kabul a week before.

With 5,000 men Akbar Khan besieged Jellalabad, his offer of 'safe conduct' was refused and Sale led out three attacking columns, with Havelock commanding the right. Coming to the front at a gallop, the guns poured fire into the massed Afghans, the columns deployed into line, moving forward at the double in the face of heavy fire, and swept the enemy out of his position, capturing his artillery, setting fire to his camp and putting him to rout.

Forcing the Khyber Pass by outflanking and thoroughly defeating a strong force of Afghans, General Pollock arrived with 8,000 men. Leaving Jellalabad on 7th September, he drove the tribesmen from the Jugdulluk Heights, then took on Akbar and 15,000 Afghans amid the ravines and precipices beyond; the Afghans fought desperately but were chased from crag to crag in a merciless pursuit. Up among the precipices there were many hand-to-hand encounters as sword and bayonet fought out the issue until the Ghilzyes were finally driven from the rocky summit by Gurkhas, hillmen themselves, effectively wielding their kukris and chasing the tribesmen from the field. Pollock's feat was extraordinary in that, with a small and inadequately equipped army, he had forced the Khyber Pass for the first time in history.

Blood kindled by what they saw around them, Pollock's force marched over the Kabul retreat route arriving in Kabul on 15th September. General Nott had been successfully holding his own in the Kandahar area where, with a much smaller force, he had decisively beaten an army of 10,000 Afghans; he drove them from Ghazni and then won a final victory near Kabul, reached on 17 September 1842. They marched out on !2th October after destroying the city's great bazaar and defeating the remaining Afghans in the area, and Dost Mahomed returned to his capital from which he had been driven three years previously.

THE SECOND AFGHAN WAR
In mid-1878 a British Mission sent to Kabul to counter an alarmingly large Russian presence was turned back at the entrance to the Khyber Pass. No apology received and the demand for a British Resident in Kabul ignored, on 21 November 1878 war was declared on Afghanistan and a force under General Sir Samuel Browne advanced on the fort of Ali Musjid, standing in a commanding position 500 feet above the deep gorge of the Khyber Pass. Mounting 15 guns, the massive fortress was connected by batteries and advanced posts to a line of fortifications and sangars (stone & breastworks) across the pass, manned by six Afghan regiments of infantry, four batteries of artillery and about 5,000 levies. Through the glasses could be seen their glittering weapons, dark faces, red uniforms and flowing robes.

The British commander sent forward jingling horse batteries of 9-pounder guns, mule-borne mountain guns and elephants dragging heavy 40-pounder guns; lines of British and Indian infantry skirmishers were thrown forward to clear tribesmen from two small villages and mountain scrub. Simultaneously he sent two brigades to turn the position – McPherson's to get behind the fort and block an enemy escape, and Tytler's to climb the Rotas heights and flank the enemy's left. Coming on the strongly held sangars the skirmishers made a furious rush over broken ground but could not take them before darkness put an end to the fighting. Night fell on Ali Musjid looking down from its height, guns silent, walls shattered and gaping by the heavy shelling. Next morning the Ali Musjid was found to be abandoned: fires burned, guns loaded and trained, while canvas tents flapped mournfully in the morning breeze; further up the Pass, at Kala Kushta, the retreating Afghans stumbled into Tytler's force and most of them, including their commander, were taken prisoner.

In anticipation of war, General Frederick Roberts VC and the Kurram Field Force had been concentrating on the frontier, and on 20th November the force of 13,000 men moved out from Kohat proceeding slowly as roads had to be made for the artillery under the eyes of hawk-nosed, dark-eyed Afridi tribesmen watching like vultures from the hilltops all round them.

The opposition likely to be encountered by the Peshawar Valley Field Force under General Browne, pushing through the Khyber Pass, and Roberts' Kurram Valley Field Force was certainly better organised and trained than that encountered in the First Afghan War of 1842. On resuming the throne, Dost Mahomed had undertaken radical steps to improve his army continued by Sher Ali from 1863–79; British drill-books were translated and new regiments formed and trained. At the outbreak of the Second Afghan War in 1878, the Afghan Regular Army consisted of 62 Infantry Regiments, each of 690 men; 16 Cavalry Regiments, each of 600 men:

 2 Elephant Batteries
    (4 guns, 2 mortars, 70 men each)

22 Horse Artillery Batteries
    (6 guns, 150 men each)

18 Mule Mountain-gun Batteries
    (6 guns, 70 men each)

 7 Bullock-drawn Batteries
    (6 guns, 70 men each)

They were centred around eight military depots:

    Kabul – 10,000

    Jellalabad – 3,220

    Sherabad – 3,200

    Kurram – 3,190

    Kandahar – 6,370

Herat — 11,220

Maimana — 2,840

Balkh — 11,820

Afghan Irregular or Militia forces, loosely loyal to the Amir, served local chieftains in a type of feudal system; light infantry — Jezailchis — formed garrisons, local militia groups were skirmishers – all brought their own weapons and horses. A large proportion were cavalry – 8,000 at Kandahar, 5,000 at Ghazni, 15,000 at Kabul and 10,000 at Balkh. Always ready for a fight, a great variety of tribesmen took part in these wars – Ghazis, Ghilzyes, Hazaras, Zermuttis, Mangals – all armed with the rifled flintlock jezail (range up to 800 yards), tulwars (sabres), knives, spears, small round shields and an assortment of home-made weapons. Ferocious and with innate fighting skills, tribesmen often proved more effective than the Regulars, 'pressed men', badly led, and with poor morale through being badly paid and cheated of much of their pay by their superiors.

The Regular Army were armed with a variety of Snider or Enfield rifles, rifled carbines and cavalry pistols; although many infantry had the old two-grooved Brunswick musket or even Tower (Brown Bess) muskets. There were few first-class Martini-Henry rifles and a great many locally-manufactured small arms, copies of Sniders or Enfields, almost as good at close range as the rifles of the Indian Infantry in the British service. Artillery were considered the most important part of the Army, the best paid and equipped arm; there were between 300 and 400 guns, fewer than a tenth being breech-loaders, the rifled ordnance included 8-pounder steel and 7-pounder iron muzzle-loaders; and 4, 6, 8, 9, 12- and 20-pounder iron breech-loaders. The smoothbores included 8-inch iron howitzers; 18- and 24-pounder iron guns; 3, 6, 9 and 12-pounder bronze guns; 8- and 12-inch bronze howitzers. Ammunition was chiefly roundshot. Their 'English Siege Train' (4 × 18-pounder smoothbores and two 8-inch howitzers) was so-called because it had been donated to the Amir, along with 29,000 muzzle-loading rifles and 5,000 Sniders, by the British government! In fact, the Afghan artillery arm was by no means as impressive as it seemed, being an unholy mixture of types and weights, many in poor condition; few gunners were adequately trained.

Like their weapons, the uniforms of the Afghan standing army were a hodgepodge of styles and types, much of it a mixture of cast-off British and Russian uniforms, and 'home-made' tunics made of red cloth brought into the country by traders. One 'Guard' unit of infantry wore a type of Highland doublet over a shapeless kilt made from red-and-white check tablecloths, revealing white pantaloons tucked in to knee-high wrinkled gaiters, the whole being topped by cast-off British white Wolseley helmets. There were regiments of Kabul infantry wearing dark brown woollen uniforms with red facings; Regular cavalry wore scarlet tunics with white facings, black breeches and boots and close-fitting black felt helmets, some horsed units termed dragoons were said to be dressed in what a contemporary author called a ludicrous imitation of British cavalry uniforms. Very few of the *Illustrated London News'* drawings of battle scenes show any of these uniforms, rather the enemy are invariably depicted as tribesmen or irregulars, wearing loose trousers of white or dark-coloured cotton, a voluminous shirt-robe with wide sleeves that reached to the knees, with a wide cloth belt wrapped around the waist; on the head a turban or skull-cap; on the feet were either brown-leather calf boots or Eastern open or turned-up-toed sandals; a poshteen, a large well-tanned sheepskin cloak worn with wool inside was universal in cold weather. Militia usually wore white national-style dress; their cavalry also in white with a red lungi (a cloth worn as a turban, often of blue check with a red border).

The Afghan style of fighting was unlikely to have changed much over the years – generally, they were said to be good shots at close range and extremely aggressive fighters when things were going well, but facing possible defeat, morale disintegrated. On their own difficult terrain they had a definite advantage over the British and Indian troops in their use of cover and concealment, and possessed a natural skill in utilising both. As against the Sikhs in the 1840s, some types of native troops were no match for the Afghan irregulars and tribesmen, being fearful of them and their reputation, particularly in a man-to-man situation.

On 26th November Roberts' force reached the Kurram fort, an oblong mud building about 120 feet by 50 feet each way, with a keep 30 feet high, walls 6 feet thick, and eight bastions each surrounded by a round tower; around the whole ran a dry-moat crossed by a drawbridge, with a covered way. Despite the interior being described as '...a succession of holes half-filled with rubbish and filth...' Roberts left his sick there guarded by artillery, a squadron of cavalry and some foot soldiers, and on the 28th sallied out to force the Peiwar Kotal. A 12-mile march brought them to where the road to the Kotal wound steeply for about two miles up to the summit, marked by a battery of guns able to rake the whole pass. On two steep hills at either side of the Kotal were gun batteries giving cross-fire, and on the right from a lofty rock the 1,000-yard-wide pass could be swept by musketry. The Afghans occupied the entire line of upper hills for about four miles, with guns on both flanks; loftier and more inaccessible hills covered their line of retreat. Roberts decided to turn the position by a night march up the Spin Gawi Pass, from which they could traverse the ridges to reach and storm the top of the ravine. Brigadier Cobbe was to make a feint frontal attack.

On an intensely dark and cold night the attackers toiled up the steep and gloomy recesses of the Spin Gawi Pass until at six in the morning the leading troops came upon an Afghan picket behind a high abatis of felled trees. This barrier and another 80 yards on were carried by Gurkhas and Highlanders, dashing through dark pinewoods in the half light, driving the enemy before them. The tribesmen resisted fiercely and actually disabled one of the four light guns laboriously dragged up the steep ascent, but eventually they broke and streamed away towards the Peiwar Kotal, the mountain-guns hastening their retreat. Five guns were pushed forwards by Cobbe to engage the batteries at the head of the Pass, and the infantry attacked through a dense pine forest until clearing the first ridge. So fierce was the Afghan resistance that the guns fired continuously until 2.30 in the afternoon, halting only when they became dangerously hot. Under heavy Afghan fire from both guns and rifles, the slowly advancing infantry surmounted a deep chasm and one and a half miles of rockstrewn track; at 800 yards from the guns they set up such a withering fire of musketry that the gunners abandoned their pieces.

The leading infantry from Roberts' flanking force came up, to charge down the road with the bayonet, causing the Afghans to abandon camp and guns and vanish into the forests. Roberts had dislodged 4,000 men and guns from a strong position at a cost of 4 officers and 90 other ranks killed and wounded. News came that the Afghans had abandoned Kandahar and General Donald Stewart now occupied this key city.

An indication of the respective merits of cavalry came at Siafoodeen on the 4 January 1879, when a 100-strong squadron of the 15th Hussars blundered into a force of Afghan horsemen in a dust storm; in the ensuing mêlée, the Hussars killed 24 and took 9 prisoners at a cost of 2 men wounded.

To protect British convoys in the Khost Valley, Roberts sent out a small mixed force of cavalry, infantry and a mountain-gun battery; near the fort of Matun they found their defensive camp surrounded by hordes of Mangals, Waziris and Kostwals, massing to attack. The 15th Hussars squadron went out and skirmished, using their short Martini-Henry carbines to good effect, but being drawn further and further away by enemy who wanted them out of the way while they stormed the camp. Tribesmen had been gathering during the night in villages near the camp, and surged over the plain to be driven back with heavy losses by the mountain-guns. The infantry went out in skirmishing order with cavalry on the flanks and burned the villages; at a cost of six men killed or wounded they cleared the area, killing at least 100 and wounding twice that number of tribesmen. Marching to Sabbri 12 miles away, Roberts heard that the camp at Matun was again threatened; hastily retracing his steps he arrived to see the valley packed with more than 6,000 excited tribesmen, who hung around sullenly but did not attack. After destroying the fort with gunpowder, the column withdrew under spasmodic attacks, covered by mountain-guns and cavalry carbines.

In February 1879 the Amir of Afghanistan died and his successor Yacoub Khan stirred up the frontier tribes so that expeditions had to be sent out against them. Brigadier Gough, with about 1,200 infantry, cavalry and four guns, came up with a large force of them in a strong defensive position at Futtehabad, but enticed them by progressively retreating artillery fire so that they came swarming out in pursuit, even attempting a flanking movement by scrambling down a ravine and coming up within 250 yards of the guns. They nearly turned the left flank of Gough's small force but his infantry effectively checked them by briskly file-firing and using their bayonets at close quarters. In spite of the Horse

The death of Major Wigram Battye in the Battle of Futtehabad.

Artillery sending shell after shell screaming and exploding among them, the tribesmen pushed on to within 400 yards of the guns. The tribesmen out in the open, Major Wigram Battye, a brave soldier with an immense reputation on the Frontier, led the Hussars and Guides cavalry, who cut and re-cut their way through the tightly massed shrieking tribesmen; when Battye was killed his Guides went berserk, scattering the tribesmen and pursuing them for five miles, killing more than 400 of them for a loss of 40 killed and wounded.

General Tytler's division was sent against the Mohmands, the Shinwarris and the Afridis and in a very successful expedition which cost the enemy more than 250 killed, some sharp fighting took place, the Afridis were dispersed and five villages were destroyed.

With the column advancing on Kabul the young Amir Yakoub Khan asked for a peace conference at Gundamuk; on 26 May 1879 a peace treaty was signed placing Afghanistan under British control while guaranteeing them against foreign (i.e. Russian) aggression; there was to be a British Resident at Kabul, and the British were to have complete command over the Khyber Pass.

General Roberts had severe reservations on the treaty, as no serious defeat had been inflicted upon the Afghan Army which remained in being; his misgivings were proved right when in early September 1879 the British Resident, Major Louis Cavagnari, with his entire staff and escort were murdered and the residency in Kabul sacked by three mutinous Afghan regiments. Roberts marched out with the Kabul Field Force (about 7,000 strong), encountering an Afghan force occupying a defile and range of hills at Charasiah, where in a spirited artillery duel at a range of 1,500 yards three Horse Artillery guns silenced four rifled pieces and the infantry routed Afghan foot soldiers; pushing on, the Highlanders with mountain artillery and Gatling guns fought a two-hour battle with some 4,000 tribesmen, finally defeating them by taking the defended hill in the rear. In this battle, less than half of Roberts' force had routed the entire army of Kabul and captured all their artillery. The victors marched into the city, accepted the resignation of the effete Amir Yacoub Khan, and executed 49 Afghans for complicity in Cavagnari's murder.

The style and ferocity of the fighting was later

THE AFGHANS

described by an erudite Lieutenant Ian Hamilton; later to become a general and command at Gallipoli in World War 1, he wrote:

'My horse has leaped over a dead tribesman. Then in the thick of it, Afghans in little knots, or else lying on their backs whirling their big knives to cut off the legs of our horses, a hell of a scrimmage in fact, until the sowars got to work in couples, one with sword uplifted, the other pulling his carbine out of the bucket and making the enemy spring to their feet and be cut down or be shot as they lay. Dust, shouts, shots, clash of steel...only a nameless little skirmish and yet it is a favourite picture amongst the many that come back to me in my dreams.'

Welded into a strong and dangerous force by Mahomed Jan, a competent and audacious leader, the Afghans made some partially successful attempts to capture the heights from which an attack could be made on Kabul. In early December, a force of 500 men led by General Massy came into action unsupported and was defeated by 4,000 Afghans, losing their guns, later recaptured by Gurkhas. Knowing the enemy to be about 45,000 strong, Roberts reluctantly abandoned his plans for offensive operations and concentrated his whole force within the Sherpur cantonment, a strong defensive position large enough to hold all the troops, the cavalry horses, transport animals, supplies and stores.

Personally supervising this withdrawal, the general breathed more easily when it was over; experience told him that:

'It is comparatively easy for a small body of well-trained soldiers, such as those of which the army in India is composed, to act on the offensive against Asiatics however powerful they may be in point of numbers. There is something in the determined advance of a compact, disciplined body of troops which they can seldom resist. But a retirement is a different matter. They become full of confidence and valour the moment they see any signs of their opponents being unable to resist them, and if there is the smallest symptom of unsteadiness, wavering or confusion, a disaster is certain to occur.'

A war beacon blazed on a ridge just above the city before daylight on 23 December 1879 and the dull roar of many thousand voices rose on the wind as the Afghans made a feint attack on the north-west angle of the defences and then put in an attack in great force from the north-east. Taking cover behind every ridge and rock, working

their way towards the defences of Behmaru, from a small village they were able to pour in heavy musketry fire; mountain-guns failed to dislodge the tribesmen, turned them back when they rushed the defences. Four guns of the Horse Artillery sent through the gorge towards the plain north of the village of Behmaru brought cross-fire to bear and drove the enemy out of the village. This reverse and their losses in attacking the defences dispirited the Afghans and they began to stream away; at once Roberts ordered every sabre in pursuit and out went the cavalry to circle to the northeast of Sherpur, cutting off the flying fugitives before they could reach the shelter of the hills. The enemy's losses were not less than 3,000 killed and wounded; the British had 5 killed and 33 wounded.

Untroubled, the garrison remained in Kabul until spring 1880 supplied by continuous columns of camels, oxen, mules, ponies and men laboriously traversing the deep and dark defiles from Peshawar to Kabul; it became a route littered by the dry bones of baggage animals, dying of toil, disease and cold, or falls over the edge of the track – by March 1880 it was estimated that 80,000 had perished.

Sir Donald Stewart's force of 7,000 infantry, cavalry and artillery left Kandahar to occupy Ghazni, and on 19 April 1880 came upon about 15,000 enemy horse and foot well positioned on a ridge near Ahmed Kheyl, 23 miles south of Ghazni. Seeing Stewart's column, the enemy left their position and advanced rapidly forward, coming under artillery fire at 1,200 yards range. So fast did they advance that the range soon had to be reduced to 400 yards and then, with tribesmen on top of them, case-shot was used, and finally guns were loaded with shrapnel with heads towards the charge, to explode at the muzzle so that heaps of dead and dying littered the ground before the guns. Simultaneously, concealed by grassy ridges enemy cavalry were pouring down two ravines to turn Stewart's left flank. Struck before they could charge, the Bengal Lancers were sent reeling back in disorder, right into the centre of Stewart's position, causing his force to assume a semi-circle with a gap in the centre. In the face of heavy musketry and artillery fire, the Afghans displayed great courage in making a fierce attack upon the British flanks and front, pouring through the gap. Despite the infantry standing firm, artillery pouring in shot at point-blank range and cavalry charging repeatedly,

33

the situation was desperate as the British right flank had been badly shaken by the desperate onslaught of the enemy whilst fierce cavalry attacks on the left flank had rolled the Indian cavalry back before their weight and impetus. The 3rd Gurkhas, formed in company-squares with open spaces between, had a surging mass of men and horses forced down upon them, but remaining cool they opened fire at point-blank range on the enemy cavalry as they swept past. At last the Afghan horsemen were halted and Stewart's cavalry, relieved from pressure on their rear, fell upon the shattered enemy with lance and sword and hurled them back to the cover of villages and orchard walls from where they kept up a parting fire while gradually leaving the field, their departure becoming a rout when pursued by Indian cavalry. The British lost 17 killed and 115 wounded; the Afghans lost 1,000 dead and more than 2,000 wounded.

Ghazni was captured without a shot being fired; then the force marched to Kabul, where they had a fierce encounter with 6,000 tribesmen, losing 2 killed and 11 wounded in routing them with a reported loss of 400 killed and wounded. Stewart entered Kabul, but early in June was ordered to evacuate the city as part of a British policy of withdrawing troops from Afghanistan.

Ayoub Khan, brother of Yakoub Khan and claimant to the throne, rallied large numbers to his standard and marched from Herat at the head of a force of Regular infantry and cavalry with 36 guns, and large numbers of tribesmen from the most fierce and warlike of the western tribes. To prevent local tribes from joining them, the Wali of Kandahar moved out with his native troops supported by General Burrows' 2,300 native infantry and cavalry with six guns; then Wali's troops mutinied, being dispersed by Burrows' cavalry and artillery, leaving the small British force to face Ayoub Khan's army now swollen to more than 12,000 infantry, cavalry and artillery commanded by Russian officers. On 27th July the Afghan army made a flank march, working their way undetected along the northern slopes of a range of hills bounding the plain where stood the British camp. Burrows ordered an advance to Maiwand three miles away, and cavalry-skirmishing took place as both forces deployed into battle formation. Ayoub Khan had seven regiments of infantry at his centre with a number of guns, 400 cavalry on the right and 2,000 Ghazis on his left. The Afghan cavalry made a feigned retreat on Burrows' right front and the British commander depleted his already weak force by dispatching two guns and a squadron of cavalry after them; next he ordered his line to advance in support thus leaving an advantageous position. He exchanged the shelter of a ruined fort and village for a position with undulating ground to his front that gave the enemy cover from his fire, and with heights from which the enemy's guns were able to play upon his front and flank troops. Although few in number, Burrows' rifled 9-pounders were superior in range and accuracy to the Afghan's smoothbore artillery but the advantage was lost when the range decreased to less than 1,000 yards.

A charge of Afghan regular cavalry on the British left coincided with the fanatical Ghazis hitting front and right causing the infantry to fall back step by step; two guns were lost, but recaptured by a bayonet charge; one gun remained in Afghan possession and was turned to fire upon the retreating British troops. Their position became a two-sided triangle with the Berkshire Regiment forming its apex; native regiments at the sides were being badly cut up by the Afghan artillery on the flanking heights. To counter this Burrows sent parties to skirmish up the hills which he should have occupied and held before the battle began, but they were beaten back. Then the Ghazis worked their way round to attack the rearguard, the baggage and stores were only saved at the cost of 100 killed and wounded. By three o'clock in the afternoon the 400 remaining men of the 66th Regiment, under fire from more than 4,000 rifles and 30 guns, fell back in good order by alternate wings, forming square twice when attacked by cavalry. Attempting to cover the left wing Jacob's Rifles were thrown back in hopeless disorder by hordes of yelling Ghazis and fled to the rear of the 66th. Stragglers from the 66th, Jacobs Rifles, the Bombay Grenadiers and some artillerymen separated from their guns put up a desperate resistance in a small enclosure; ammunition ran out and desperate hand-to-hand fighting took place. During this part of the action a British gun that had escaped the enemy fired so quickly and with such deadly effect that it became too hot to be serviceable and was captured.

Burrows attempted to retreat along the Kandahar Road but was badly disorganised by thousands of terrified camp-followers; the cavalry were still making sporadic charges, and gunners stuck bravely to the last remaining gun until cut down. From then on it was a confused and disastrous flight, until 100 officers and men of the 66th Regiment made a determined stand in a garden against almost the whole Afghan army, fighting until only 11 men were left with the regimental pet, a little white dog, scampering among them; then, ammunition gone, the small party charged out and stood back to back in the open until the last man was shot down. Burrows led the few survivors in a fighting retreat for 16 miles towards Kandahar, his remaining cavalry making repeated charges to beat off pursuers. Seven miles from Kandahar, the fugitives met a small force who covered their disorderly retreat. They lost 1,302 officers and men and all their guns; two Victoria Crosses were awarded, two senior officers were court-martialled and honourably acquitted; General Burrows was removed from the Brigade staff.

General Primrose, in command at Kandahar, withdrew his 3,000 men into the citadel and prepared for assault; Ayoub Khan threw up siege works, deployed his 10,000 men and opened fire on the city with his guns and those captured at Maiwand. To halt firing from a village near the citadel, an ill-conceived sortie was made and completely repulsed with 200 casualties, including most of the senior officers.

On 8 August Sir Frederick Roberts set off from Kabul to march 318 miles to Kandahar through mountainous country peopled by fierce and war-like tribes who might well seek to bar his way; his force consisted of nearly 10,000 men with more than that number of horses, mules and other baggage animals, plus thousands of native camp-followers. Extending fully six miles on the road, the column marched 16 miles a day under conditions of the strictest march discipline. After travelling 240 miles in 17 marches, Roberts relieved the garrison of Khelat-i-Ghilzie and on 31st August, after some rearguard skirmishing with tribesmen, was close enough to Kandahar to send out a reconnaissance in strength,

opposed by large bodies of the enemy allowed to come within 200 yards and then mowed down by heavy file-firing. The cavalry and two mountain-guns held 5,000 Afghans at bay on the right flank, the cavalry dashing in and scattering them after they had been shaken by artillery fire. So heavy were the Afghan attacks that Gurkhas and Highlanders were forced to form in company-squares; their independent file-firing shattered the attacking Afghans who gave way and were pursued by Gurkhas and Lancers.

Roberts attacked Ayoub Khan's army, strongly entrenched on a precipitous mountain ridge, by a frontal attack that took the village of Gundi-Mulla; then 72nd Highlanders and Sikhs steadily advanced under a hot fire from garden walls and houses, to the low spur of hills short of Paimal. Fighting among the loopholed walled enclosures was desperate, the Ghazis hurling themselves on British and native infantry, dashing their shields against bayonets and grappling with the men, trying to wrench their muskets away. After most severe fighting the infantry pressed on, sweeping the enemy through closely wooded gardens and orchards to take the village of Paimal. Now they encountered Regular soldiers fighting from an entrenched camp commanding an open space of ground; Afghan guns on the Baba Wali Kotal wheeled round to increase the heavy fire poured upon the advancing troops, screw-guns of the mountain battery replied. Highlanders and Gurkhas stormed forward to drive the enemy out of their entrenchments and take the ridge that overlooked Ayoub's camp in the entrenched village of Mazra. Quite defeated, the Afghan force fled in all directions, leaving 32 guns behind, and losing about 1,200 men. British casualties were 40 killed and 228 wounded. The pursuit by the cavalry was greatly hampered by broken ground.

The battle of Kandahar was the last action of the Third Afghan War; in September the Kandahar Field Force was broken up and General Roberts returned to India.

3　The Ashantis

Prior to its annexation by the British in 1902 Ashanti was a powerful native kingdom of western Africa, a principal district of the British colony of the Gold Coast on the Gulf of Guinea. By 1800 the importance of the slave trade far outweighed that of the gold, ivory and other produce of the West Coast of Africa which had originally attracted European traders. On the Gold Coast the traders established themselves in defended settlements on the coast, where the Fanti people acted as go-betweens for the slave suppliers further inland.

Dominant among these were the Ashanti. They occupied the forest land between the coast and the more open country of the Northern Territories. They were militarily well organised and had a fully deserved reputation for cruelty. Their first clash with the British was in 1823 when they raided the Fanti who appealed to the Governor of Sierra Leone for help. The Governor was defeated and killed but in 1826 was avenged by a British force who drove the Ashanti back into their forests at the battle of Dodowah. By 1844 the British presence was regularised by a treaty with the tribal chiefs of the coastal region.

Whereas the coastal peoples were friendly and traded peacefully with the whites, the warlike Ashantis resented the British dominance of the Gold Coast area, not only because it interfered with their plans for expansion of the Ashanti union but also because Britain's abolition of the slave trade had ruined the market for their principal export. Faced with a superabundance of slaves, the Ashantis increased their practice of human sacrifice to take care of the surplus. By 1863 there was open hostility between the British and Ashantis; however, there was no serious conflict until 1873, when the Asantehene (King of the Ashantis) Kofi Karikari launched a full-scale attack on the coastal tribes, the Denkera and Fanti, who were under the protection of Great Britain, and soon defeated. As the Ashanti warriors ravaged the surrounding area, the neighbouring tribes lived in terror, having intimate knowledge of the Ashantis' extreme cruelty to enslaved captives, as well as their especially fearsome witchcraft.

In June 1873 an Ashanti army swarmed across the River Prah to reach Elmina, being joined by tribes in its neighbourhood. A small party of Marines and Marine Artillery landed from the ships on the coast and prevented the invaders entering the town. Britain became painfully aware that she was again becoming embroiled in another of those little wars which her extensive colonial possessions regularly obliged her to enter, and recognised the fact that she was faced with the choice of abandoning her interests on the Gold Coast or taking punitive action against 'King Koffee', as the public called Kofi Karikari. An expedition, officially designated 'Special Service on the West Coast of Africa' was organised

Warrior of Elmina.

36

under command of Major-General Sir Garnet Wolseley.

On 6 October 1873, the London *Times* published the following commentary by its military correspondent:

'Preparations for the Ashantee War.

'History teaches us that warfare with a semi-savage nation is marked by certain peculiar characteristics, which require to be fully recognised and provided for. The savage does not fight by the rules of modern tactics. He knows nothing of those intricate manoeuvres which characterize civilized warfare, and in general his idea of victory is connected with the number of foes he has slain, or the number of scalps he has taken. His weapons are comparatively rude, and have little effect except in hand-to-hand fighting. Thus a battle between two opposing savage forces partakes of the nature of an indiscriminate mêlée. In scientific warfare the absolute number of slain is a matter of secondary consideration. Modern battles are won more by moral than by physical effects. We employ engines that terrify as well as kill, and we find it more advantageous to kill a few, provided the rest run away, than to slaughter a number while the remainder stand fast. Thus, a flight of rockets – a comparatively harmless warlike engine – might cause a regular "skedaddle" among a set of savages without the loss of a single life.'

Thus, Sir Garnet was sent out to punish the Ashantis for their temerity, commanding a small force of white soldiers – Scots infantry of the 42nd (Black Watch); Welsh Fusiliers of the 23rd Regiment; a battalion of the Rifle Brigade; sailors and Marines of a Naval Brigade; and two battalions of the West India Regiment; some native infantry; a few Royal Engineers; and a battery of mountain-guns crewed by native artillerymen. They were to fight a campaign in completely alien territory of dense jungle against vastly superior numbers of fierce native warriors on their own terrain; their commanders (some of whom had fought in the Crimea 20 years earlier) had to employ completely unfamiliar dispositions and tactics; medical facilities were primitive, almost horrific; while climate and conditions caused sickness and disease – as formidable an enemy as the Ashantis themselves.

Before marching out, Wolseley issued a memorandum detailing advice on general health and the mode of fighting to be expected; revealing in its thoroughness, it describes the theatre of operations as a great forest of gigantic trees in a bush undergrowth of varying thickness that can, in places, be penetrated by men in skirmishing order, but often requiring paths to be cut with the sword-bayonet. All fighting was to be done in skirmishing order with small tactical units of quarter-company sections, and detailed instructions are given for the precise methods of fighting. 'Fighting in the bush', wrote Sir Garnet, 'is very much like fighting by twilight with no one able to see further than a few files to left or right.' Sir Garnet describes Ashanti tactics which are invariably the same in that they employ their superiority in numbers by encircling enemy flanks with long thin lines of skirmishers, hoping thereby to demoralise – the soldiers were not to be concerned about this as their general had plans for meeting all such eventualities.

'Each soldier must remember that, with his breechloader, he is equal to at least twenty Ashantis, wretchedly armed as they are with old flint muskets, firing slugs or pieces of stone, that do not hurt badly at more than forty or fifty yards range... they have neither guns nor rockets, and have a superstitious dread of those used by us.'

Method of firing and conservation of ammunition is stressed, together with method of advancing in short rushes, cheering; and emphasis that all positions once taken must be held – 'In warfare of this nature there can be no retreats.' The memorandum ends with a typical Victorian-period exhortation:

'It must never be forgotten by our soldiers that Providence has implanted in the heart of every native of Africa a superstitious dread and awe of the white man, that prevents the negro from daring to meet us face to face in combat. A steady advance or a charge made with determination always means the retreat of the enemy. Although, when at a distance, and even when under heavy fire, the Ashantis seem brave enough, from their practice of yelling, singing, and beating drums in order to frighten enemies of their own colour, they will not stand against the advance of the white man. English soldiers and sailors are accustomed to fight against great odds in all parts of the world. It is scarcely necessary to remind them that when, in our battles beyond the Prah, they find themselves surrounded on all sides by hordes of howling enemies, they must rely upon their own British courage and discipline. Soldiers and sailors, re-

Ashanti elders and warriors.

member that the black man holds you in superstitious awe. Be cool, fire low, and charge home; and the more numerous your enemy, the greater will be the loss inflicted upon him, and the greater your honour in defeating him.'

Perhaps this was a morale-raiser, or maybe Sir Garnet had not done his homework, because earlier wars with the Ashantis had revealed them as courageous and fierce warriors capable of defeating – if only by sheer weight of numbers – disciplined troops sent against them. Certainly it was known that they were perhaps the most barbarous of all enemies encountered in Victorian colonial wars, through their custom of having thousands of slaves and prisoners slaughtered at their many festivals to ensure that departing kings and lords had a happy 'after-life'. However, Wolseley's plan proved to be simple but effective – after securing the coast with the aid of the Navy, he would march in defensive formation through forests and across rivers to the Ashanti capital Kumasi. Garrisons were to be left along his supply route; the Royal Engineers employed in cutting paths, building bridges and destroying villages, usually under fire so heavy casualties might be sustained. It was a straightforward strategy based on overwhelming firepower, with

Kumasi as the goal.

The Ashanti nation was formed of eight clans, each with its own territory, the whole forming a confederation; clan chiefs and elders assisted the king (the Asantehene) to govern, although he was a relatively despotic monarch who derived his awesome powers from his Golden Stool, a never-sat-upon symbol of authority. At the time under review the total Ashanti Army probably totalled 50,000 men and consisted of six major groups centred on the capital Kumasi – the main body was Adonten; Benkum and Nifa the left- and right-wings; Kyidom the rearguard; Cyase the king's bodyguard; and the Ankobea were the militia guarding Kumasi. There were three other major military groups, each ruled by one of the Nyafohene or Kumasi-based chiefs – they were the Oyoko (Royal) clan; the Konti clan, and the Ahramu clan. There was another military group organised similarly to the National Army, feudal in nature and formed of troops of chiefs (Amahene) governing outlying conquered territories – they were the Mampong (the most powerful); the Juaben; the Gyaman; the Bekwai; and the Kokofu.

The soldiers, the Asafo, were organised into units called Guns, and grouped under captains (Asapohene) who were more ornately dressed, wearing a helmet adorned with a pair of ram's horns and a double plume of eagle's feathers; they wore skirts, gilt and red charms suspended from a necklace, horsetails on their arms, and a leather waist-belt bearing a short knife and a razor in coloured sheaths, a razor-strop and a four inch square leather pouch; hanging from the belt, a pair of bilateral thin gold chains attached to the tops of high leather boots. The Caboceers, nobles who led their own armies, wore white turbans sometimes wrapped around the ram's horn helmet; while jacket and loincloth exposing the belly; and leather boots; sometimes they rode a horse in war, with an over-blanket emblazoned with Arab texts, and a leather head-piece; they carried a long spear, a box and a quiver of arrows.

Ashanti soldiers were simply dressed – sometimes they fought almost naked with a collection of knives fastened in a necklace and used a bow and arrows if they did not have a musket, powder and slugs. Their long flintlock rifles were called 'Danes' after the European who first supplied them; they were plentifully supplied with powder and slugs, mostly smuggled into the country by European traders. Spears were sometimes carried but no shields; side-arms consisted of various types of knives and swords – the native afona (resembling a machete), Muslim scimitars or European-made swords and Navy cutlasses. They wore a variety of clothing – white shirts and skirts, solid coloured or patterned in irregular oblongs of colour; others wore tattered European uniform-tunics with ankle-length skirts. There are pictures of the Gyase, the king's bodyguard, wearing light-coloured 'vests' with dark dots and a white belt bearing a cartridge-box. Equipment consisted of a hunting-belt, sometimes a native 'haversack'; or a leather or cloth belt with cartridge-box and knife in an animal-skin sheath. Some wore a shako-type high 'box' hat, similarly bearing horns as a mark of rank, but also for signalling and adding to the general din of battle.

Undoubtedly the Ashanti warrior was a fierce and barbaric foe, formidable in his own jungle, and adding to the list of unusual foes encountered by the long-suffering British soldier during Victoria's colonial wars. It is recorded that the Ashantis fought with great courage and resolu-

tion, resisting stoutly and attacking through the far-echoing bush at a fierce run, beating drums and blowing horns, and in such masses that the whole bush moved and swayed. They had no idea of making a silent advance and their well-advertised sallies were always met with hails of bullets, shells and rockets, yet usually they advanced to within 20 paces of the muzzles of British rifles before being forced back. In greatly superior numbers and in their own wilderness admirably suited to their peculiar method of fighting, they were a formidable foe and could have triumphed had they been allowed to make a real massed charge. Their old and worn-out muskets, firing rough lead slugs, compared badly with the breech-loading Sniders of the Regulars, and even the muzzle-loading Enfields of the native levies could fire faster, yet at times so rapid and well-sustained was the fire coming from unseen foes in the bush that it was thought they were discharging muskets loaded for them and handed to the men at the front by loaders in the rear.

The Ashantis used enormous charges of power in their muskets, dropping down on to the powder three or four slugs of roughly chopped-up lead. The noise of their explosion was almost as loud as Wolseley's small guns, the sound broken up by the trees in a singular manner, to result in a strange and confused reverberation, mingled with the hissing sound rising from the storm of bullets and slugs, mingled with that of the rockets. It was fortunate that the Ashantis used such heavy charges as it caused the muskets to throw high, and slugs whistled harmlessly over the heads of the troops, covering them with showers of leaves cut from trees overhead.

That it could all have been much worse was suggested by the correspondent of the *Standard*, a daily newspaper of the period, who wrote:

'The sale of bad powder, and seven-and-sixpenny Birmingham guns does little harm; but surely we should prevent traders from supplying modern arms to African savages. Had the King of the Ashantees got 50,000 Sniders or other breech-loaders to place in the hands of his troops, what must have been the dimensions of our expedition? Instead of three regiments of whites, we should have required twenty, and our loss would have been awful. And yet it is quite possible that this is the sort of war we may be called upon, ere many years are past, to wage with Dahomey, and that Britain may be obliged to spend countless

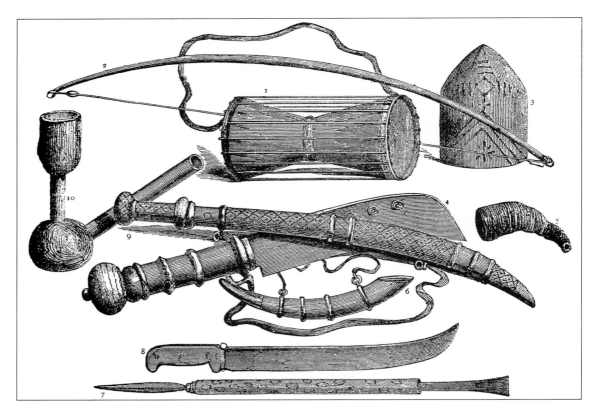

1. War drum 2. Bow 3. Native cap 4. Knife of office 5. Powder-horn 6. Powder-flask 7. Arrow 8. Native knife 9. Native sword 10. Kro boy's pipe

millions, and thousands of lives, because some mercenary trader will sell a hundred thousand breech-loaders at a profit to himself of five shillings a rifle. The savages are as brave as we are; and if they had breech-loaders, rockets, and cannon, the advantages which the climate and country give them would more than balance our superiority in drill and discipline. In view of such a contingency, no time should be lost in making it a penal offence to import into Africa any weapons save the old flint-and-steel guns. France and Portugal should be asked to co-operate in the matter; and though it is possible that a few guns might be smuggled in, yet the high rates which traders would be compelled to charge, in order to run the risk, would put them out of the reach of all but the wealthiest natives; and would thus ensure us against having to repeat the Ashantee campaign against tribes armed with weapons as good as our own.'

The best plan of action that could have been used by the Ashanti against Wolseley would have been guerrilla warfare against the tenuous British line of supply, but this was a type of fighting foreign to the Ashantis who would have been incapable of carrying it out, even had they guessed Wolseley's plan of campaign beforehand. It is believed the Ashanti Army had had some training from Europeans and Muslims in their king's service – more of such training might have led to a different campaign result; as it was, even their most skilful generals, such as Assah Moquantah who had been successful against such tribes as the Fanti, could not cope with British firepower. In fact, so fearful did they find it that at Prahsu, Wolseley's headquarters, in January 1874, one of a group of Ashanti envoys bearing peace proposals from King Kofi Karikari blew out his brains after a purposefully frightening demonstration of the power of the Gatling.

Wolseley's march to Kumasi was through dense forests of gigantic trees, some more than 200 feet high, laced together with creepers supporting bush so thick as to literally choke the earth with its density and luxurance; broad-leafed plants, creepers and trailers twisted and intermingled with each other as to almost defy the power of the sun and caused a perpetual twilight of golden spears of light and speckled shadows valiantly penetrating vistas of graceful plantains waving smooth shining green leaves. Native war-paths trodden into semi-ditches were the only way through in single-file, and two persons meeting in opposite directions had difficulty in passing each other, the more so as long use wears down the soft moist earth until the tracks are converted into ditches two or three feet deep, forming primitive shallow trenches in which men could lie and fire with a modicum of shelter. This was particularly useful when one of the many Ashanti ambushes was sprung and had to be beaten off. Certainly for the soldiers these tracks or paths hacked out with machetes or swords were the only way through the jungle, but the Ashantis scorned lacerations of their bare flesh to creep on all fours through the leafy tangle. There were semi-clearings here and there where the ground was covered with breast-high low brush, together with knee-deep swamps with masses of bright flowers carpeting their fringes. Most of the fighting occurred close to villages where the system of African cultivation afforded good cover to the natives, who cleared the ground by fire, then sowing in the ashes and, when the soil was exhausted, abandoned the area for another. On these deserted fields arose lofty vegetation, impenetrable except to naked natives who crawled through it on their faces.

It is never pleasant to come under fire, but even worse when it comes suddenly from places that a moment before had given no indication of human life, and every forward movement seemed to disclose the presence of Wolseley's men to the perfectly concealed enemy. Fortunately, the enemy missiles were slugs incapable of penetrating even the clothing at much more than 50 yards range, although sometimes the sheer solidity and impact of the slugs tore away great chunks of flesh or caused fractures of bones; usually however, the Ashanti slugs inflicted wounds that required only a day or two of disablement; had it been otherwise the expedition would very quickly have been without officers and reduced to minimal numbers.

The British force replied by pouring in volleys from their Sniders and Enfields, Rait's

mountain-guns firing canister at 50 yards range with a booming roar, and the rockets' tremendous rush from their troughs made an uproar that seemed to shake the whole forest; the storm of shot sweeping through the bush, shredded away showers of twigs and leaves until the twilight landscape became draped in lurid white and yellow smoke pierced by red musketry flashes. Despite the terrifying impact of shells and rockets, the Ashantis remained steady in their leafy lairs, patiently enduring the heavy fire while maintaining their own so that it was difficult to conceive that men armed only with old muzzle-loaders could keep up such an unslackening roar; their yells and beating of drums were unceasing and rose in wilder chorus as each volley of grape, canister or rocket tore at their green hiding places. Usually they never showed even their heads, but here and there, inspired by their own noise and encouraged by their women posted behind them, they rushed madly out in a wild onslaught. Invariably met with a volume of fire too crushing to be withstood, they fell back out of sight – to sing again, drum some more, and continue madly firing their raucous muskets. It was rarely possible to drive them from their lairs and usually, after an hour or so of musketry exchanges, the Ashanti fire ceased and it was presumed they had fallen back; cautiously the troops went forward to see great gouts of blood spattered on all sides, discarded clothing and damaged or abandoned muskets, and a few bodies; without such signs it was hard to conceive that any enemy had been present, the nature of the terrain making it impossible to conjecture on the enemy's strength or his losses. The roar of fire was so general and continuous that none of the three columns had much idea where the others lay; each of them sent messenger after messenger back to Sir Garnet, with his staff at the village, complaining that adjacent friendly groups were firing upon them. Possibly true, as the bush was so bewilderingly dense that all ideas of points of the compass were lost and men fired in any direction from which shots came. To counter this, bugles constantly sounded regimental calls to inform of their whereabouts, blending and rising over bird-like calls echoing eerily through the bush as the Ashantis signalled to each other and kept up their spirits by means of traditional war-cries and sounds. Heralding an attack, the sounds multiplied until hundreds of deep voices broke into the Ashanti war-song, a

Ashantis resisting Wolseley's advance on Kumasi.

barbaric, spine-chilling chant quite unlike anything the British had ever before heard; innumerable horns, modulated in tone, played a wild accompaniment with pulsating tom-toms beating a rhythmic background. Suddenly it ceased and as though on a signal and with a startling roar hails of musketry came from unseen weapons in the bush, the Ashanti muskets, booming and full-voiced as small artillery-pieces, pouring out fire that raised rising clouds of white smoke, the only indication of their presence. 'Never was a battle fought admitting of less description,' says an eyewitness.

'It is impossible, indeed, to give a picturesque account of an affair in which there was nothing picturesque; in which scarcely a man saw an enemy from the commencement to the end of the fight; in which there was no manoeuvering, no brilliant charges, no general concentration of troops; but which consisted simply of five hours

of lying down, of creeping through the bush, of gaining ground foot by foot, and of pouring a ceaseless fire into every bush in front which might contain an invisible foe. Nothing could have been better than Sir Garnet Wolseley's plan of battle, or more admirably adapted for the foe with whom we had to deal. Wherever he attacked us, he found himself opposed by a continuous front of men, who kept his flank attacks at bay, while the 42nd pushed steadily and irresistibly forward. To that regiment belong, of course, the chief honours of the day; but all did excellently well.'

The victory at Amoaful virtually decided the campaign, costing Wolseley about 250 casualties, a heavy proportion of a small force; the Ashantis carried off their dead and wounded so numbers could only be conjectured; nevertheless large numbers of bodies were seen and it was thought their losses must have been around 2,000. They fought with extraordinary courage and resolution; although enormously outnumbering Wolseley's force the terrain was admirably suited to their type of fighting; they were wretchedly armed, their old and worn-out muskets were poor weapons indeed compared to breech-loading rifles, guns and rocket-tubes.

Because of the climate, impending rains and the sheer horror of the blood-soaked capital Kumasi, the force only remained there for a day before burning it to the ground and withdrawing to the coast.

Sir Garnet Wolseley's victory, although splendidly organised and gallantly put into execution, was little better than a flourish of trumpets in that it had no permanent effect on the Ashanti nation. A glint of civilisation penetrated Kumasi for a moment, and when the expedition returned to the coast the Ashantis were left to their fetishes, human sacrifices and slave trading.

Subsequently, the Treaty of Fomena was signed; under the terms of this agreement, the Ashantis relinquished all claims to Denkera, Akim, Assin, Adansi, and the coastal forest, and promised to give up their practices of slavery and human sacrifice, and to pay indemnities. His people were rankled by this humiliation and, later in 1874, Kofi Karikari was de-stooled – that is, deposed as ruler.

For 20 years peace reigned but the Ashanti did little or nothing to comply with the terms of the treaty. In 1894 they were offered the benefits of becoming a British Protectorate, but judging the benefits to involve only the abandonment of a way of life to which they were attached, they refused. In 1895 another force went to Kumasi to compel Ashanti compliance with the Treaty of Fomena. As in 1874, British troops were used. The capital was entered without resistance and Prempeh, the Asantehene or King of the Ashanti, was banished to the coast. This was bitterly resented by the Ashanti but they were in no posi-

tion to do anything about it. In 1897 Ashanti was declared a British Protectorate and a Resident with a Gold Coast Constabulary escort was established in Kumasi. A very fine fort, barracks and a jail were built and peace reigned. Meanwhile Ashanti resentment smouldered and in 1900, without warning, a well-organised revolt broke out.

In 1899 it was announced that Sir Frederick Hodgson, the new Governor of the Gold Coast, would visit Kumasi the next year. To the Ashanti it offered the opportunity they had been waiting for. If the Governor were kidnapped he could be held as a hostage against the return of Prempeh and the restoration of Ashanti independence. It was unlikely, because of the South African War and the Boxer Rebellion in China, that any British troops could be spared to restore the situation. The Ashanti held locally enlisted troops and constabulary in contempt but after 1874 had a very healthy respect for British volleys and British bayonets. The stage was set for revenge.

The Governor set out from Accra on 13 March 1900, clearly expecting no trouble as he took Lady Hodgson with him and the escort was limited to an NCO and 20 men of the Constabulary, plus some European staff, servants and porters, some 400 in all who entered Kumasi on 25 March 1900. On 18th April Major Morris, Commissioner of the Northern Territories, hearing the Ashanti tribes had risen and were threatening Kumasi, set out on a 350-mile march through the jungle with less than 200 men, a 7-pounder gun and a Maxim, en route picking up another 60 men. Brushing aside resistance at Sekodumasi and other places, where the disciplined firepower of repeating rifles and the Maxim scattered the natives, he reached Kumasi on 15th May. Here they were trapped without much food and ammunition; after some sorties, the party left on 23rd June to make a fighting retreat under constant harassment until reaching friendly territory. Under Colonel Willcocks, with a force sent from Nigeria, operations to put down the rebellion continued until late November 1900.

4 The Baluchis

Sind lay in the valley of the River Indus, between India and Afghanistan in what today is Pakistan; by all accounts in 1843 it was not a particularly pleasant place as Upper Sind is notorious for heat, frequently 130°F in the shade; air full of dust, water stinking and brackish and rife with malaria of a malignant kind. At this time it was a native kingdom with chieftainship divided among the Amirs of Kyrpur (Upper Sind); Hyderabad (Lower Sind) and Mirpur on the borders of the eastern desert. Its population was slightly more than a million, formed of four distinct elements – Sindians proper, Hindus, Baluchis of the Plain, and Baluchis of the mountains. In 1838 when the British Army marched to Afghanistan through Upper Sind, the Amirs had been forced into compliance with British demands, and the resulting signs of hostility caused General Sir Charles Napier to be sent with a new and more stringent treaty.

Napier was undoubtedly one of the most extraordinary soldiers of the nineteenth century; a much-wounded Peninsular War veteran 60 years old at this time, he was a bewhiskered, bespectacled eccentric whose utterances seemed to fit him for his task. He believed that 'the great recipe for quieting a country is a good thrashing first and great kindness afterwards; the wildest chaps are thus tamed...' And 'the human mind is never better disposed to gratitude and attachment than when softened by fear...'

A contemporary source describing the situation in Sind, wrote:

'These Ameers governed Scinde by the sword alone. The Beloochees were their paid mercenaries, who were at full liberty to mutilate or kill any Scindian or Hindu at their pleasure or caprice. They disliked the presence of all foreigners, restricted commerce, and though the soil of Scinde is fertile, and the people naturally industrious, under their barbarous misrule it was the most poverty-stricken land in all Asia.

'Like William in England, after Hastings, these Ameers, to form hunting-grounds, laid waste in sixty years a fourth part of their fertile land in Scinde. They were slave-dealers, and infanticide was an organised system among them.'

The military strength of the Amirs was variously estimated at from 30,000 to double that number of warriors of considerable martial prowess; similar in weaponry and fighting-style to their Northern compatriots, the Pathans, Baluchis were said to be 'the best swordsmen in the world'. In addition to the sword, they were armed with matchlock muskets, long knives and round convex shields. Not particularly prepossessing (being regarded as a mark of effeminacy cleanliness was not a Baluchi virtue), by custom tribesmen wore all-white (but invariably filthy) clothing – a long ankle-length robe resembling the large, loose angarka worn by Pathans, loose cotton pantaloons, and a long cotton sash (lungi) used as a cummerbund around the waist or as a shawl-type covering worn over the shoulder; on the head a turban wound round a small cap, usually red – their only concession to wearing all-white; and curved-up sandals (chaplis) of leather or palm-leaves. Convention decreed that most Baluchis wore their hair long, in oily curls, with the obligatory heavy beard and whiskers.

Characteristically, Napier could hardly wait to settle things with the Amirs, and when informed that a force of at least 25,000 were mustered at Meanee, on 17 February 1843, he marched against them with 2,200 men, all native units except 500 men (mostly Irish) of HM 22nd Regiment. The Baluchi could be seen in a dry riverbed about 1,000 yards away; under heavy artillery fire Napier's small force assembled with his 12 guns on the right; in columns of regiments they advanced under fire to within 200 yards of the enemy, deployed into line and charged. What followed is vividly related in an account published at the time:

'The Beloochees, having their muskets laid ready in rest along the summit, waited until our troops were within fifty yards ere they poured in

Sir Charles Napier's cavalry chasing a Baluchi force in Sind, 1843.

44

Battle of Dubba, March 14th, 1843.

their fire. The rapid pace of the British, with the steepness of the slope, deceived them in aiming, yet the loss was great. Reaching the river-bank and looking down at the closely-packed mass of weapon-waving tribesmen waiting to receive them, the men halted and staggered back, in utter amazement at the flashing forest of sword-blades that glittered in their front.

'Thick as standing corn,' says Napier, 'and gorgeous as a field of flowers, stood the Beloochees in their many-coloured garments and turbans; they filled the broad deep bed of the ravine, they clustered on both banks, and covered all the plain beyond. Guarding their heads with their large dark shields, they shook their sharp swords gleaming in the sun, their shouts rolling like a peal of thunder, as with frantic gestures they dashed forward, with demoniac strength and ferocity full against the front of the 22nd. But with shouts as loud, and shrieks as wild and loud as theirs, and hearts as big and arms as strong, the Irish soldiers met them with that queen of arms, the bayonet, and sent their

foremost masses rolling back in blood.

'The Beloochees would not yield ground, their screams and shouts could be heard over the pealing musketry that filled the air as the native swordsmen, shields held high and blades drawn back, strove to break through the British ranks. Closing in dense masses, the rear urging on the front, again the Beloochees came on, and amid the rolling of musketry, shouts and yells, the dreadful rush of their swordsmen was seen along the whole extended line and such an unequal fight ensued as seldom occurs in modern war. With sword in hand, and round shield braced on arm, these wild warriors – sprung from the men of the Gedrosian deserts – came pouring on, in the fierceness of their valour, and the utter recklessness of existence, striving to break into the scarlet ranks, but striving in vain!'

'No fire of small arms,' says Sir William Napier (colonel of the 22nd), 'no thrust of bayonets, no sweeping discharges of grape from the guns, which were planted in one fearful mass on the right, could drive these gallant soldiers back. They gave their breasts to be shot; they leaped upon the guns by twenties at a time; their dead rolled down the steep slope by hundreds; but the gaps in their masses were continually being filled up from the rear; the survivors of the front rank still pressed forward with unabated fury, and the bayonet and the sword clashed in full and frequent conflict.'

Then Napier ordered the Bengal and Sind cavalry to attack the Baluchi right; crossing the river bed to the plain beyond, they charged along the enemy rear, causing a momentary falter. It was enough for the 22nd to redouble their efforts and push the Baluchis back into the deep river-bed; then, doggedly and reluctantly, they began to retire on all sides.

'For three hours had that living tide of valiant Beloochees held their ground against that still more valiant little band, when they began to give way, and slinging their broad shields upon their backs for protection, began to retire, with their fierce dark faces half turned to their pursuers.'

'Upon those retiring shields volley after volley rattled, and many a bullet found a deadlier billet, until our men grew tired of slaughtering, or their pouches became empty.' Yet the Beloochees, 'those stern and implacable warriors,' says Napier, 'preserved their habitual swinging stride, and would not quicken it to a run, though death was at their heels.' It was a soldier's battle with no quarter asked nor given and casualties were heavy:

'Our losses were 6 European officers, 60 sergeants and privates killed; 14 officers and 200 privates wounded; but the casualties of the Be-loochees were enormous. A careful computation gives it at 6,000 slain; and 1,000 of their corpses formed one vast hecatomb in the ravine alone.'

Napier wrote to his brother Henry: '. . . when I saw their masses, each strong enough to have smashed us, I saw no safety but in butchery; it was we or they who must die.' Only three un-wounded prisoners were taken.

A month later, reinforced to 5,000 men and 19 guns, Napier attacked 26,000 Baluchis in a skil-fully chosen position with an unturnable flank resting on the River Fullailli at Dubba near Hyderabad. In another desperate battle that cost 270 officers and men (the long-suffering 22nd los-ing 147) to the Baluchis' 5,000 dead, Napier utterly destroyed the power of the Amirs and cleared the territory of lawless hordes of marauders.

'Numerous, bold, desperate, and rapid in movement, it took some hard fighting and much toil to achieve this. Doodiah Khan, chief of the Jackranees, and Toork Ali were the most formid-able of these outlaws; but all were subdued in the end. The Scindian people were delighted with this change of masters; and the warlike Be-loochees, whose swords were no longer required, kept grimly and disdainfully aloof.'

The Baluchi armies Napier met in Sind were quite undisciplined – it was his dash and vigour plus the enthusiasm he engendered in his troops that won the day. Singular in an age when arche-typal generals could always be relied upon to appear and win a war for the Queen, Sir Charles Napier deserves the last word: 'We have taught the Baluchi that neither his sun, nor his deserts, nor his jungles, nor his nullahs can stop us. He will never face us more!' And in this respect, Napier was a true prophet.

5 The Boers

The First and Second Boer Wars were clashes between two vastly diverse fighting traditions, when the Dutchmen of South Africa, highly mobile irregulars fighting on familiar fields, took on a British Army that found difficulty in shaking the centuries-old dust of the parade ground from their boots. For almost a century there had been a clash of Boer and British interests in South Africa, culminating in 1877, when the British annexed the Boer Republic of the Transvaal, two years later declaring it a Crown colony. Sir William Lanyon, Administrator of the Transvaal, badly underestimated the strength of Boer feelings, less than a week before the revolt, saying: 'The Boers . . . are incapable of any united action, and they are mortal cowards, so anything they do will be but a spark in the pan.' Determined to fight for their independence, in December 1880 the Boers openly revolted, taking up arms against Britain when at Bronker's Spruit a Boer commando unit ambushed a small detachment of white-helmeted British redcoats, marching behind their band across the open veld. The Regulars' volleys of rifle fire that invariably blasted natives from their path had little effect at long range against concealed Boer marksmen who brought down 155 out of 259 men in ten minutes, forcing the remainder to surrender. It was almost a duplication of similar actions 100 years before during the American Revolution, when Regular troops had been mown down by concealed farmers, all masters of their weapons.

Sir George Pomeroy Colley, High Commissioner for South-Eastern Africa, led out a force of just over 1,000 British Regulars, including some cavalry and four guns, to disperse a Boer force on Laings Nek, a ridge forming a natural boundary between the Transvaal and Natal. Despite showing considerable bravery, in a badly handled action Colley's force suffered a severe defeat, losing 198 casualties – the 58th Regiment had to bury 75 officers and men out of a total strength of 494, barely saving their colours. It is ironical that the very last foemen to see British colours in the field were un-uniformed Boer farmers, because never again were they permitted to be taken into battle. The Boers lost 14 killed and 27 wounded; they showed great humanity towards the British wounded left lying in the field. In his dispatches after the battle General Colley wrote:

'Of the numbers of the Boers and their losses it is difficult to form any reliable estimate. Judging, however, by the numbers who actually showed at the points attacked and by information obtained from various sources, I should put their number at about 2,000. Considering the excellent cover under which they mostly fought, I cannot suppose that their losses were heavy. I must do my adversaries the justice to say that they fought with great courage and determination. A good deal of the fighting was at short ranges of twenty to one hundred yards, and the Boers showed no fear of our troops, but rather advanced to meet them. I have also to acknowledge the courtesy shown by some of their leaders in giving facilities for the care and removal of the wounded. I shall hold this camp until I receive reinforcements sufficient to enable me to renew the attack.'

Ten days later, after the confident Boers had intercepted his lines of communication, Colley took a small force with two mountain-guns to the Ingogo River area but they were driven back by accurate fire from the Winchester repeaters or Westley-Richards cap-rifles of the Boers, who had no artillery; they lost 139 officers and men against the Boers' 8 killed and wounded. Despite his two defeats, Colley now led between 400 and 500 men by night to the top of Majuba Hill, the highest point in the area; disturbed at seeing them on the hilltop when daylight came, the Boers soon recovered to set up a murderous fire and clawed their way up the steep slopes. They made such skilful use of dead ground that their marksmanship demoralised Colley's men who, outnumbered and plagued by the accurate fire, eventually broke and fled down the precipitous slopes, leaving General Colley dead behind them. An untrained bunch of 180 Boer farmers had assaulted a seemingly impregnable position held

Boer sharpshooters near Ladysmith.

by more than double their number of regular soldiers commanded by one of Britain's leading generals, and completely routed them.

Majuba Hill, where, with most officers and NCOs down, the British Regulars, seasoned veterans of the North-West Frontier and the Afghan Campaign of the previous year, broke and fled, possibly confirmed a military theory that when veterans panic the result is far worse than among less-seasoned troops. There British soldiers, rigidly trained to fight shoulder-to-shoulder in two-deep firing lines, were lambs ready for the slaughter against the almost uncanny marksmanship of the hidden Boers. In this style of war the accepted formations of Regular armies could not cope, because the small company unit did not have high enough standards of morale and physical courage.

A peace treaty was hastily signed, but this minor war in which the British had been humiliated had settled nothing; the Boers had gained confidence and British pride was dented – not a good augury for future peace. Even Queen Victoria believed these 'horrible people' should

be taught a lesson, and the opportunity came in 1899, when the Boer Republic of the Transvaal and the Orange Free State renounced Imperial rule and firmly refused to accept the principle of one large dominion of South Africa united under the British Crown. Subsequently Kruger mobilised his commandos on 27 September 1899, and when his ultimatum became effective at 5.00 p.m. on 11th October, Britain found herself at war with the Boer Republics. In a sense it was not unwelcome as Britain was determined that a lot of irritating uncouth Boers should not disturb Imperial peace, as it would be embarrassing in other parts of the world – particularly India – if word got round that a few thousand armed and rebellious farmers could shake the British Empire. It was considered inconceivable that this wild and undisciplined army could hope to withstand the finest parade-ground army in the world – but in the event the Boers, well versed in the use of horse and gun, fighting on their own familiar terrain and employing every available male from 16 to 60 years of age, became an invariably elusive, invisible and deadly enemy. Lacking a uniform, they did not look very impressive, but from the youngest to the oldest, they were expert shots and, through a long history of wars with natives, possessed an innate knowledge of tactics suitable to local conditions.

The total number of Boers at the height of the campaign was probably about 50,000, including Dutch rebels from Natal and Cape Colony, who did not compare as fighting men with the tough frontiersmen. From 16 to 60, each Boer was a member of a local militia grouped into commando units of various sizes (according to the population of the district, and varying from 300 to 4,000) to form an army made up entirely of mounted infantry capable of bewildering mobility. In larger districts commandos were split into units named after their originating city or town. The only Regular force in the Boer Army was the Staats Artillerie, about 700 strong; plus the paramilitary South African Republic Police (ZARPs) with about 2,000 men.

Victor Pohl, son of an Orange Free State farmer, was only 13 when the war began; later he recalled the scene when a commando gathered to go out into the field:

'Soon there were gathered a large number of farmer-soldiers, hefty, clear-eyed, bronzed, and good-natured men from the open veld... Sitting their horses like cowboys, they wore what they had stood in when they were called up, and their rifles and bandoliers were slung carelessly on their persons according to individual inclination. A raincoat or blanket, or both, were rolled tightly and fastened to the pommel or tail of each saddle, and in most cases saddle-bags stuffed to bursting with boer-rusks, bread, and biltong (dried meat), completed their outfits. To an outsider this motley and unwarlike gathering would have appeared to be without leaders or discipline, for the Boer leaders did not differ in appearance from the rest of the slouching burghers. And yet when they addressed the men they were listened to with earnest attention, although not with parade-ground rigidity. What these men lacked in military discipline was largely made up for by their independence of thought and action and their sense of responsibility. Moreover many of the men were deeply religious, and all these qualities, combined with their profound faith in their cause, their reliance on themselves and their Mausers, and the knowledge that they were fighting for their homes and country, made of this undisciplined crowd a formidable army, one to whose prowess the civilized world was to pay tribute.'

The Boer style of life as farmers and hunters

taught them to be skilful with the rifle, and from boyhood each man's acquaintance with cover and terrain produced an irregular firepower capacity from concealed positions capable of causing devastating casualties to close-order formations.

More than 70 commandos and similar groups fought in the Boer Army during the Second South African War of 1899–1902, including foreign volunteers, and can be grouped as follows:

Transvaal Commandos: Bethel; Bloemhof; Boksburg; Carolina; Ermelo; Gatsrand; Germiston; Groot River; Heidelberg; Heilbron; Jeppstown; Johannesburg; Klerksdorp; Krugersdorp; Lichtenburg; Luneberg; Lydenberg; Marico; Midleburg; Piet Retief; Potchefstroom; Pretoria; Rustenberg; Standerton; Swaziland; Utrecht; Vryheid; Wakkerstroom; Watersberg; ZARPS (Zuide Afrikanische Republika Poliz); Van Damm's, Transvaal, Johannesburg Pretoria Police; Zoutspansberg;

Orange Free State Commandos: Bethlehem; Bethulie; Bloemfontein; Boshof; Brandfort; Caledon River; Dewetsdorp; Edenburg; Fauresmith; Ficksburg; Frankfort; Free State; Harrismith; Hoopstad; Jacobsdal; Kroonstad; Ladybrand; Moroka; Philippolis; Ramdan; Rand Police; Rouxville; Senekal; Smithfield; Ventersburg; Vrede; Wepener; Winburg;

Country of Commando Unknown: Fordsburg; Middenvelder;

Foreign Volunteer Units: Blake's (1st), Irish Brigade; Lynch's (2nd), Irish Brigade; Chicago, Irish-American Volunteers; American Volunteers; Hollander Corps; German Corps; Italian Corps; Scandinavian Corps; Russian Corps (Don Cossacks).

The largest foreign contingent was the Dutch, with 250 men in various commandos and another 400 in the German Corps; there were 400 French, 300 Americans, 200 Irish, 200 Italians, 225 Russians and 150 Scandinavians, in national legions and in commandos. Quite unlike any others in the world these military units were formed of sub-units of perhaps 150–200 men under a field-cornet, in turn composed of sections of 25 men or so, under a corporal. The commandant of each commando was elected, often more for political reasons than for any military expertise; a popular commandant attracted more men than did an unpopular one and Boers would leave a commando and join another if they lost faith in their leader. Like all militia and irregulars, they had the habit of leaving and riding home when they felt like it, particularly if it was near to harvest-time. Discipline was virtually unknown, and although a Boer could be compelled by law to serve in the local commando he could not be forced to obey orders; military decisions were made only after long discussions when everyone had their say. Both as individuals and collectively Boers lacked disciplinary control and only a gifted few of their leaders had any concept of tactics or strategy. The traditional Boer tactics were, in fact, to keep themselves mobile and, if possible, the enemy immobile; this they had learned from numerous wars fought with the native Africans.

In loose organisation, groups of commandos united to form an 'army' for a specific operation or area; thus the activities in the Tabanyama and Spion Kop areas in January 1900 were conducted by the commandos of Boksberg; Carolina; German; Heidelburg; Krugersdorp; Pretoria; Rustenburg and Utrecht – with two 75-mm Creusot field-guns; one 75-mm Krupp field-gun, and a pom-pom on Tabanyama; a 75-mm field-gun on the koppie from which Botha commanded the battle; and a Krupp 75-mm and a pom-pom on the ridges to the east of Spion Kop. Immediately on the outbreak of war, commandos began to cross the border of Cape Colony and ride into the province of Natal, where about 14,000 Boers, under Commandant-General Piet Joubert, rode in bitter cold through the mountains and down into the plains, past that symbol of past British humiliation – Majuba Hill. 'As far as the eye could see,' one of them wrote, 'the plain was alive with horsemen, guns and cattle, all steadily going forward.' Family grocers, wives, children, even native servants travelled with Boer Commandos, living with them in laagers or camps; to them, war was a family affair. Acting as rallying points well behind the battle line, laagers of supply wagons were used by the Boers who, accustomed to travelling light in open country and being more mobile than the British, had their laagers captured in very few cases.

Fighting for their independence, the Boers were very patriotic and commandos carried into battle the Transvaal or Orange Free State flags – whichever was applicable; the former was com-

General Joubert.

monly called the 'Vierkleur', being red, white and blue (from top down) with a wide green border running from top to bottom at the pole edge. The Orange Free State colours – from the top down – orange, white, orange, white, orange; with transverse red, white and blue stripes in an oblong at the top left-hand corner (pole side).

Boers provided their own horses, although in most battles the commandos fought on foot with their mounts corralled in some convenient clump of rocks nearby. None wore uniform, in action they appeared just as when they left the farm, in dun-brown or black civilian clothing with the customary slouch-hat of varying colours although black seemed popular; older men and traditionalists wore black claw-hammer coats and low-crown top hats, officers trimmed with crêpe. Shoes, boots or soft veldschoen; with one or more bandoliers over the shoulders and crossed on the body; some had home-made waistcoats with sewn-in bandoliers in rows – pictures indicate three rows of seven pouches each holding five bullets (105 bullets in all). They also wore three-pouch bandoliers around the ankle, containing nine bullets.

Only the Staats Artillerie and the Police Commandos wore recognised uniform; in the field the Transvaal Artillerie had tunics and trousers mouse-coloured, off-white, cream or light khaki with dark blue collars and shoulder-boards.

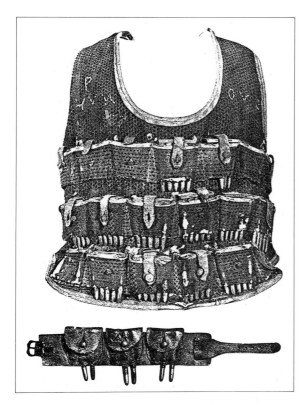

Home-made waistcoat and bandolier.

Orange Free State gunners wore an all-khaki uniform in the field, with orange collar and shoulder-boards. Both had slouch (bush) hats. Damm's Police Commando (ZARPs; Transvaal Police, etc.) wore dark brown corduroy jacket; grey or khaki trousers; khaki bush hat, brown leather belts and riding boots; possibly a black bush hat. Almost everyone had a beard which, becoming unkempt in the field, added to their untidy appearance, but what the Boers lacked in smartness they made up for in determination – their military effectiveness was not measured by polished leather or gleaming brass, but by skill with rifle and riding.

It was said at the time: 'Let no man despise the shooting of the Boers, they are strictly marksmen.' And they certainly made telling use of their German-made state-provided repeating Mauser rifle, with its faculty of allowing pre-loaded clips to be inserted and firing to be almost continuous; using smokeless powder and sighted up to 2,200 yards, they were more accurate and harder to pinpoint than the British sol-

dier's Lee-Metford. When the Boer government purchased these rifles they refused bayonets, feeling it disgusting to fight too close to the enemy; being at a distinct disadvantage against bayonet-armed troops they hated close-quarters fighting and always tried to avoid it. This does not mean Boers never fought hand-to-hand; tough, fit and courageous, they acquitted themselves well at Spion Kop and Inniskilling Hill. Believing cold steel used by humans on each other to be inhumane, the Boers were greatly incensed when British Lancers got among the fleeing burghers at Elandslaagt early in the war. Not surprisingly, as they were armed civilians and not trained soldiers, a lot of Boers were distinctly unhappy when under shell-fire.

Probably the most surprising aspect of the Boer Army was their artillery, up-to-the-minute modern guns purchased from European armaments manufacturers for just such a war as this. Until long-barrelled quick-firing 4.7-in 12-pounder guns were brought ashore from warships, mounted on land-carriages and handled by Royal Navy gun-crews, the British had no guns to match the Boer's four Creusot 5.9-in (15-cm) guns (known as 'Long Toms') capable of hurling a 96-lb shell a distance of four miles. Initially written off by the British as 'immobile fortress cannon', they were manoeuvred rapidly and competently by their crews, who showed great ingenuity in working them without the usual elaborate platforms and mountings, sometimes firing from the top of a boulder-strewn hill believed accessible only to little mountain-guns. Then there were the devastatingly effective 75-mm Krupp field-pieces, their extreme range of 6,600 yards outranging the British 15-pounder howitzer. Botha, the Boer commander at Spion Kop, said his shells 'told with terrible effect upon the unfortunate Tommies on the narrow ledge of the hill...'; there is little doubt that Boer artillery fire decided the battle.

The weapon the British soldiers dreaded more than any other was the Vickers-Maxim 'pom-pom', dubbed thus because of the noise made when firing 37-mm explosive shells, one round every two seconds, in bursts of about 20, at ranges of up to 2,750 yards with timed fuses, or 4,400 yards with percussion fuses. Possessing devastating effect on morale, the little 1-pounder shells wiped out complete gun-crews and carelessly grouped bodies of infantry; they were particularly telling at Magersfontein and Colenso.

The Free State Artillery.

Numbers and distribution of Boer artillery were as follows:

Transvaal Staats Artillerie: 1,000 men; 22 Vickers-Maxim 37-mm pom-poms; four 5·9-in (15-cm) Creusot guns; four 4·7-in (12-cm) Creusot howitzers; six 75-mm (15-pounder) Creusot guns; four 75-mm Krupp howitzers; eight 75-mm Krupp field-guns; four other (type and size unknown);

Orange Free State Staats Artillerie: 300 men; six 75-mm Krupp field-guns; two Vickers-Maxim 37-mm pom-poms; four other (type and size unknown);

Guns Captured from the Jameson Raid: Six Krupp field-guns (probably 75 mm); six Maxim machine-guns.

Then there were guns captured from the British; one 7-pounder mountain battery (four guns) captured at Mafeking from the armoured train *Mosquito*; four field-guns (probably 15-pounder Armstrongs) captured at Stormberg; two 7-pounder mountain guns captured at Naauw-poort; ten 15-pounder Armstrongs (with 13 wagons of ammunition) captured at Colenso.

The Staats Artillerie of the two Republics were their pride and joy; the gunners were recruited and trained before the war (some overseas and some by foreign instructors – many gunners were German or Swedish volunteers); they were provided with uniforms and regular pay. Frequently they showed they were worthy of their distinctive standing – General White's dispatch after the battle of Elandslaagte expressed admiration of the dogged courage of Boer artillerymen – their guns frequently silenced by overwhelming weight of British fire, they persistently returned and reopened fire. At Talana Hill in Natal, Boers of Louis Mayer's commando dragged five or six guns up the hill under cover of darkness; on opening fire they were engaged by 12 RHA guns and silenced in about 20 minutes. The Boers, not being so highly trained and having inferior equipment, could only fire slowly and less accurately, and very few of their shells exploded due to them being 'plugged shell' with a plug in the hole intended for the fuse so, to all intents and purposes, they were old-fashioned solid-shot. When the hill was stormed the Boers fought tenaciously to save their guns and managed to carry off every one of them with their wagons, dragging them down by sheer manpower to the clump of rocks below where horse-teams awaited.

The rigid drills and customs of the Royal Artillery brought guns into action neatly spaced in rows of six, making them extremely difficult to conceal. Even though the guns were using smokeless powder, the still air and sun of South Africa caused a firing gun to generate a faint haze, and after a few minutes of rapid fire six closely concentrated guns were covered by enough of a haze to betray and pinpoint their position clearly. The Boers, with far fewer guns at their disposal, dispersed them singly, carefully concealed along the whole front so that the slight haze created by a single gun was almost impossible to detect, making the British artillery fire at random. Battery commanders invariably sought to position their six guns on hard ground, which allowed Boer high-explosive shells to burst with maximum effect, greatly magnifying the casualties caused by a single shell.

In laudable attempts to provide their infantry with the closest possible support, British artillery tended to deploy their batteries too far forward so that Boer rifles took a heavy toll of both gunners and horses, frequently causing them to be withdrawn. This was particularly the case at Colenso, where British guns unlimbered at 1,000 yards from the Boer trenches, only for the gunners to be mown down by hails of Mauser bullets and the devastating 'pom-pom' shells. In a gallant but abortive action heavy casualties were sustained by gunners and supporting infantry until the survivors were made prisoner and the Boers carried off ten guns. In defence of those in charge of the British artillery, it must be agreed that however closely they had studied the role of artillery in previous wars, there were not many practical lessons of use against a surprisingly tough enemy on battlefields whose extent contrasted greatly with the overcrowded terrains of Europe.

General Cronje, obviously aware that rows of prominent buildings or low hills hold a magnetic attraction for gun-layers, sited his gun-pits at Moddar River in carefully concealed positions 200 yards in front of a range of low hills; alternative gun-pits were dug elsewhere for his guns to move to when their positions were pinpointed. For much of the day shells burst harmlessly in their rear but eventually the superior number of guns told and the Boers withdrew, leaving behind one of their heavy guns that had been knocked out. There was a gross overestimation of the effectiveness of shrapnel, which, although devastating to infantry or gun teams caught in the open, did little damage to men in trenches or sheltered by rocks and earthworks. There were many instances of Boer positions being thoroughly 'combed' by shrapnel, only for the assaulting British infantry to be mown down by well-concealed Boers, who had hardly suffered any casualties.

To the British, whose military leaders invariably came from the upper classes (with the notable exceptions of Field Marshall 'Wullie' Robertson and General Hector McDonald) Boer generals looked exactly the same as the mass of ragged farmers they led. It was to be expected, because they were Citizen-Generals who led the Boer Nation; but before the struggle had reached its end there were very different types of Boer general in the field, separated from Cronje and Joubert in age, ability and character by more than a generation. At the start of the war the Boer generals were relatively old men – Piet Joubert, commanding the Transvaal forces, was a 68-year-old lawyer with all the careful and unaggressive traits of his profession. He was determined to avoid casualties even at the cost of dramatic victories – thus, despite frantic pleas from younger commanders to go for Durban, he lay leisurely siege to Ladysmith. 'He was a kindly, well-meaning old man,' noted one frustrated young Boer fighter, 'who had done useful service – but he gave the impression of being bewildered at the heavy responsibility now resting upon him.'

The patriarchal General Cronje, whose military knowledge came from biblical studies rather than from military textbooks, was a natural master of modern warfare on his own selected terrain. His entrenchments were sophisticated and unique in that, contrary to all established practice, they were frequently on forward slopes, sometimes in three rising tiers so that every rifle could simultaneously be brought to bear. Boer fire control was excellent; at Modder River the Lancer patrols and the leading infantry formations were allowed to approach within 500 yards before a devastating fire opened on them. Going to earth, seeking cover in every little shallow and behind every anthill or rock, the sweating British infantry were pinned down without food or water throughout a blazing African day. During the night Cronje stole away to an even stronger position at Magersfontein.

Joubert's death in 1900 accentuated the general gloom caused by General Piet (Honest Piet) Cronje's surrender at Paardeburg a few weeks before. Like Joubert, Cronje had a distaste for decisive action and wasted valuable time by besieging valueless Mafeking. Roberts, one of the few British commanders to appreciate the limitations of infantry when up against entrenched modern weapons, outflanked Cronje and herded the Boer Army into a river-bed at Paardeberg. It could have been a bloodless victory had not Kitchener, left in operational command,

Louis Botha.

would have made their mark in any army at any time; all were to be a thorn in the flesh of the British for months to come.

The cherished and hallowed traditions and the memories of the British Army came to nought in South Africa where there was no inspiration to be gained from the hissing, well-aimed bullet fired by an invisible foe, nor any stimulus to be gained from the cries of battle, the wind-rippled colours, or lines of men manoeuvring to drums and bugles on the sun-baked veld. Those in command of the British Army in 1899, displaying a total ignorance of the military lessons of the previous half-century, attempted to fight a major war with outdated, outmoded tactics and weapons. As constituted, the British Army was singularly ill-suited in almost every respect to cope with the Boers, who were an organised, skilled and determined enemy armed with modern weapons, impossible to defeat with the tactics that were successful against ill-armed and undisciplined natives. The majority of the British soldiers had campaigning experience and all, from the generals down to the men in the ranks, shared a complacent conviction that the undrilled and quaintly dressed farmers would soon take to their heels when they came up against the disciplined Regular regiments of the British Army.

In the early days of the war first-class British infantry, in formations resembling those of Waterloo, were launched in hopeless frontal assaults against the concentrated power of modern rifles competently handled by superb marksmen in carefully prepared positions. Although numbers were small by Continental standards, proportionate losses were very heavy. It took some time for the generals to realise the futility of sending men in close order over open ground against hidden riflemen, but then the British infantry began to advance in extended order in short rushes, sometimes to be successful against even the heaviest fire. Soon it was discovered that the Boers, typically for partially trained Irregulars, were very sensitive to outflanking movements. Their tactics of digging themselves in on features of great natural strength invulnerable to frontal assault positively invited outflanking movements by cavalry and horse artillery. But the Boers were no fools, and, aware that such a position once enveloped was doomed, they were very alert to flanking movements that might turn their main position; on the slightest

lost over 1,000 men in a completely unnecessary frontal assault on the Boer position, before Roberts withdrew all troops and subjected the unhappy Boer commandos (including women and children) to such an artillery pounding that this main Boer Army surrendered, virtually to concede the war. On 27 February 1900, Cronje was forced to surrender with 4,000 men.

Joubert's death and Cronje's surrender were bitter blows to the Boers but cleared the way for younger and more audacious commanders who, aware that the military balance had already shifted decisively against them, devoted their slender resources to a protracted guerrilla campaign. Joubert's successor, Louis Botha, was a 38-year-old farmer who symbolised the Boers' unorthodox approach to warfare, relying on his own personality to maintain the spirits of his hard-pressed men. The other young generals were Koos de la Rey, Christiaan de Wet, and Jan Smuts, all extremely capable commanders who

suspicion of such an occurrence they would slip away at night to another equally strong defensive site. This was a simple matter for the Boer farmer on his hardy little horse with well-worn saddle and bridle, carrying a blanket and a pair of bags for rations and spare cartridges with his rifle and bandolier round his shoulders.

Recent wars had affected British military thought in that it was believed the subsequent immobilisation of Regular infantry in entrenched positions lowered the morale and blighted aggressive spirit; and that such defences were only valuable to troops with insufficient training and experience to fight in open country. The American Civil War, the Franco-Prussian War, the Russo-Turkish War were cited but the most recent example of only a year past in Cuba, when only the dash and courage of the American infantry enabled them to defeat Spanish soldiers armed with repeating rifles and behind cover, was completely ignored. The British pundits triumphantly pointed out that each of these defensively inclined armies had lost their war. But had the untrained, irregular Boer farmers emerged from their entrenchments and advanced *en masse* across open country it would certainly have been the shortest cut to a Boer defeat. The Boers did not refuse to fight it out through lack of aggression but because they were fully aware of the potentialities and limitations of both their own troops and of the British. Skilfully, they husbanded their slender manpower as they made rapid adjustment to battlefield situations, such as quickly learning that soft earth cover (i.e. trenches) was far more satisfactory than hiding amid rocks and kopjes where bursting shells caused destructive rock splinters to lance in every direction. The Boers were always ready to make a speedy withdrawal and took good care not to be caught in the open. Choosing a good defensive position, they dug trenches or rifle-pits, bunched horses behind adjacent cover for a quick getaway, and fought as long as possible to cause maximum casualties to the attackers. This caused Kitchener to grumble that '...they won't stand up and fight fair'. A young English officer asked what Boers looked like replied, 'Can't say...been fighting 'em for six months but haven't seen one yet.'

The 10–17 December 1899 became known to the British as the 'Black Week' through three humiliating defeats at Magersfontein, Colenso (with ten guns lost) and Stormberg – on all three

fields the British Empire was utterly defeated by a pair of nearly-bankrupt Boer Republics. At that time, Magersfontein was arguably the most appalling reverse suffered by British arms in any conflict since the American War of Independence. The Boer commander positioned his men in trenches at the *foot* of the ridge instead of on *top* where everyone expected them to be; this gave them a field of fire from which they could blaze away and hardly miss the close-rank attackers. The British commander Lord Methuen initially combed the ridge with a battery of horse artillery and naval 4.7-in guns (hauled into action by 32 bullocks). The hail of shrapnel and high explosive did not provoke a single answering shot because Cronje had entrenched his riflemen and his guns some 200–300 yards forward of the ridge, protected by a thick apron of barbed wire hung with tin cans. This was followed by a night advance of the Highland Brigade, densely packed in quarter-column with guides carrying ropes to preserve perfect alignment, who stumbled into the Boer trip-wires some 400 yards in front of the concealed trenches to unleash a devastating hail of fire that caused 500 casualties within ten minutes. For the rest of the day, the Highland Brigade lay on the open veld under a heavy fire and a pitiless African sun, without food or water. When they pulled back at nightfall they had lost a quarter of their total numbers, including their commander General Wauchope.

After the capture of Pretoria in mid-1900, the Boers turned to guerrilla warfare; their forces infuriatingly still at large and seeming to move as freely as desired, to mingle with the population or disappear into the vastness of the veld, reappearing with dramatic suddenness to attack an unsuspecting column or isolated stronghold. While the British were endeavouring to round up the hard-riding and elusive commandos of De Wet and Louis Botha, small groups of British infantry in widely spaced blockhouses had to be supplied by wagon convoy. These caravans were particularly vulnerable to the Boer tactic of charging in, firing from the saddle, to overrun the convoy and either destroy it or take prisoner all those who were not killed in the first rush. The captured supplies maintained the commandos in the field for nearly a year. As a considered policy, the British burned Boer farms and imprisoned families, claiming it destroyed the guerrilla's base of supplies, his place of rest, and his source of information. The Boer horsemen were

A Boer outpost.

in the habit of leaving a commando and returning home for a short break, gathering information, and returning with food and a rested horse.

When the dragging war was finally ended, over 400,000 British and Dominions troops had been engaged against less than a quarter of that number; 22,000 British troops had died, the majority from disease.

South Africa was perhaps the last great theatre of war where imaginatively handled, adequately trained and equipped cavalry had the ability to make a decisive mark on the course of the campaign. It was a terrain that permitted wide-sweeping cavalry raids like those of the American Civil War, striking at the long lines of communication necessitated by the heavier supplies (such as ammunition) required by both

sides. Fortunately, the Boers did not have sufficient men adequately to exploit such possibilities!

The Second Boer War was unique in the area over which it was fought and the state of technology that provided the weapons. Earlier, without accurate artillery or automatic weapons, the Boers would have stood no chance in an era of smoke-enshrouded short-range slower musketry; ten years later vast improvements in field communications, plus the advent of aerial reconnaissance and armoured cars, would have made such a war impossible.

It was also the last war fought during the long reign of Queen Victoria and the Boers of South Africa were her final enemies. When the aged Queen drifted slowly from sleep into death on 22 January 1901, in South Africa De Wet the Boer commander was concentrating his forces in preparation for a fresh invasion of Cape Colony.

6   The Burmese

Before invasion by the British East India Company's army in 1824, Burma was truculent and expansionist, perhaps the most powerful monarchy in South-East Asia, and likely to devour Bengal. As with other ancient kingdoms coming up against the British, Burma was given a hard sharp shock by contemporary technological methods of warfare; nevertheless, it required three wars over 60 years – 1824 to 1886 – before being subdued. Perhaps it was lack of British application coupled with adverse environmental conditions rather than Burmese military prowess that made it such a long-drawn-out business. Perhaps it was not expected to be otherwise – in March 1824 when war was declared, British soldiers in India were said to have been delighted – Ensign F. B. Doveton wrote: 'Never shall I forget the shouts of joy with which we welcomed the intelligence of a war with the Burmese. Here would be glory for the young soldier . . . perhaps even an opportunity to sustain a flesh wound, in the easiest possible manner.'

Burmese lack of sophistication was revealed when their greatest general, Maha Bandula, curious to inspect at close quarters one of the 'shells' so terrifying his soldiers, ordered men to fetch one that lay nearby, sputtering and smoking and obviously a dud. Before reaching him the burning fuse was consumed and the carriers blown to pieces – although noted for courage Bandula was unnerved by the occurrence. During the Second Burmese War of 1852, when a Burmese force made a surprise attack upon Martaban, the gunboat *Feroze*, arriving at a point three and a half miles from the White Pagoda sheltering the enemy,

' . . . threw in shot and shell with such precision that the Burmese were forced to seek a more distant spot for safety, while their handsome pagoda was all knocked to pieces . . . a body of them, sorely bewildered to find that our shot could reach them at such a distance began to entrench themselves near another little white pagoda, and deeming its vicinity doubtless holy and safe, they hoisted on it a showy flag. To

Lieutenants Stewart and Baird on board the Feroze, this became a mark at once, and a single shot sent it down in tatters, together with the whole summit of the pagoda, which fell amid the yells of the infuriated Burmese.'

The *Moulmein Times* reported of the subsequent day:

'We understand that the whole Burmese force was commanded by the notorious Dacoit chief and robber, Moung Shoay-loang, and that he had been sent from Ava to retake Martaban, or forfeit his head in case of failure. Wednesday last was, according to the guardian angels of Moung Shoay-loang, considered a lucky day for the exploit; but with what success has been seen.'

Unable to combat the fearful British guns, the Burmese fought in their traditional way by hastily throwing up a ring of bamboo forts to hem in the invader. Glory-seeker Ensign Doveton said of this:

'Stockades sprang up like mushrooms in every direction, so that, look which way we would, there was ever a pleasing variety from which to pick and choose whenever our general wished to relieve the monotony of the cantonment by the excitement of a sortie.'

It was known that:

'The troops of the king of Ava were not very much inclined to come to close quarters with their enemies at any time. Like the Ghoorkas of Nepaul, they preferred getting behind stockades, or wooden barricades, concealed by a leafy screen, which they raised rapidly and ably, rendering them most formidable in point of strength; and they defended them with great perseverance. The province of Rangoon, or Henzawaddy (as it was called by the natives), was well adapted for their irregular mode of warfare. With the exception of a few considerable plains, or rice-grounds, it was covered with a thick jungle, with no roads, but numerous creeks and rivers, which were great impediments to a strange army. There were footpaths through the woods, totally inapplicable, without great labour, for military purposes, and they were impassable in the rainy seasons.'

When hostilities ended, Major Snodgrass wrote:

'...the war...being of a more serious and protracted nature than any in which our Eastern Empire had been engaged for a long series of years; distinguished from all others by the obdurate and determined perseverance of the enemy; and characterised by a series of difficulties, obstacles, and privations to which few armies have been for so long a period subjected.'

Not natural warriors, the Burmese displayed other attributes, as when Bandula, far to the north threatening Bengal with the rainy season upon him, marched his army of 60,000 men over the difficult hills of Arakan, through jungle transformed into a watery nightmare by constant rain, flooded rivers, leeches, mosquitoes and other natural enemies, to arrive before the British at Rangoon. In his *Narrative of the Burmese War*, Major Snodgrass says: '...the Burmese is...half amphibious in his nature...expert with a chopper...unencumbered with... equipage of any kind and carrying a fortnight's rice in a bag slung across his shoulders, he is at all times ready to move'.

Commanders were not noted for their powers of leadership, but Soomba Woongee, sitting down to dinner when told of the approach of the British, cried: 'Drive the audacious strangers away!' Later, he set an example not very common with Burmese commanders by putting himself at the head of a few determined men and attempted in vain to rally his fleeing troops; the prolonged resistance only increased the slaughter, and at length Soomba was killed.

Contemporary illustrations of the first Burmese War show semi-naked soldiers, clad only in a drab striped/checked robe; some wore flat turbans, and they were armed with native swords (dahs), spears, and an occasional matchlock. Regular soldiers wore conical gilded hats said by the British to: 'make many of them striking objects for musketry practice, as they strove to escape...by swimming in the water'. In 1852 Rangoon was defended by picked men from Ava, wearing red uniforms and gilt hats, who fought with great spirit until driven out. A heavy British bombardment was withstood with great firmness, fire being returned with muskets, jingals and light artillery – although it was written at the time:

'Whether inspired by courage or not, the Bur-

Burmese soldiers.

mese soldiers must fight, as the king holds their wives and children in his hands as hostages for their fidelity; and in the former war, Bundoola resorted to the infernal device of chaining his gunners to their cannon, that they might never cease firing till victory was won, or death laid them low.'

Carried over the heads of high-ranking officers were chattahs (umbrellas of office), sometimes gleaming golden in the hot sun. A white chattah is carried over the head of King Mindon of Burma, riding on an elephant, in a print of 1865 showing the king and his soldiers in a procession in Mandalay. The soldiers are dressed in red tunics over a baggy red/white checked 'loincloth'; below it blue trousers with a red stripe tucked into calf-length white gaiters, and sandals; a red conical hat extending back beyond the head, with a white 'tip' resembling a candle on a cake. Others wear blue tunics with black edging, the same red/white 'loincloth' and black/white mottled trousers; gaiters and sandals; black rimless 'bowler-hat' with white bandeau extending up and back in two 'rabbits ears': others wear dark red or brown tunic, patterned red, red/white or red/yellow trousers; gaiters and sandals; on the head, brown rimless 'bowler' hat with yellow bandeau and 'ears'. All are bearing musket and bayonet; officers(?) carry swords over the shoulder; and there is a leading group in more fanciful uniform with wide collar extending over the shoulders; 'plaid' hanging down back; golden 'temple' tall hat with red earpieces; they carry spears and seem to be an elite unit. Many Burmese dead were said to have been athletic men, each wearing a charm.

An elite body of Burmese troops were the king's 'Invulnerables' who '...amply provided with charms, spells and opium, in the ensuing operations afforded much amusement in their "dance of defiance", committing all manner of ludicrous extravagances, with the most prodigal exposure of their persons'. They took part in an attack on a British position at Rangoon:

'At last the time arrived pronounced by the astrologers to be favourable for an attack upon the great pagoda, still the principal point of the British position. At midnight, that attack was made by the "Invulnerables", who had, it was understood, volunteered for the occasion. They emerged from the jungle in a compact body; and, rushing towards the pagoda, encountered a small picket thrown out in front of the British, which retired skirmishing with the enemy, till they reached the stairs of the building, at the summit of which the troops were drawn up; their silent and firm demeanour was strikingly contrasted with the voluble fierceness of the Burmese, who advanced, uttering terrible threats and imprecations against the strangers if they did not immediately leave the sacred temple. They continued to advance, boldly and rapidly, along a narrow path, which led to the north gate of the pagoda; when, suddenly, vivid flashes from the cannon's mouth illuminated the dark atmosphere, and showers of grape and volleys of musketry arrested the onward progress of the assailants. They stood a few minutes; but soon their sense of "invulnerability" departed, and they made for the jungle. No doubt they invented a plausible tale to account for their failure. That failure had one good effect; it prevented them from volunteering upon any more such dangerous encounters, and protected the troops from the harassing movements that had so frequently deprived them of a night's rest.'

Recruiting for the Burmese Army was encouraged by the ageless hope of plunder, causing men to flock in and rally round the standard. On one occasion, each man was paid £20 sterling to encourage him to enlist. The tributary Chan tribes were commanded to contribute their quota and it is recorded that their chiefs embodied, equipped and disciplined an army of 15,000. The Burmese Cavalry arm was almost exclusively composed of horsemen from Cassay (distinguished by the national appellation of 'the Cassay Horse'), or Manipur, a state lying between Burma, Assam and Cachar, and subject to Burma. Riding exotically caparisoned ponies, these people were said to possess supreme skill in the management of their mounts.

In 1852 the Burmese Army was about 50,000 strong. A large proportion were musketeers; irregulars were armed with muskets, bows, spears and the dah, a short native sword with a blade 18 inches long which was always kept very bright and clean, and handled well. They had jingals, a small piece of artillery throwing a ball of from 6 to 12 ounces, mounted on a light carriage handled by two men, or on swivels and fired from walls. They were well provided with implements for erecting stockades and throwing up entrenchments. The energy and engineering skill of the Burmese were suprising – no sooner were positions taken up, than the men began to work with their entrenching tools, and in about two hours their line had disappeared,

'and could only be traced by a parapet of new earth gradually increasing in height, and assuming such form as the skill and science of the engineer suggested. The moving masses which had so lately attracted the anxious attention of the troops, had sunk into the ground; and by any one who had not witnessed the whole scene, the existence of the subterranean legions would not have been credited. By a distant observer, the hills, covered with mounds of earth, would have been taken for anything rather than the approach of an attacking army; but to those who had watched the whole strange proceeding, it seemed the work of enchantment. The trenches were found to be a succession of holes, each capable of containing two men. They were excavated so as to afford shelter both from the weather and the fire on an enemy. Even a shell, lighting in the trench, could at most kill but two men. As it is not the Burmese system to relieve their troops in making these approaches, each hole contained a sufficient supply of rice, water, and fuel for its inmates; and, under the excavated bank, a bed of straw or brushwood was prepared, in which one man could sleep while his comrade watched. When one line of trench was completed, its occupiers, taking advantage of night, pushed forward to where the second line was to be opened; their place being immediately taken up by fresh troops from the rear, and so on.'

The Burmese troops – Regulars and Irregulars – speedily formed a cordon round the British cantonments,

'capable, indeed, of being forced on every point, but possessing, in a remarkable degree, all the qualities necessary for harassing and wearing out in fruitless exertions the strength and energies of European or Indian troops. Hid from view on every side in the darkness of a deep, and, to regular bodies, an impenetrable forest, far beyond which the inhabitants and the cattle of the Rangoon district had been driven, the Burmese chiefs carried on their operations, and matured their future schemes, with vigilance, secrecy, and activity. Neither rumour nor intelligence of what was passing within their posts reached the British cantonments: beyond the invisible line which circumscribed their position, all was mystery or vague conjecture.'

Occasionally war-elephants with howdahs bearing musketeers were encountered; at one action,

'British cavalry under the protection of horse-artillery, charged and rode up to the elephants, who seemed by no means disposed to give way to their comparatively pigmy antagonists. When their drivers (mahouts) were shot, the unwieldy animals, finding themselves no longer under restraint or control, turned their tails upon the foe and walked leisurely back to the fort.'

One can read that, during the periods of hostilities, arsenals throughout Burma were kept in constant employ repairing old arms and making new. Most guns were the usual Eastern ornate type, including 18-pounders, brass and iron guns, and carronades, and many jingals or wall-pieces. Grapeshot was made-up of badly formed iron bullets and bits of metal packed in canvas bags, dipped in dammer (resin) from the East Indian isles.

The defensive works of the Burmese were often immensely strong, such as those at Donabue assailed unsuccessfully by General Cotton's force of about 1,000 men. Major Snodgrass who took part in the attack described:

'... the stockade as extending for nearly a mile along a sloping bank of the Irawaddy, its breadth varying from 500 to 800 yards. This work was composed of solid teak beams, from fifteen to seventeen feet high, driven firmly into the earth. Behind this formidable wooden wall, the old brick ramparts of the place rose to a considerable height; they were connected with the front defences by cross-beams, and afforded a firm and elevated footing to the defenders. Before the right face, or that lowest down the river, two strong outworks were constructed. The advance of a hostile force was still further impeded by a ditch of considerable breadth and depth; the passage of which was rendered still more difficult by the insertion, along the sides and bottom, of spikes, nails, sword-blades, and similar obstructive materials. Beyond the ditch were several rows of strong railing; and there was a formidable abatis in front of all, except on the side next the river. On these works upwards of 150 guns and swivels were mounted. The place was defended by a garrison of 15,000 men. It is thought that if he had passed the whole fortress and taken the works in flank, he might have succeeded, as the movement would have rendered most of the enemy's guns useless. The men were landed, however, and the attack made, on the outworks in front of the right face, which were first reached by the flotilla. One of these works was carried; but at the next the resistance was so stubborn, and its effects so fatal (150 of the assailants being killed and wounded), that a retreat was ordered. This retrograde movement was made so precipitately, that the wounded were left behind. As soon as the troops got on board the flotilla, the boats returned about ten miles down the river, being much tormented by the Burmese war-boats. The next day they were horrified by seeing rafts floating down the river, bearing the wounded who had been left behind the preceding day, and whom the Burmese had crucified, and thus sent adrift. This proceeding, revolting to every humane feeling under any circumstances, was doubly barbarous in the Burmese; for their wounded at the first stockade had been kindly and carefully treated by the British surgeons, and had liberty given them to go where they pleased.'

When the Second Sikh War ended, the Governor-General in India, with troops to spare, decided the truculent Burmese must be brought to heel, as they were failing to abide by the 1826 Treaty. On 12 April 1852, General Sir Henry Godwin's 8,000 men easily took Martaban after a furious bombardment; next day when similarly treating Rangoon, some Burmese soldiers jumped into the river to escape the bombardment 'as if resolved on becoming targets for practice...' wrote an English officer. On 14th April 20,000 Burmese were swept from their main redoubt, the Shwe Dagon Pagoda; Colonel

William F. B. Laurie took part in the action, and wrote: 'It was amusing to see them chevied through the bushes, across the plain where the artillery was drawn up, by the European soldiers. Crack! crack! crack! – away they ran, as if a legion of evil spirits were after them.' In May, with 8,000 men and the fearful artillery, Godwin overcame 7,000 Burmese at Bassein, and by June almost the entire province of Pegu-Lower Burma was occupied. Lord Dalhousie, the new Governor-General of India, complained: 'But the beasts don't give in... there is no symptom of submission and I now give up all hope of it.' Prome fell in October, but still the Burmese refused to recognise '... their actual inferiority to the British power'. In December, his patience at an end, Dalhousie annexed Lower Burma, proclaiming it to be a portion of the British Territories in the East. *The Times* pronounced it 'generally inglorious', costing 3,000 British dead and a million pounds.

Ascending the Burmese throne in 1878, King Thibaw consistently revealed anti-British feeling, culminating in secret negotiations with France over rights in Upper Burma; subsequently the alarmed British Government presented an ultimatum in October 1885, which was rejected by Thibaw, and on 10th November General Prendergast left Rangoon by river for Thayetmyo with a force of 12,000. Said to be 'not a war at all... merely a street row', the Third Burmese War surprised the Burmese who thought it would never happen and were not prepared for it, their army being scattered all over the country. After three weeks Thibaw requested an armistice, agreeing to comply with all the points of the ultimatum. But the Burmese Army refused to surrender, melting into the jungle to carry on guerrilla warfare, joined by large numbers of civilians, roaming the countryside like firebrands, in dacoit bands ready to support any successful side but, until one came along, destroying everything in their path. The British tended to consider anyone who fought them to be a dacoit, including patriots and followers of princes; indeed, the dacoit was sometimes a brigand, but equally he was a rebel following a local chief claiming kinship with the fallen Alompra dynasty. Disrupting everyday life and administration (twice they set fire to occupied Mandalay), there were enough of them active a year after occupation to require 32,000 British soldiers and 8,500 military policemen in Upper Burma. Captured, more than a thousand of them were brought into Mandalay and branded – to 'save the formality of a trial when arrested a second time'.

It took some years to pacify the country, to suppress the bands of desperate, resolute and ruthless men who harassed peaceful inhabitants by vicious and murderous raids that kept the British forces ever on the move, marching here and there to break up a gathering, storm a stronghold or defend a sorely beset village; scarcely a day passed without an engagement to mark it. Eventually, such notorious leaders as Yakut, Boh Thaee and Boh Toke were killed in action or executed but the rebels, repeatedly defeated, had many refuges in the wild countryside and reunited to form fresh bands. Finally, when the dacoits were under control there still remained the hill tribes, wild men who had never paid more than nominal allegiance to Mandalay – the Chins, Lushais, Kachins and Karens – and there was organised resistance in the remote Shan states. The Siglo tribe laid waste 25 villages and were not quieted until a punitive expedition had gone out against them and burned a few villages in North-West Frontier style. Large-scale operations were superseded by a network of small British outposts, each dealing quickly and effectively with trouble in its area, until the Shans were subdued.

By 1891 the country was largely pacified, although during the three following years the Kachins gave a lot of trouble; armed in the most primitive fashion with bows, spears, dahs and a few flintlock muskets, they were a wild tribe of blackmailing marauders who preyed on travellers and plundered caravans. In 1893 a column of 580 men and two guns went into the Karen hills against the great chief Sawlapan at Sawlon; in efficient style he was defeated, dethroned and a suitable successor appointed. There was also an expedition against Tashous, leader of one of the Chin tribes, and this too ended in success. As late as 1900 more than 20,000 soldiers and police were still needed in Burma and at least one rebel leader, Bo Cho, eluded them until 1920.

7   The Canadians

Queen Victoria's first year on the throne was disturbingly marked by trouble in one of her largest and most rapidly developing colonies, where the rebellion in Lower Canada could have become another American revolution. After the Napoleonic Wars a series of depressions in the United Kingdom caused the greatest westward migration of British people since the settlement of the American colonies 200 years earlier, and between 1825 and 1850 the population of Upper Canada rose fivefold, from 158,000 to 791,000. Canada was changing so fast, both socially and economically, that inadequate government caused constitutional strife in both Upper and Lower Canada. The reform-minded immigrants of the former – labourers, frontiersmen, Nonconformists – were led by William Lyon Mackenzie, a newspaper writer consumed with violent antagonism towards privilege. Lower Canada's Reformers were older residents, French Catholics and 'Patriotes', more conservative than radical but united in their antagonism to being controlled by an English-speaking Protestant oligarchy. Their leader was a well-born and educated French-Canadian lawyer, Louis Joseph Papineau, a distinguished orator who had been prominent in the Province's politics since 1815, the year of Waterloo. Under different leaderships they might have united in achieving their aims of a Canadian Republic in place of the British connection, instead they went their own ways. Early in November, in Montreal, a revolutionary party known as the Sons of Liberty were routed in conflict with a loyalist Doric Club, and arms were taken up in open violation of the law.

Sir John Colbourne, commander of the military forces, was a veteran soldier who led the decisive charge on the evening of Waterloo, and – not a man to be overtaken by events – the fortifications at Quebec were repaired and thoroughly armed, horses were purchased for the artillery, magazines of provisions and ammunition were established, barracks built; and enlisted Napoleonic War pensioners, settled in Lower Canada. Because Canadians boasted they could travel better in winter than could the soldiers, Colbourne had 100 15-man sleighs built and snow-shoes made for the soldiers. By mid-November 1837, Montreal and surrounding countries were in a state of revolt, and it became known that ringleaders Papineau, Dr Wolford Nelson and 'General' Brown with large numbers of followers were at the villages of St Denis and St Charles, beyond the Richelieu.

Colonel Gore was sent with troops to St Denis, but the severity of the Canadian winter forced them to withdraw after being thrown back in a hot, five-hour battle. Simultaneously, Colonel Wetherall moved out with about 600 men and two 6-pounder guns from Chambly in severe weather towards St Charles through the rebel-infested Richelieu Valley; on 25th November they stormed the place, with 3 dead and 18 wounded. The rebel leaders had fled to America and command at St Charles had been assumed by Thomas Brown, one of the few British 'Patriotes' and a journalist with no military experience; he had less than 200 men armed with 'flintlocks in all conditions of dilapidation, some tied together with string...' and two 'small rusty fieldpieces as useless as two logs'. The defenders had 42 men killed, many of the rebels shot or bayoneted and 16 taken prisoner. Brown escaped to the United States, where he stayed until the amnesty of 1844.

On 28th November at Point Oliviere they advanced to attack another body of rebels entrenched behind an abatis of felled trees. After exchanging a few shots the insurgents lost heart when they saw the soldiers form up for the attack and ran from the field, leaving two cannon behind them; there were five prisoners. This did not completely suppress the rebellion and losses were incurred in guerrilla warfare amid snow and frost of a severe winter.

Gore was sent reinforcements and took the village, burning the houses and recapturing his lost gun and some of his wounded men. The news of his initial repulse had encouraged an insurrection at St Eustache, a village in the country of the Two Mountains, where 800 rebels with a 3-pounder gun under a Swiss, Amury Girod, and a doctor, John Chenier, had seized the convent and fortified it. Contemporary reports indicate that this garrison did little to prepare for the inevitable attack: 'there were courageous men among them but their chief aim was to steal, drink, eat, dance and quarrel...' On 13th December Sir John Colbourne marched out of Montreal at the head of 2,000 men with artillery. Arriving at St Eustache, they found the rebels occupying the church, convent, presbytery and an adjacent house; Girod had fled and only about 250 men remained to resist the soldiers. The Royal Scots and the Montreal Rifles seized defensible houses in the main street to carry on a brisk exchange of musketry with the fortified rebels; from the rear of the village the artillery opened fire on the church. A party of the Royal Scots, after a furious struggle, forced their way into the presbytery, bayoneted the defenders and set it alight; hidden by smoke, grenadiers stormed the church, killing and bayoneting those who resisted and taking many prisoners. 'Patriotes' leapt from windows of blazing houses, still firing as they fell; Cheniot was killed and Girod fled, but shot himself later when in danger of capture. Colbourne returned to Montreal with 120 prisoners and a large white rebel flag, bearing a big black eagle with the inscription 'Free as Air'. Thus died the rebellion, but French-Canadian resentment lived on.

Meanwhile, in Upper Canada a band of rebellious farmers led by Mackenzie threatened Toronto for two days before being dispersed in half an hour by a hastily raised Loyalist force; Mackenzie and other radicals fled to the United States.

Contemporary illustrations of the fighting depict lines of troops facing and firing upon men in irregular lines, in undisciplined imitation of the soldiers. They are wearing fur caps, varicoloured long coats, legs bulky with blanket wrappings or crude gaiters; some wear belts and cross-straps supporting a haversack or pack, and here and there a short sword. Obviously they are non-military personnel – in other words, civilians.

Trouble flared up again in October 1838, when signs of new disturbances were evident; Sir John Colbourne called out the Volunteers and took steps to defend the frontier. A revolutionary uprising began in the counties on the Richelieu River where large bodies of disaffected 'habit-ants' gathered in the hope of being joined by sympathisers from America. On 4th November at Napierville, 15 miles from the United States boundary, Robert Nelson was proclaimed President of the Canadian Republic, and two days later led his 4,000 followers into the United States without attracting new adherents as they had hoped, so recrossed the frontier on 7th November. They were attacked by soldiers and routed, leaving 11 dead on the field; Nelson, who had remained behind at Napierville, went to Odelltown and attacked a small British force in a Methodist church; meeting determined resistance, the rebels retired with 50 men killed.

On the same day, a column under General Macdonell left Montreal. On reaching Napierville Macdonell found the insurgents had left *en masse*. He dispersed some gatherings at St Edouard and St Rémi, a little to the west. An insurgent camp which had been formed near Boucherville, under Mailhot, broke up on the advance of the 66th Regiment. Another party of rebels was dispersed at Beauharnois on the 10th by a detachment of the Napierville force under Colonel Carmichael. This was the last act in the revolt in Lower Canada, which collapsed after lasting one week.

The situation as seen by a privileged onlooker is revealed in a letter written on 17th November by Lady Colbourne, the Commander-in-Chief's wife:

'I am more hardened to warfare, for certainly there can be no reasonable doubt that the state of affairs has been infinitely more perilous, and every day proves how much more extensive, much more secret, much more deeply laid, all the plans of the enemy have now been.

'I was surprised to find that in different affairs at least 10,000 men at arms have already been conquered and dispersed. La Colle, Beauharnois, Napierville, Odelltown, Boucherville and all the country round quieted, but actually that number in arms, without counting the abominable 800 Yankees at Prescott (Upper Canada), who this morning we learn have cost us more lives than all the rest put together, and sadly distressing it is to Sir John, of course, that he was obliged to draw the force from that neighbourhood before it was attacked. Such a reinforcement, however, went immediately that not one, it is to be hoped, can escape from the mill where they have now stationed themselves, and from which nothing but heavy artillery can dislodge them.

'Sir John, with all the force he could take with safety to Montreal, was absent from Thursday (8th) to Tuesday (13th), and the fatigue, &c., all went through from the horrible state of the roads, the weather, &c., was very great, but the troops have borne it famously, and Sir John, they all say, seemed to stand it better than almost anyone. I flattered myself he would have some days, at least, of comparative rest, when in less than an hour James comes in, "Well, Sir, your campaigns are not over so soon as you think; 800 Americans have landed, and Colonel Gore and Colonel Wetherall are downstairs with the despatches, waiting to see you." Before, his fear was that they must be coming over in much greater numbers, and, in so disaffected a part of the country, might get a kind of stand. We have lost, I am sorry to say, 45 killed and wounded, two officers killed – the loss much greater on the other side. It is very dreadful to rejoice at such things as we are obliged to now, and I am constantly obliged to recollect what horrors they intended for us when I hear of the misery occasioned by the march of the troops through the rebels' land, and to confine my pity to the poor women and children who fly to the woods and return only to find all destroyed, for it is impossible to prevent it, or to keep proper discipline, except with the regular troops. "Ordered expressly by Sir John Colbourne not to be burnt", they say is to be seen written in white chalk in all directions, but it is useless. The volunteers will revenge themselves in a degree; but not more, Sir John says, than must be expected, and with nothing of the cruelty that was openly intended, had they been the victors.

'Prisoners are coming in from arrests and skirmishes every day. We have now between 600 and 700, and the jail cannot hold them. The court-martials must begin directly. My husband decidedly thinks that the worst is past. We are strong enough if all the States were to invade us instead of this vile portion of cut-throats.

'From the confessions of the chiefs, had they not been disturbed and detected sooner than they expected, it would have been bad indeed.'

Another letter was dated the 18th November:

'I must give you the good news just arrived from Prescott. As soon as the heavy artillery, 18-pounders, could be procured from Kingston, the 83rd, commanded by Colonel Dundas, and the armed steamboat by Captain Sandom recommenced the attack, I told you was suspended, on the Americans, who had taken up a very strong position in a windmill and adjacent houses. They bore the second battering for more than an hour, but then surrendered. About 100 prisoners, 16 wounded, six pieces of cannon, quantity of powder, &c. Two or three hundred had contrived, in the nights previously, to make their escape, and amongst them their leader, a Pole – but fortunately he had been taken. I trust this example will make the Yankees more careful how they pay us another visit.

'I believe I told you of all the combustibles, &c., found on board the "Princess Victoria" steamboat, which was the only one for some days communicating between Montreal and La Prairie, and conveying all our troops backwards and forwards; a man also secreted. It has now been discovered that she in flames was the appointed signal for their great rising, &c., to commence. One of their chief plots was to take possession of all the boats, and one or two have always been suspected as to captain and crew. So Sir John took quickly possession of them and put strong guards on board.

'The courts-martial commence trying the 700 prisoners here tomorrow. How I wish it was all over. They all pass close to our windows. It is curious and most melancholy to witness the different expression of their countenances.'

Martial law declared, all who could prove they had been forced to take up arms were liberated. Courts-martial were convened on 28th November for rebel prisoners, and with only a dozen tried four were sentenced to be hung, six transported and two acquitted. It was not thought that these sentences would be carried out but after the first had been hanged, the attitude of prisoners changed remarkably as they saw the solemnity and power of the law. From Britain the Whig government sent the Earl of Durham out to investigate; in Lower Canada he immediately perceived the root of the trouble: 'I expected to find a contest between a government and a people,' he wrote. 'I found two nations warring in the bosom of a single state: I found a struggle not of principles but of races...' To strengthen the government of the colony, an Act of Parliament was passed in 1840, making one province of Upper and Lower Canada.

The Irish potato famines of the mid-nineteenth century caused many Irish to emigrate to the United States of America, along with their politics and hatred of the British, through the Fenian

A half-breed camp.

Movement dedicated to the establishment of a republic in Ireland. On the night of 31 May 1866 these fanatics surged over the border into Canada, 1,500 jobless Irish-American veterans of the recently concluded Civil War crossing the Niagara River from Buffalo and landing at Fort Erie. They camped on the borders of New Brunswick, won a sprawling brawl with Canadian Militia who had nine killed with no territory lost or won; the defeated Irish went back over the border on hearing that reinforcements were coming up. Four years later the Fenians came again, this time from Vermont into Quebec, to be soundly defeated in a battle on the Trout River not far from Montreal; the survivors again retreating to the United States. Seemingly, the objectives of these abortive expeditions were to establish an Irish republic in British North America from which to wage a vengeful campaign against Britain.

Potentially more serious than the threat of the Fenians was the revolt which occurred in 1869 in the wild untamed forests of the almost unpopulated North West, the immense territories of the Hudson's Bay Company where lived only Indians, a few traders, and the Métis in their Red River Colony. Also called Boisbrules (French, 'burnt wood') for their dark complexions, these people were the part-Indian descendants of the early French fur traders of North West Canada. In November 1869 the Company surrendered to the Crown all its rights in Prince Rupert's Land and the North West Territory; on 15 July 1870 the area was declared a new Province of Canada, called Manitoba. Unfortunately, no one thought to ask, or even tell the Métis, the French-speaking French-Canadian inhabitants of the Red River Settlement and these people, with their strong French and Roman Catholic culture, did not want to become Canadians and resented being taken over by the British, English-speaking and mostly Protestant Canadians. Fearing for their lands and their half-nomadic, buffalo-hunting existence, they threatened violence and prevented by force the governor of the new province from taking over his new domain – by order of the 'Comité National de Métis'. Their demonstrations were planned by Louis Riel, son of French and half-breed parents, a 25-year-old educated man of considerable energy and shrewdness. He gathered around him some 500 armed and strictly disciplined Métis guerrillas and on 2 November 1869 seized Fort Garry, a Hudson's Bay Company fortified post on land now part of the city of Winnipeg, and began seeking other settlers to help in creating a provincial government. The Company's officials were not ill-disposed towards the rebels, and Garnet Wolseley blamed the French Catholic priests, claiming that they 'openly preached from their altars resistance to the Canadian Government...' and that Riel's rebel flag had been made by local nuns. The Ottawa government tried conciliatory measures. Commissioners were sent to interview Riel, who had assumed the title of President, and sat under a flag the design of which was fleurs-de-lis and shamrocks. Besides having hauled down the Union Jack and substituted his own flag, he had

Louis Riel.

more than half-a-hundred loyal subjects of the queen under lock and key. The commissioners made little effect on the half-breeds. Riel sent a delegation to Ottawa to demand that the Métis be permitted to retain their customs, language and religion and, with support from sympathetic French-Canadians, these demands were granted. Then Riel made a mistake by overzealous use of the powers bestowed upon himself and the desire to commit his followers irrevocably by summarily executing a young English Canadian, Thomas Scott; thus ensuring that there would have to be military measures taken against him. Sure enough a military expedition was mounted, under the leadership of the deputy Quartermaster-General in Canada, that archetypal British Victorian general, Sir Garnet Wolseley, whose force of 1,200 men included a number of British Regulars – to impress the United States with Britain's continued commitment to Canada.

Riel appears to have completely discounted the very existence of the expedition, which had to fight hard against the forces of Nature if not against active resistance from the Métis. Without the loss of a single man, taking three months they covered 1,280 miles of ever-changing scenery under most arduous conditions. Tracing the route on the map cannot fail to impress – from Toronto to Georgian Bay by locomotives, up the Great Lakes in churning steamers, through the woods on wagons, wracking over corduroy roads, and then by portage, river and lake on to Fort Garry.

Reaching Point Douglas on 24th August, they disembarked and formed into battle order, advancing on the enemy camp until seen by the astonished rebels who immediately took to their heels by the fort's south gate. With them went Louis Riel, escaping to the United States after long marches barefoot and floating across rivers on fence-rail rafts. Safe in America, Riel became a schoolteacher in Montana, but Canada had not seen the last of him. Had Riel's project succeeded it could have whipped up a great Indian war that would have seen the massacre of unprotected settlers and their families, and many months of bitter fighting before it would have inevitably been defeated.

To escape the civilisation imposed upon their own lands in Manitoba, many of the Métis moved west to Saskatchewan, but it overtook them again, as the buffalo disappeared and white farmers moved in. Local Indians were becoming increasingly restive through their over-sudden transition from hunter and horse-thief to rationed loafer on a Reserve. The Wood Indians, Crees and Chipwayans, in the far north, lived on fish, game and the barter of furs with the Hudson Bay post. They also had been relegated to reserves, a system they disliked. The great chiefs 'Big Bear' and 'Poundmaker' had bands they could not feed. The emissaries of Riel were busy among them, with promises of a millennium of pork and flour from the plunder of the Hudson Bay stores and settlements – 'no police, plenty whisky'. These blessings were to be obtained with the aid of their brethren from the United States and the evergreen Fenian Brigade. They were also told King George's red soldiers could not help the Canadians, as they were fighting the Russians.

In 1884 the Métis sent four delegates with five rail tickets to Montana and Louis Riel returned with them. After unsuccessfully trying legal means to secure title to their lands, he organised in 1885 a provisional government which inevitably brought him into conflict with the North West Mounted Police, unfamiliar authorities formed during his years of exile. The atmosphere

encouraged rebellion as the long familiarity between Police, Indians and Métis had bred contempt, accentuated by the way in which Riel had been amnested and allowed to return from the United States after, 15 years before, seizing power in Red River County, proclaiming himself president, turning out the governor sent by Ottawa, imprisoning those who opposed him, and executing Scott, a loyalist. Now he was allowed to roam the countryside and hold seditious meetings, causing the half-breeds to view authority with supreme contempt.

The first clash occurred near Duck Lake on 26 March 1885, when Superintendent Crozier from Battleford with 53 Mounties, 41 soldiers and a 7-pounder gun was routed with severe loss by a large party of Métis led by Gabriel Dumont, a celebrated old buffalo-hunter. At about the same time, Indian Crees murdered nine white settlers at Frog Lake; in the vicinity of such small settlements as McLeod and Calgary in Alberta groups of relatively unarmed settlers were terrorised by about 2,500 Winchester-armed braves of the Bloods, Blackfeet, Peigans and Sarcees, urged on by half-breeds and disaffected whites to plunder and ill-treat them. Later it was said that the Indians were swayed by a belief that North West Canada was to be sold to the United States and only those involved in outbreaks would get any of the purchase money.

The Mounties retired to Battleford, to which all the whites in the territory poured to shelter in the stockade. Taking a few days for a journey that had occupied Wolseley three months 15 years before, General Frederick Middleton shipped to Saskatchewan 5,000 Canadian Militiamen by the newly constructed Canadian Pacific Railway. After some preliminary engagements, they arrived before Batoche, Riel's HQ. It was fighting made colourful by oaths, shouts and jeers of excited Métis, mingling with the vibrating warwhoop of Big Bear's Indians, in full warpaint, demonstrating their natural skill at warfare. They excelled at concealment, fighting from rifle-pits and trenches with loopholed-logs for head cover and a firing step, concealed by branches stuck in the loose excavated earth. At Batoche the overwhelming forces of the government, employing the latest weapons, were more than a

Canadian militia in an affray with Cree Indians during the Louis Riel Revolt, 1885.

match for the rebels, as shown by two newspaper reports of the time. *The New York Herald* reported on 11 May 1885:

'The Grenadiers advanced, skirmishing through the bush, on the right of the trail, the Gatling Gun being pushed forward down a declivity, toward Batoche, now plainly visible in the valley below. Here "A" Battery unlimbered on top of a ridge, sending shells into the enemy, and while doing so were surprised by a number of rebels, who crept up through the bush, not being discovered until twenty yards distant. They made a dash for our guns, firing and yelling as they ran. Captain Howard, who operated the Gatling, saw the danger, and, with cool daring, ran his gun a couple of yards in front of the battery, and, opening fire, literally mowed the rebels down. In dismay, those who were not killed, turned and fled like deer, making for the bush.'

Similarly, from correspondence of the *Toronto Mail*, May 1885:

'The rebels suddenly rose from the ravine right in front of us and opened fire. The guns were ordered to the rear, and the Gatling, which Howard had been working so well, rained down a fusilade; but our position was too high, and the bullets flew over the ravine, and did no harm. This was a ticklish moment, and our men were thrown into some disorder. Howard, however, worked like a Trojan in the thick of it and kept the rebels from charging us. We should have lost many lives, and probably our guns, but for the Gatling.'

Battleford was relieved; Louis Riel gave himself up on 15th May; the Crees who perpetrated the massacre at Frog Lake were captured on 2nd July; the Indian leader Big Bear was sentenced to life imprisonment, but was soon released with a full pardon. But Louis Riel was tried, condemned to death, and hanged on 16 November 1885 – had he been released after a term of imprisonment he would perhaps have been elected a member of the Canadian parliament, where his undoubted oratorical talents might have eventually gained him a knighthood.

8   The Chinese

The Victorian era had just begun when Britain fought the first of three major wars with the Chinese, against a semi-medieval nation simultaneously struggling against dragging itself into the nineteenth century; the third conflict, coinciding with the last months of the old Queen's life, saw Britain as part of an eight-nation International Force battling against a fanatical secret society and the Chinese Imperial Army, armed with the most modern weapons – yet still quaintly tinged with archaic Oriental influences.

It might well be thought that the Opium War of 1839/42 was a characteristic Victorian moral project, waged by Britain to free China of the curse of opium – in reality it was the exact reverse. The British Empire was the world's greatest producer of opium and, as China was its main market, encouraged addiction as a means of securing a monopoly, which it went to war to protect against a Chinese Emperor endeavouring to stamp out the trade. Seen in the context of its time, it was also all about disagreeable celestial arrogance that refused Britain the usual courtesies of diplomacy and trade, unacceptable to Britain as the greatest Empire of the day. After naval skirmishes in the Canton Estuary where a few British frigates scattered a large Chinese fleet of war-junks, the British Expeditionary Force arrived in June 1840, when 20 warships carrying 4,000 troops destroyed by bombardment and a landing the port of Tinghai on Chusan Island.

Contemptuous of the barbarians who would run 'on display of the celestial terror', whose quaint uniforms were so tight they would fall and be unable to get up, so weakened were this 'insignificant and detestable race...by the ravages of our climate', the Chinese had no concept of what they were facing. Disregarding ritual and using muskets instead of bows was taken as a sign of English weakness; conversely, the British thought Chinese soldiers harmless and effeminate, because they carried bows and wore protective leather skirts. *Britain's Sea Soldiers – A History of the Royal Marines* records:

'The Chinese bows here referred to are most powerful weapons. Two or three were brought home and are now in the R.M. Officers' Mess at Plymouth. They appear to be made of a species of horn spliced together, and when unstrung, spring back and curve in exactly the opposite way to when ready strung for use. It must take a powerful man with considerable skill to use them effectively.'

Chinese artillery was archaic and included some exquisitely cast bronze guns dating from the fourteenth century; the batteries defending Canton River – in forts Taikok on Taikoktow Island and Shakok on Chuenpi – were formed of a variety of guns lashed to large wooden blocks that slid on the stone floors of the forts. Later, it was found that the gunners had sold much of their powder to British smugglers and were using a mixture of 30 per cent gunpowder and 70 per cent sand. The Chinese navy was a mass of outdated junks, and their Marines were reputed to be perpetually seasick. However, Sir Hugh Gough, the British commander, revealed a certain foresight when reporting on the Chinese as a military nation:

'...looking to them to repel an aggressive attack, are very contemptible, but they are neither wanting in courage nor bodily strength to make them despicable as a foe in a defensive system of warfare. In short, I conceive the Chinese at present a totally unmilitary nation, with capabilities of making a very formidable one. The Chinese system is not one to which the British soldier is accustomed, but if the Chinese have not bravery and discipline, they have cunning and artifice. They have had ample time to prepare and we may be well assured that their system of strategem will be called into full play on the present occasion.'

The British force occupied major seaports up to Ningpo against little resistance, but had to fight when approaching Canton where 3,000 Tartar 'Manchu' troops, the elite of the Emperor's army, were entrenched, with field-guns on the flanks – Gough noted later that the Chinese persistently allowed their artillery to be outflanked and so rendered useless. After silencing guns of the forts by bombardment, about 1,000 British infantry and Marines attacked frontally, the Chinese unused to such aggression broke and fled, after slight resistance. Some were cornered in the forts and, believing the British grossly mistreated prisoners, fought to the death. In an action lasting 90 minutes, the attackers lost 38 men wounded only; the Chinese between 500 to 600 killed, many wounded and 100 prisoners – most casualties were in the forts where they had run after their morale had earlier failed. The guns in the forts were found to be useless, Chinese matchlocks little better, and the majority of soldiers were armed with such outdated weapons as pikes and swords – a few carried only brass gongs. Further actions took the remainder of the Canton forts; the Chinese commander Admiral Kuan was killed, and his body given a military salute by the British who respected his bravery.

In time it was discovered that the best tactics were to lull the Chinese into believing they had a considerable superiority in numbers, thus drawing them on and into effective musketry and artillery fire, rather than attacking their positions *en masse* when they would turn and flee. When cornered, Chinese soldiers, invariably superior in numbers although outclassed and outarmed, fought with considerable courage; it was marked how they allowed scaling-ladders to be placed and stormers to enter embrasures of the forts before resisting with sword and spear against bayonet and cutlass. The commander at Canton, Admiral Kuan, had trouble preventing his troops from deserting, pawning his clothes to raise a two-dollar bonus for each man.

Of the enemy, Colonel Mountain, later Adjutant-General HM Forces in India, wrote:

'The fact is, their [the Chinese] arms are bad, and they fire ill, and having stood well for a while, give way to our rush, and are then shot like hares in all directions. The slaughter of fugitives is unpleasant but we are such a handful in the face of so wide a country and so large a force, that we should be swept away if we did not read our enemy a sharp lesson whenever we come in contact. The Chinese are robust, muscular fellows and no cowards, the Tartars desperate; but neither are well commanded nor acquainted with European warfare. Having had experience of three of them, I am inclined to suppose a Tartar bullet is not a whit softer than a French one.'

British Marines played a leading part in all operations, a typical action being described in *Britain's Sea Soldiers*:

'From time to time more war junks were destroyed, and on the 25th and 27th May an attack was made on a large force of those vessels... the crews of the junks took refuge in houses, and opened a heavy fire with gingalls on the boats crews as they were endeavouring to tow off the biggest junk, and destroy the rest. The only thing to be done was to land the Marines who created a diversion by charging into the streets of the city. It was a perilous duty, and they were lucky to escape with only nine men wounded. A similar expedition was undertaken against a fleet of junks in Fatshan Creek on 1st June, by 250 men with twelve officers and twenty-two N.C.Os. The junks, heavily armed, were in a position to sweep the channel as the British flotilla advanced and were supported by the fire of a fort perched on a hill on the left of the attack, and a six gun battery on the opposite side. Arrived at this point the Marines were landed and attacked the fort while the gunboats engaged the junks. The hill was steep, which proved a protection to the stormers as the volleys of grape shot discharged by the Chinese guns swept over their heads as the gunners were unable to give their pieces sufficient depression. Finding their fire unavailing, the Chinese rolled down 32 pound shot, and threw showers of stink-pots, and three-pronged spears. Commodore Elliott who had also landed, a midshipman, and Captain Boyle, who was in command of the Marines, ran a neck and neck race for the fort. When close up Captain Boyle fired his revolver at a Chinaman who he noticed aiming his matchlock at him. Panting from his run up hill, he missed him, whereupon the Chinaman rolled down two huge shot at him, and hurled a trident at the midshipman. But it was his last effort, a bullet from the Commodore finished his career. The Chinese gunners stuck to their posts till the Marines were within fifty paces of the embrasures; then they made a bolt down the back of the hill.'

The Jingalls or Gingals were a favourite

Types of Chinese soldiers, 1840–1.

Chinese artist's impression of the fighting in 1842.

Chinese weapon, 'resembling enormous breech-loading muskets of about one and a half inches calibre, mounted on swivels, and carried by two or three men. Their breech action is practically the same as that of the pateraroes which formed the quick-firing armament of both men-of-war and merchantmen in the seventeenth and eighteenth centuries. The breech end of the barrel is prolonged into a kind of trough, in which a short cylinder of thick iron, called a chamber, can be laid. This cylinder is closed at the breech end, and provided with a touch hole. At the other end it is coned so as to fit closely to the rear of the barrel when fixed in position for firing by a wedge or "key". These chambers, fitted with a handle, for lifting in and out and supplied ready loaded, two or more to each weapon, enable a fairly rapid fire to be kept up for a short time.' Two of these Gingals were brought home from China by the Battalion in 1860, and are now to be seen in the RM Officers' Mess at Plymouth.

The British remained in winter quarters in Ning-po, where they were attacked in March 1842, when the Chinese suffered the most decisive defeat of the war, witnesses reporting the carnage from a howitzer firing at 50 yards range in a street packed with Chinese soldiers to be the most devastating seen since the Peninsular War. To prevent the killing of native citizens of the town, the Chinese commanders had forbidden the use of cannon – mistakenly thought to apply to all firearms and the volunteer-attackers from the Golden River region of Western Szechwan Province carried only knives! Perhaps the confusion arose from the wording of a Chinese document ordering the attack:

'Our water braves must board the steamers and men-of-war and take them. In the attack upon the English robbers our soldiers ought to use only their swords and nothing else. The foremost must step forward and cut off the heads of the enemy. As soon as these are in their possession another file ought to advance and do the same; and thus they must go on until their army is annihilated. We must advance with a strong phalanx to strike terror, we must not fight but kill them outright; let the daggers do this work – this is the proper weapon for spreading destruction.'

There was little attempt at secrecy, it seemed general knowledge that the attack was planned for the Day of the Tiger (10th March) and at the Hour of the Tiger (between 3.00 and 5.00 p.m.). Early in the day citizens were leaving the town, drawing hands across throats and pointing at British soldiers; later they sought vantage points to watch, unmoved, the fate of their countrymen. Subsequently, the British moved northwards, held up briefly at Chapu by 300 ferocious Tartars who,. rather than submit, killed themselves and their families in a variety of grisly ways. Shanghai fell, then Chinkiang, where General Hai-Lin cracked under the strain and burned himself to death on a pyre of official papers. On 29th August 1942, the Treaty of Nanking was signed and the Opium War was over; for Britain it was a complete success, making her master of the Far East; for China it was a disaster, the 4,000-year-old last Empire of the ancient world had succumbed to Western capitalism.

Severely handicapped by archaic weaponry in the struggle against nineteenth-century invaders, knowing nothing of contemporary warfare and armed mainly with the fuse-matchlock, recently acquired although long obsolete in the West, and the bow, China struggled sporadically through the years that followed. Their command structure left much to be desired, as the Abbé Hue reveals:

'The renowned General Yang, in command of a Chinese Army, when the battle commenced he tied up his beard in two knots, to keep it out of his way; he then posted himself in the rear of his troops. There, armed with a long sabre, he poked his soldiers to the fight, and mercilessly slew all who had the cowardice to retreat. This way of commanding an army may seem very strange; but those who have lived among the Chinese will be sensible that the military genius of General

A Chinese military despatch, 1854.

Yang was based on a knowledge of his troops.'

Not surprisingly, the Royal Marines featured in many actions, and at Canton in 1857, Lieutenant W. H. Poyntz RM recorded various incidents:

'One very lovely night a curious spectacle was to be observed from the city (of Canton) walls, truly characteristic of the Celestial Empire. A considerable army came on to attack us...the path or track by which they advanced was cut into steps...nearly every soldier carried a lighted lantern on the principle of, I suppose, "taking care of number one, and no light how can see?" They kept at a respectable distance and a few well-directed rockets and shells from the city walls soon doused their glims...it was a novel and picturesque sight and would have been highly appreciated at Cremorne or Vauxhall Gardens.'

And:

'...the Chinese were in a very strong position...congregated in great numbers behind a wall, with sandbags and straw thrown up before it...they made almost their best stand there, as they held it for nearly two hours...we mounted the breach by scaling ladders...and were first within the walls. It is most extraordinary that the Chinese make so little opposition when the men are scaling the ramparts. They let our people get inside before offering much resistance. We took prisoners a lot of Tartar soldiers...they had no arms...so we let the poor devils loose.'

And:

'At Chusan the harbour literally bristled with guns and gingals. The Chinese seemingly worked on the theory that the more of everything, the better results. Hence the guns were handled on the precept the more powder the more execution – and so it proved to the defenders themselves, when the guns were loaded to the muzzle and burst, as might have been expected.'

But Chinese artillery could be well-served. In 1859 the Canton garrison sallied out to attack a Chinese position at Shek-Tseng, across a deep unfordable river and unassailable except by a narrow wooden causeway leading to an island where there were a dozen Chinese guns, well manned and making very decent shooting.

A bronze gun captured from the Chinese in August, 1860.

Not much changed from when they fought Gough, Chinese infantry wore loose cloth jackets, usually brown or yellow, baggy blue trousers and a quilted cotton loose top-robe or surcoat, on its back was the word *yung* (meaning brave or courage); while the front bore the symbol of their branch of the service; hats were conical and of hammered iron, or 'mandarin' style of cloth or felt, those of the leaders embellished with a red plume. Cavalry, usually Tartar tribesmen, wore light-coloured tunics over a long darker-coloured robe, blue trousers tucked into Tartar boots, and a characteristic Chinese hat of black silk. Red horsetails decorated spears and lances, they used wooden saddles, large circular-soled stirrups and a single rein; they handled their small wiry ponies well, could fire and reload in the saddle at the gallop, and were hard to hit because of their speed and loose formations. They were armed with muskets, bows, lances, swords, and round shields. The infantry, manoeuvring in badly-drilled columns, were armed with iron smoothbore matchlock muskets, with a match of hemp or coir, bows, and swords; many of them were irregulars, carrying a mixture of bows, self-loading crossbows, spears, pikes and swords.

Artillery was a hodgepodge of calibres and types, some of European manufacture, others Chinese-cast; generally they were antiques and of variable performance because of the inferior black powder used. Details of their home-produced artillery is revealed by a gun taken at

the Taku Forts in 1860, published in the *Illustrated London News* at that time, when captured artillery-pieces had arrived at the Royal Arsenal, Woolwich. The text reads:

'Through the kindness of Colonel Sir Henry James, R.E., R.F.S., Director of the Topographical Branch of the War Department, we are enabled to present our subscribers with an Engraving of a gun that was captured during the operations in China in August last. A consignment of between 200 and 300 of them arrived recently at the Royal Arsenal, Woolwich, in the transport Chersonese. Many of these are highly interesting specimens of workmanship, as showing the progress made by the Celestials in the construction of heavy ordnance. The one which forms the subject of our Illustration is a very large and heavy bronze gun, mounted on an imposing-looking siege-carriage. Its principal dimensions are as follow:– Length from muzzle to base ring, 10 ft.; ditto, extreme, 11 ft 6 in.; diameter at breech, 26 in. Its calibre is 8 in., or as nearly as possible the same as one of our own 68-pounders; and it weighs not less than 5 tons 19 cwt. The construction of this gun is peculiar, as it has been cast upon a tube of wrought iron about 2 inches thick; and this latter now forms the interior of the bore.

'The carriage upon which the gun is mounted is of teak; its construction is rough but substantial; and the wheels are decorated with a profusion of iron nails with large rounded heads. At the extremity of the trail there are small iron trucks, to enable the gun to be moved with greater ease.

'Twenty-three of the guns are very similar in size and weight, though no two of them are exactly alike in pattern; and the metal of which they are made also varies, being, in some instances, almost pure copper.

'There are about fifty small and very neatly-made brass pieces, each weighing about 39 lb. The remainder of the guns are of iron, and are very various in size and pattern, some of them being fastened into rough wooden beds. One of them is a rather remarkable specimen of a breech-loader; but the rest of the apparatus belonging to it is wanting. Another is furnished with two rings. A bamboo passed through each of these enables the gun to be easily carried by four men. The whole of these iron guns were found in the forts; but none of them appear to have been used in any of the late actions.

'It is worthy of remark that among the guns captured were several British naval pieces which fell into the hands of the Chinese after the Peiho affair of June, 1859. These, it appears, were all mounted in the north Taku Fort, and took part in the defence.'

In the open, the most effective gun seemed to be the Gingal, and Chinese rockets impressed Royal Marine Lieutenant W. H. Poyntz:

'Unlike an English rocket although fired in the same way. It is a thick arrow with a heavy iron barbed head which causes it to descend with great force; said to be poisoned so that the wound is extremely dangerous. They make capital practice with it . . . I think I may say it is about their best weapon. You can see these rockets quite plainly, but from their zig-zag flight they are extremely deceptive.'

In June 1858 the Treaty of Tientsin was signed, confirming the surrender of the Chinese and opening up more ports to trade and British vessels; but its virtual repudiation led to Admiral Sir James Hope, on 25 June 1859, attacking the Taku forts at the mouth of the River Peiho, blocked with cables, chains, floating booms, rafts and iron stakes planted in the riverbed. Shallow water allowed only 11 small gunboats to be used and the Chinese fort-guns, served so rapidly, steadily and with true aim that they could have been crewed by trained European artillerymen,

Storming of the Taku forts, 1860.

soon disabled six of them and severely battered the others. In early evening a landing party of 600 sailors and Marines attempted to storm the South fort across 500 yards of mud and weeds, cut up by ditches and pools in which men sank to their waists. The struggling attackers were belaboured by round-shot and grape, balls from swivel-guns and muskets, rockets and even arrows. Forced to withdraw in gathering darkness, they were heavily fired upon by the ghastly blue light of fireballs and rockets; the force lost 68 killed and 300 wounded.

By the following August an avenging force of 18,000 British and French troops under General Sir Hope Grant assaulted Taku forts from the landward side or rear; the commander's dispatches reveal the strength of the position:

'These forts . . . are all constructed on the same plan, having redoubts with a thick rampart heavily armed with guns and wall-pieces, and having a high cavalier (a raised work overlooking the other fortifications, and mounted with guns having a higher command) facing seawards, the guns of which were all turned towards us. They

Tartar cavalry near Peking, 1860.

have two unfordable wet ditches, between which and the parapet sharp bamboo stakes were thickly planted, forming two belts each about 15 feet wide, round the fort, an abattis encircling the whole, and further covered by pieces of water, which force an advance to be made only on a narrow front.'

The Chinese resisted fiercely with artillery, gingals, matchlocks, spears, hand-grenades, fireballs, stink-pots and jars of lime, standing to their guns until the stormers were actually in the embrasures; a British officer believed this to be because the men were tied to their guns! So strong was the opposition that it was rumoured their Mongol commander, Seng-ko-lin-ch'in, was an Irish adventurer Sam Collinson, a well-known Anglophobe. The defenders were Mongol soldiers of the Imperial Guard, considered the best troops in the Empire, having in their ranks elite gunners and bowmen, in whose hands the bow became a wondrous instrument and several Marines were killed under the walls by arrows. Fierce hand-to-hand fighting wiped out many of the garrison, Chinese losses being at least 1,500 against the Allies 200 or so; three forts surren-

dered and no less than 600 guns were taken. The Allies marched into Peking, and burned and looted the Summer Palace.

In the 40 years that followed, the undisputed ruler of China was the Empress Dowager Yehonala, appointed Regent in 1862 and assuming nominal control of the government in 1872, a formidable and ruthless woman who deeply resented the greedy Westernisation of China. Towards the end of the nineteenth century her hopes of defeating the foreigner lay in a recently-formed secret society whose banners proclaimed: 'Support the Manchus. Exterminate the Foreigners'; they practised Shen Ch'uan (Spirit Boxing) – from this came the name Boxers (I-ho-ch'uan – Fist of Patriotic Union). Fanatical extreme nationalists reputedly immune to fear and pain, they left a bloody trail of murdered Christians and missionaries of all nationalities, thus arousing the ire of the many countries with interests in China. Fevered armed men surged into Peking, to put under siege the British Legation sheltering nationals from the other Legations – Americans, Austrians, French, Germans, Italians, Japanese and Russians. A relief force made up of troops of those nations was hastily assembled from warships laying off Taku and set out from Tientsin, but were forced to turn back. Then followed severe fighting around Tientsin before an International Relief Force of 17,000 formed from troops of eight countries – the largest contingents coming from Britain, Japan, Russia and the United States – arrived and set off on 4 August 1900 to fight the Boxers in Peking. Reaching the City on 14th August – the 54th day of the epic siege – they relieved the Legation; on the city walls were hoisted flags of the eight powers forming an army of more nations going united to war than at any time since the Crusades.

An Imperial Decree forbidding the Imperial Chinese Army to fire on Boxers served to ally them – the *History of the Royal Marines* records this:

'From this time forth the little garrison of the Legations had not only to deal with the fanatical but ill-armed Boxers but with the comparatively well-equipped Imperial regular troops, who, up to this time, had shown themselves rather more friendly than otherwise.'

'The Boxer rabble were distinguished by their blue jean jackets and loose trousers tied at the ankle with red strings, red sashes and waistbands, and in some cases red caps. Their leaders wore yellow instead of blue, and were also denoted by numerous black flags ornamented with various devices, and mottoes. Most of them carried murderous looking 7-foot halberds, others swords and spears of all kinds. The regular Chinese Infantry, who from this time forward reinforced the Boxers, were a very different and more formidable proposition. Their uniform was usually dark blue, grey or black, with white, yellow, black or red facings. Their coats were made very loose and in the centre of both back and front was affixed a large circular piece of parchment upon which was inscribed the wearer's regiment, army and all other necessary particulars of his identity. These placards formed excellent 'bulls-eyes' for the Marines, so that eventually John Chinaman found it advisable to 'take his coat off' when going into action. These troops had had the advantage in most cases of having been trained by European instructors – they were well armed with Mauser and Mannlicher

A Boxer soldier.

rifles, and had it not been for the contemptible quality of their officers, the defence of the Legations would have been almost hopeless.'

Disliking Western weapons, the Boxer halberds were of Oriental design; some carried wicker or brass shields. Most of the Imperial troops in Peking during the Boxer Rebellion were from the Rear Division of the Chinese Guards Army (Wu wei chun), made up of Yung (or Brave Ones) units from Kansu Province in Western China. Many had not been issued with the standard uniform of blue jacket with yellow lace and black silk 'Mandarin' hat; instead they wore a red (yellow decorated) collarless coat over a front-split red/yellow 'apron', with tapered red trousers, bound at the ankles, and sandals; a dark red patterned low turban on the head. Other infantry units wore a Westernised dark uniform, with a voluminous 'sailor-type' peakless hat, and jackboots; artillerymens' uniforms were typically oriental with full trousers (probably blue) taken in below the knee, a yellow/red jerkin/vest over a blue shirt; a green turban; black stockings and white slippers.

Their guns were the usual assorted collection but included B/L Krupp guns; 3- and 6-pounders; pom-poms and native gingals; the Imperial Horse Artillery had 12- and 15-pounders and did some useful work; there were also some 7-pounders and smoothbores at Peking. A British officer wrote of them: 'The "Heathen Chinee" proved a really good gunner, his artillery practice is marvellous, directly he had found his object.' At this time the Chinese Imperial Army were equipped with Mannlicher 1888 rifles with a range of 2,500 metres – superior to any hand weapon of the Allies, and proved themselves, both in armament and courage, to be much more formidable than had been expected. Their attackers showed great bravery, especially in the way banners were kept flying – as soon as a bearer was killed another took his place. Among the banners captured at Peking was a black silk flag bearing Chinese characters for 'artillery,' and a white banner with a red inscription, 'Presented by the Dowager Empress to General Ma'.

Arising from the Legation siege comes an interesting comment on the random Chinese rifle firing:

'June 27 – the men, however, seemed for the most part to fire quite at random, and storms of bullets flew high over our heads. It was curious to speculate where they all went: one would naturally suppose that scores of innocent people in the city must have been hit by stray shots. There were many conjectures as to the cause of this ridiculous waste of ammunition. One, mentioned by Dr. Morrison in his account of the siege in *The Times* was that the soldiers wanted to kill, or rather frighten away, the devils which protected the Legations, just as they fire off crackers to drive away evil spirits at any festival or leave-taking. Another theory, started, I believe, by Dr. Coltman, was much more worldly minded. It was that the soldiers emptied their cartridges in order to sell the brass cases. It was said that, when first the troops were supplied with foreign weapons and ammunition, they used to empty the powder out of their cartridges for the same purpose, and the practice became so universal that it had been made a capital offence. But the refutation of this theory laid on the surface, the ground outside the Legation barricades being littered with cartridge cases, which the Chinese had not taken the trouble to carry away. A most interesting solution was suggested by Mr. Cockburn. He said that in 1881 when China seemed to be on the eve of war with Russia, Gordon wrote a memorandum advising the Chinese how to meet the foreigners. He told them in that paper to avoid meeting the enemy in the open, but to worry them night and day, especially by making as much noise as possible at night, in order to keep them continually on the strain, for he said that the demoralisation produced by anxiety and want of rest would be of greater service to the Chinese than many victories.' (From *The Siege of the Peking Legations*, by Revd Roland Allen, MA, Smith, Elder and Co., 1901.)

A contemporary witness wrote: 'Hordes of barbarians armed with the deadly weapons of civilised warfare.'

9   The Dervishes

Most typical of all Victorian campaigns was that in the Sudan when sun-helmeted British County Regiments and straw-hatted Naval landing parties tried unsuccessfully to snatch Gordon from beleaguered Khartoum in 1884/5 and then avenged him 13 years later. Where the 'sand of the desert was sodden red...with the blood of the square that broke...' and the Victorian soldier saw his foe as 'a pore benighted heathen...but a first-class fighting man...' His respect, freely given, was more than justified for, with the Zulu (although never as organised), the generically named 'Fuzzy-Wuzzies' in appearance and fighting ability were among the fiercest natural warriors in the world. Their arena was the Eastern Sudan, an arid scrub desert stretching 1,400 miles from the southern frontiers of Egypt to Uganda and the Congo (Zaïre), where from 1880 to 1884 the nomadic tribes had been united by Mohammed Ahmed ibn Al-Sayid Abdullah, the self-styled Mahdi, whose gapped front teeth were a Sudanese luck-symbol – the Guided One of the Prophet – preaching Holy War to establish the Islamic faith across the whole of Northern Africa.

Although the Arabic name for the Sudan means 'Land of the Blacks', in colour the 600 tribes and 56 main tribal groups ranged from very black to light brown, divided into several major peoples – Beja in the area round Suakin, the Ababdeha in the north, the Bisharin south of Wadi Halfa and north of Debba, the Kababish, the Hassaniyeh and the Shaguyeh near Khartoum. South of Khartoum was the homeland of the Baggara people and near Abu Hamed the Amara were the major tribe. Each was subdivided, thus the Hadendowah were part of the Beja and the Taaisha were a division of the Baggara – then there were Beja-Hadendowah; Baggara-Taaisha; the Jaalin; the Donagla; the Batahin; the Berberin; the Barabra; the Allanga; the Duguaim; the Kenana; the Awadiyeh; the Hamr-Kordofan; the Darfureh; the Monassir; the Sowarab; the Hau-hua-hin; the Robatab; Base and Shukreeyah. The Mahdi's recruiting ground was the entire male population of the Sudan.

Numbers rapidly increased with an escalating series of victories over Egyptian forces sent to quell them, by hurling themselves on the enemy when least expecting attack. Each triumph brought recruits from the defeated force with their arms and ammunition; hauls from the annihilated Hicks Pasha and Baker expeditions included Krupp field-pieces, mountain-guns, Nordenfeldt machine-guns, and thousands of breech-loading Remington and Martini-Henry rifles.

By 1884 the Mahdi could call on thousands of horse and foot, a swelling horde of loyal fanatics clad in jibbas, rough robes with varicoloured patches symbolising virtuous poverty; this col-

The Mahdi.

lection of regional armies became generally known as Dervishes, although to the Mahdi and his followers they were always the *Ansar*, an Arabic word meaning helper or follower. The Mahdist army was centred on first Kordofan, then Khartoum or Omdurman, organised around the flags of his three main Khalifas; these 'flags' (rayyas) were semi-permanent forces augmented by tribal levies, divided into separate commands in different provinces. The Khalifa Abdallahi recruited the Baggara Arabs and other tribes from the West around the Black Flag (al-Rayya al-Zarqa'). The Khalifa al-Sharif's Red Flag (al-Rayya al-Hamra') contained warriors from the riverain peoples north of Khartoum, including Ja'aliyin and the Mahdi's own Danaqla. The Green Flag (al-Rayya al-Khadra') of the Khalifa Ali wad Hilu was drawn from the Dighaym, Kianan and al-Lahiwiyin Arabs of the Gezira region between the Blue and White Niles. Wherever the main army gathered, warriors were attached to one of these three flags, under their own amirs. The internal organisation of the various flags had groups of 20 men or so under a *Muggadam*; each force of 100 men under a *Ra's Mi'a*, grouped into several hundreds under the flag of an *Amir*, organised around one of the major flags. The basic tactical unit was the *Rub*, numerically flexible and ranging from several hundred men to a few thousand, but usually between 800 and 1,200; *Rubs* were subdivided into an administrative and three combat units – spearmen; riflemen; and cavalry, usually Baggara.

In 1883 a force of riflemen was formed of black Africans from south and west who had been in the Egyptian Army, or served in private armies of ivory and slave-traders; called the *Jihadiyya* it was developed and commanded by Hamdan Abu Anja. Armed with Remington rifles, it was a semi-autonomous group with different sections assigned to each flag and province. In 1892 the Jihadiyya was superseded as the main rifle-force by the Mulazimiyya, recruited from former jihadiyya, Western Arabs and recruits from the Nuba Mountains and the South, numbering about 10,000 to 12,000 and mostly armed with breech-loading rifles. From that year the main army was organised round the Mulazimiyya and the Black Flag.

The outward and visible sign of adherence to the Mahdiyya was the short, rough-cloth, patched jibba, reaching to the knees and well short of

Jihadiyya riflemen.

the wrists, irregularly patched as a necessity; later the varicoloured patches became ordered and meaningful. In the early days, the Mahdi decreed that the Ansar should wear this crude garment of the poor and lowly, with siraval (white trousers), sayidan (sandals), karaba (girdle of straw), taggia (skull-cap), imma (turban) wrapped around the taggia with a tail (aziba) hanging free behind the left ear, a style as important a badge of Mahdiism as the jibba; and sibba (beads). Jibbas were basically coloured white or greyish-white and patched in symmetrical designs with rectangular pieces of coloured cloth, two or three in front, one on each sleeve, and one on each side of the jibba's skirt; sometimes there were coloured rectangles under each arm and collars were bordered by a triangular patch. The most common colours for patches were – black, dark and medium blue, various shades of red, turquoise, and green; black patches often being edged with yellow and blue patches with red;

cuffs, hems and collar-edges could be trimmed in red, blue, black or yellow. Manufactured in Omdurman, jibbas were often issued to warriors at the start of a campaign, but it is unlikely that units were uniformly dressed with the same type. Amirs dressed much the same as the ordinary warrior, although jibbas were sometimes more ornate and they usually had their patches ornamentally embroidered and the 'club' shaped breast pocket was similarly decorated. Amirs were always mounted, usually on fine Arab horses, their saddles had high cantles and pommels, bridles were decorated with brass studs and coloured horse hair; the horses' faces and rumps were often coloured with fly-fringing. Subordinate officers wore less ornate jibbas than did Amirs, but enough to distinguish them from their men. Amirs Mahmud, Osman Digna and the Khalifa Sharif invariably wore simple jibbas, and at Omdurman the Khalifa Abdullah is reported as wearing a blue-patched jibba with a blue waistband, riding a donkey under a parasol.

The usual Ansar head-dress was a white imma (turban) wrapped around a white or solid-coloured taggia (skull-cap); some wore the taggia only, or went bare-headed. The Beja, Bisharin and some Baggara wore their hair long, frizzed and stiffened to stand out as much as 8 in from the side of the head, then brushed to pile up with a long wooden skewer through the top part. Other groups shaved heads except for a long tuft from crown-centre covered by a small straw-plaited or cotton taggia, sometimes covered with a cotton puggaree, the loose end wound under the chin and around the neck. Beja 'Fuzzy-Wuzzies' and Bisharin wore ankle-length white cotton trousers, or loincloths worn 'dhoti-fashion' around the waist, with a loose cotton scarf over the shoulders tucked into the waist-band.

Exotic illustrations show Dervish cavalry wearing elaborate chainmail; however, it was not worn in battle and perhaps the only unit thus dressed were the 200 Baggara of the Khalifa's bodyguard, who were said to wear chainmail and greaves, red sashes, and red turbans wound round iron helmets and under the chin; their horses wore brass headguards.

Each Amir's command was based on his flag, containing lesser amirs and leaders who also had their personal standards. Generally about 4 feet by 3; black, blue, green or red, or a white background with coloured borders and letters, they bore passages from the Koran in Arabic on one

Osman Digna.

side only. Staffs were decorated with brass balls, fist-topped globes or crescents, and horse-tails: the Khalifa's famous black flag was attached to a dark-red leather-covered staff 17 feet long.

Most Dervish warriors carried the 10-foot long, broad-bladed thrusting spear, plus short throwing spears, and the long straight double-edged razor-sharp sword with simple metal cross hilt; the red leather scabbard, under the armpit close to the body, was attached by metal rings and crocodile-skin binding to a sling worn over the left shoulder. Short daggers in red leather sheaths were strapped to the upper arm under the jibbah; Beja and Bisharin tribesmen carried wicked knives with hooked blades broadening towards the tip. Shields were usually elliptical or round, with a raised conical boss, made from rhinoceros, crocodile or elephant hide and reputed to deflect a bullet; they were seldom carried, except by the Beja. Firearms were restricted to the Jihadiyya and the Mulazamiyya, trained

Dervish coat, sword and shield.

rifle-bearing infantry, who initially bore captured Remington breech-loading rifles or percussion muzzle-loading muskets, but by the time of the Dongola Campaign all had either the Remington, Martini-Henry, Italian bolt-action magazine rifles, or the Belgian Alboni. Some of the Mulazamiyya carried flintlock pistols, and Amirs occasionally had revolvers; riflemen did not carry any edged weapons except when low in ammunition, as they were in 1898 in Equatoria. Their musketry was reasonable although accuracy was impaired by a tribal habit of shortening the barrels of captured rifles, and they tended to fire high; after the war with Abyssinia, musketry standards deteriorated through heavy casualties, lack of ammunition and wear-and-tear of firearms. Riflemen wore no special uniform, having round waist or shoulders one or two locally made bandoliers decorated by strips of coloured leather; those with muzzle-loading muskets carried cartridge-boxes and powder-horns.

The Mahdist army had an impressive number of cannons, some quite modern, served by four chiefs and 152 Egyptian-trained artillerymen; but apart from reasonably effective fire from

forts along the Nile against river-steamers in 1885 and 1896/7, little use was made of them. At the time of Omdurman they were known to have either in the arsenal, in mud-forts along the river, or mounted in captured river boats – 63 guns, made up of 35 brass mountain-guns (howitzers); 8 Krupp field-pieces; 12 assorted muzzle-loaders including Remington (possibly a machine-gun); and a 'French' gun; plus six multi-barrelled Nordenfeldt machine-guns. At the Battle of Omdurman in 1898, there were 19 guns present – 13 mountain-guns; one Krupp gun; the Remington gun, and three Nordenfeldts. Only five of them were actually known to have fired from a hill overlooking the battlefield – a war correspondent noted their performance:

'More than forty rounds were fired from these Dervish field guns, but the shells did little, if any, damage as, although the fuses were beautifully timed and the projectiles burst at an excellent height above the ground, the range was too long, and they all fell short. Moreover, after the fight some fragments of these shells were picked up and found to be made of very thin brass casing; so that the damage they could have inflicted, even had they reached our lines, must have been inconsiderable.'

They fell short because locally-made shells had a range of only 500 yards – captured shells (in very short supply) could reach 2,500 yards – with few facilities for ammunition manufacture and local saltpetre poor quality, they could only make shells of light copper, with little shrapnel effect.

Three river-steamers had been acquired by the Ansar, two – 'Ismailia' and 'al-Safia' — left behind by the Egyptians had each been armed with a mountain-gun; 'Bordein' was one of the boats sent by Gordon to meet the Camel Corps at Metemma and scuttled when the British retreated; raised and refitted by the Mahdists, it remained unarmed.

Following Wolseley's successful campaign against Arabi Pasha in 1882, the British government refused to intervene against the Mahdi in the troubled Sudan. Subsequently, the Egyptian Government sent Colonel W. Hicks, a retired Indian Army Officer with a force of 10,000 ill-organised Egyptian troops recruited from Arabi's defeated army in to the Kordofan Desert in November 1883; near el Obeid, the force was

Beja/Hadendowahs.

utterly destroyed. Next, General Valentine Baker, head of the Egyptian Police, went out with a rabble of 4,000 policemen and peasants; attacked at El Teb by Osman Digna's 1,000 tribesmen, in utter confusion the Egyptians were slaughtered by a far smaller force armed only with spears and swords. Deeming themselves in honour bound to save the garrison at Khartoum, the British government sent out General Charles Gordon, a former governor-general of the Sudan, who promptly became besieged in the city.

General Sir Gerald Graham led a force of 4,000 British infantry and cavalry with eight 7-pounder guns and six Gatlings against Osman Digna, now much reinforced, and with two Krupp guns from the Hicks massacre manned by pressed Egyptian artillerymen. In early March 1884 at El Teb, in a convincing demonstration of the superiority of discipline backed by modern rifles, artillery and machine-guns over numbers and fanatical courage, Graham defeated Osman Digna who lost over 2,000 killed. A few days later, Graham again triumphed at Tamai, beating off some 9,000 tribesmen and killing more than 2,000; British losses in both battles were 144 killed and 257 wounded; the campaign was then brought to a close.

These encounters taught the British at first hand what it was like to come up against the fanatically brave and ferocious Ansar. From the moment a few flags appeared over a crest, then solid masses of tribesmen came into view, the bushes became alive with riflemen who swarmed invisibly through the scrub, revealed only by little smoke puffs rising above mimosa trees. The muffled roar of a vast crowd hung on the still, hot air, chanting 'La Illah illa'llah wa Muhammad rasul Allah!', backed by the incessant beating of drums. Contemporary accounts tell how disconcerting this could be: 'they had a knack of making their drums sound as if they were many miles away and the next moment they rose from the grass a few feet away from you'; a black cloud moving so rapidly forward that it astonished the watching British soldiers. Seemingly well-drilled, they manoeuvred in big phalanxes, each headed by a superbly mounted and well-attended Amir; jogging forward and increasing in momentum in time with drum-beats, keeping up with, the galloping horses of their excited Amirs, standing in the stirrups and crying encouragement.

Their tactics were based on surprise and shock,

with riflemen screening sword- and spear-armed warriors, softening-up the enemy with their rapid fire; concealed in the scrub and making use of cover to get close before launching an attack, they came forward very fast in wedge-formation that inevitably widened the breach once the point had penetrated enemy ranks. Requiring neither drilling nor organisation, the wedge is a natural formation arising simply from the bravest rushing to the front. At Abu Klea, masses of Dervishes rushed silently down on the left-front corner of the square, the ground quivering under the furious drumming of bare feet; they fell in waves as volleys crashed into them without stopping their charge. Trying to halt the onrushing Dervishes, soldiers sliced off the heads of bullets, but even the huge wounds caused by such expanding missiles did not stop the courageous tribesmen. They hit the square with a spine-shaking impact, forcing the left face back onto the rear of the square's front face; once within, the avalanche was broken by frightened camels forming a living traverse and the centre became a maelstrom of desperate conflict, with camels, horses, uniformed soldiers and naked tribesmen welded together in a hacking, slashing, surging mass. The rear rank, forced up onto a steep little ridge within the square, were able to fire over the heads of front-rank men, into the heaving confusion of camels and Dervishes, until they began wavering. Then slowly and reluctantly, they walked away from the square, turning backs upon it as they sullenly retreated into the scrub, leaving the surrounding ground white with the jibbahs of the great piles of dead behind them. Following up, there was the ever-present danger of wounded tribesmen lying in the scrub feigning death, shooting or slashing at all who came within reach.

Frantic firing soon caused dense clouds of smoke to hang on the still air, blending with dust to conceal the Dervishes and allow them to approach unseen, bursting like spectres from the haze flourishing broad-bladed spears and cross-hilted swords, or creeping and crawling beneath the muzzles of rifles and guns, to suddenly erupt like malevolent jack-in-the-boxes, hacking and slashing with 5-feet long swords, razor-sharp and capable of lopping off a man's arm or slicing off the top of the skull.

Cavalry always had a hard time against them

The Desert Fights, 1884.

as the Dervishes flung themselves to the ground and tried to hamstring passing horses with sickle-bladed knives; lancers thrust until lances broke or could not be withdrawn from a body, then they cut with sabres, but found it impossible to reach crouching or lying men. Later, General Stewart ordered the Hussars to convert Arab spears into lances by weighting the heads with rolls of sheet iron. Dervishes did not break with the shock of a cavalry-charge's impact, as undisciplined savages were supposed to do – they attacked horses with rifle butts, swung long heavy swords at mounts and riders, and hacked at horses' legs with broad-bladed spears.

Towards the end of 1884 the British government belatedly sent Sir Garnet Wolseley to relieve Khartoum; he sent the River Column of 2,000 up the Nile by boat, to take to the desert and meet General Stewart's Desert Column of 2,000 men, marching across the Bayuda to Metemmeh on a more direct route to Khartoum. After desperate battles at Abu Klea, where 174 men were killed or wounded in five minutes of

The Dervish warriors.

fighting, and at Abu Kru where Stewart was killed, they reached the Nile, to meet four armoured river-steamers sent down by Gordon from Khartoum. Two of them made an epic river-journey, discovering at Khartoum that the town had fallen two days earlier when Gordon was killed.

Moving out from the supply port of Suakin, General Graham's force fought memorable battles at Hasin and Tofrik, where the square was momentarily broken with 100 killed and 140 wounded. By April 1885, after horrendous casualties, most of the tribes had deserted Osman Digna and this part of the campaign was practically at an end. In January 1885 Earle's River Column struggled on until recalled, but Earle himself was killed; Wolseley arrived in Suakin, announced the campaign was to end, and in June 1885 returned to England as the Mahdi died of typhus, succeeded by the Khalifa Abdullahi.

By now the Egyptian Army had been reorganised and strengthened by British units and for three years fought successful actions at Ginnis on 30 December 1885, at Saras in April 1887, at Toski in August 1889 – an action marking the turning point of the Mahdist invasion of Egypt. In 1888/9 the Jehadia, said to be 85,000 strong, won a war against the Abyssinians so costly that the Khalifa could never again amass such a large army.

Kitchener's Dongola Expedition of 1896/8, when inflicting crushing defeats on the Dervish army at Firket, Atbara and Omdurman, discovered that although they still fought as redoubtedly as ever, they had not appreciably altered since the battles of the early 1880s and their ageing Remington rifles and spears were no match for modern artillery, machine-guns, repeating rifles, nor even the hard-hitting Martini-Henrys of the new Egyptian Army. Nevertheless, it was still one of the most powerful African armies at the end of the nineteenth century. The Amir Mahmud, trapped with 12,000 men in an angle of the Nile and Atbara, entrenched themselves behind a thorn zariba enclosing a stockade and triple-trench amid bush thick with thorn and scrub-grass, dotted with a honeycomb of holes and pits. Showing no signs of life, the tribesmen lay there under a heavy bombardment until British and Egyptian infantry stormed in, when suddenly out of the very ground erupted dusty black figures, fighting like demons. Unable to withstand the crashing musketry volleys, they were driven onto the dry sand bed of the river, soon thickly carpeted with bodies; Madmud himself was captured.

Now the Khalifa, unacquainted with battle since 1885, with the exception of Osman Digna, had only untried or undependable commanders, but instead of awaiting attack in the hilly area around his capital of Omdurman, he obligingly flung his Ansar army at Kitchener's well-defended zariba on the banks of the Nile. Said to be about 40,000 strong, it was formed of the *Khalifa's Guard* of about 1,000 men in two *Rubs*, one with Remingtons, the other divided into Khashkhashkan, wearing red waistcoats over jibbas and armed with percussion elephant-guns on tripods; Mushammaratiya, tall natives with long spears; and axe-armed Bultagia. The *Mulazamiyya*, under Uthman Shaykh al-Din, 10,000 riflemen in 18 *Rubs*, subdivided into 8 to 10 standards each 100 strong. The *Omdurman Garrison* led by Ibrahim Khalil, 2,500 in 500 standards divided into three main and three lesser Rubs, half armed with rifles. *Uthman Azraq's 'Flag'* of 8,000 men under six Amirs. *Green Flag* (Abdallah abu Siwar) 2,500 in three tribal *Rubs* under five Amirs. *Black Flag* led by Amir Yaqub, 12,000 men in 51 standards, with less than a thousand firearms. And finally, the 7,000 natives of *Uthman Diqna*. This savage and courageous army was described by Winston Churchill (who fought there) and others as: 'a mighty army, its huge banners flying, drums beating and spears flashing...in the clear morning air the pageant was truly magnificent, a splendid panorama of 40,000 barbarians all moving forward to do battle with the largest Army which Great Britain had placed in the field for forty years...' An *Illustrated London News* correspondent mentions the sound of the Dervish Army as 'a loud continuous murmur of prayer chanting culminating with increased drum tempo in the whole line sweeping forward with a mighty roar'.

The unceasing blast of fire from the zariba and the river gunboats raked the ever-attacking Ansar with devastating effect, causing them to disintegrate as they pressed forward over piled bodies; the Amir Bhaikr Bedri (a leader of known courage) was said to have rubbed his face in the sand out of fear of the dreadful bullets and shells. By mid-morning it was all over with the Ansar wiped out as few armies have ever been – losing 11,000 killed, 16,000 wounded and 4,000 prisoners from 40,000. The Anglo-Egyptian army of 22,000 men, lost 48 killed and 382 wounded. For more than a year, the Khalifa, Uthman Diqna, Shayk al-Din, Ali Wad Helu and a small but faithful band hid in south-west Sudan until tracked down and destroyed by Wingate and two Sudanese regiments recruited mostly from ex-Mahdists; only Uthman Diqna escaped.

10 The Egyptians

In Egypt in 1882 Arabi Pasha set himself up as a virtual dictator of the country, supported by many of his countrymen brought to his banner by the impassioned demands he made for the foreigner to be driven from the country. As a major power, Britain found it impossible to recognise his control of Egypt and, in June of that year, found herself fighting for the Khedive against his own minister of war. Claiming descent from Husseyn, the youngest grandson of the Prophet Mahomet, Sayed Ahmad Bey Arabi – Arabi Pasha – leader of the Egyptian Nationalist Party, was 48 years of age when defying the guns of the British Fleet sent to Alexandria to overawe him. Entering the army as a private he rapidly rose to the rank of Lieutenant-Colonel and, after being reinstated when cashiered after a false charge, became the most popular soldier in the army. In 1881, at the head of the Cairo garrison, he marched to the Abdin Palace, secured the fall of Riaz Pasha, a prominent politician, and obtained a pay rise for the army, subsequently becoming under-secretary for war in the Egyptian government and being created a Pasha. Having declared support for the powerless Khedive, Britain sent Admiral Sir Beauchamp Seymour's Mediterranean Fleet to lie off Alexandria for some weeks, but without the authority to land and stop the rioting and massacre of Christians in the town. Growing bolder, Arabi Pasha (known to the British sailors and soldiers as 'Horrible Pasha') set his engineers and their plentiful labour forces to strengthen the forts around the harbour and throw up substantial earthworks, besides mounting heavy guns. A Naval Officer correspondent of the *Illustrated London News* wrote: 'A few days ago Egyptian troops were exercised at shelter-trench making...and now a very creditable series of earthworks protects their guns, some originally pointing landwards now command the harbour. Probably not far short of 150 guns of all kinds might now be brought into play against a hostile fleet.'

On 10 July 1882 the British presented an ultimatum for the surrender of the forts, otherwise they would be bombarded from the sea; on rejection, the Royal Naval battlefleet cleared its decks for action. It consisted of eight battleships mounting 60- and 80-ton guns, and 11 small gunboats armed with 64-pounder and 7-in rifled guns, besides Gatlings mounted in their foretops. Against them, the forts were plentifully equipped with 18- and 12-ton guns and many smaller calibre weapons. Fire was opened at 7.00 a.m. on 11th July and continued throughout the morning; the defences were quickly obscured with clouds of smoke and dust and occasionally magazines were set off with shattering roars. Onlookers reported that it seemed scarcely possible for men to stand their guns under such fire as was

Arabi Pasha.

90

A Krupp field-gun in the earthenworks, Alexandria.

poured on them, admiring this unexpected obstinacy of the gunners remaining so long at their posts, fighting their guns gallantly as their batteries crumbled about them. The Egyptian artillerymen revealed courage and determination equal to that which might be displayed by any army in Europe; their officers set a fine example by springing upon the parapets in most exposed positions, selecting targets and directing fire. Alas, the technical ability of Arabi's gunners was unworthy of the officers who led them so gallantly, and the British fleet had only 10 men killed

Cuirassier of the Guard, Cairo.

Ismailia at the mouth of the Suez Canal. General Graham took 2,000 men and a few guns into the very heart of the desert to secure the precious water of the Sweetwater Canal at Kassassin. At this time Arabi Pasha had about 60,000 fighting men disposed at the likeliest places all over the Delta – in the neighbourhood of Alexandria, at Cairo, and at Tel-el-Kebir, a commanding point on the railway between Ismailia and the capital. It was an army made up of different races and ethnic groups – negroes of the Sudan, Arabs of various tribes, and large numbers of Bedouin tribesmen; a fairly high proportion were ordinary peasants or fellaheen, forcibly conscripted by Arabi. A war correspondent of the *Globe* wrote that, at Mahuta, there were many dead wearing brown felt head-coverings of peasants, besides numerous woven palm-leaf baskets used to carry provisions. Wolseley did not consider it a formidable army, but feared that Arabi might arouse Mohammadan fanaticism to a pitch that could transform the scale and scope of the struggle.

The Egyptian military system was adapted to secure maximum strength in wartime, or minimum when the army was on a peacetime footing; every soldier passing through the ranks could be recalled, and a large portion of the male population could be mustered in the ranks in times of necessity. Raids were made on villages for levies of fresh men, who received arms and ammunition, but no uniform and little training, whole companies being summarily drafted from one battalion to another if suspected of disloyalty. At the time of the Arabi Pasha rebellion the Army was weaker than at any period in its history, its strength being only six regiments of infantry (9,000 men); two regiments of cavalry (1,000); one regiment of Field Artillery (600); one regiment of Coast Artillery (700) totalling in all only 11,300 men, but all old soldiers. Large numbers of veterans must have been recalled to the Colours and numerous fellaheen (Egyptian peasants) dragged from their homes and formed into regiments which could have had little power of cohesion or confidence in each other.

The rebel Egyptian infantry wore tunics and trousers of coarse white cotton cloth; tunics had a low round-fronted standing collar, six buttons in a single row, with badges and buckles all of brass bearing the star and crescent. Loose trousers and white canvas gaiters worn over black

and 27 wounded, although one ship received 27 hits. By one o'clock all fire from the forts had ceased and no resistance was offered to a landing party that spiked guns and burst the barrels of those guns not put out of action by the bombardment. An Egyptian officer of the garrison later said that about 900 were killed and wounded of the 8,000 who manned the forts. Rioting, murder and incendiarism raged unchecked for two days in the city until permission was received for a force of sailors and Marines to be landed; they fought a street-by-street, house-by-house battle with the looters until peace was restored.

Far from subduing Arabi, the defeat spurred him to greater resistance, so a force under Sir Garnet Wolseley was sent to destroy him; collected from Britain, India and the Mediterranean garrisons of Cyprus, Gibraltar and Malta, by mid-August 40,000 men were lying in transports in Alexandria Bay. Deluding Arabi that the bulk of the force were going to land at that place and seek battle at the fortified lines of Kafrdowar, Wolseley landed a feint force, while the convoy sailed eastwards to disembark on 20th August at

An Egyptian infantryman, 1882.

leather shoes; all equipment was black leather including straps on field-pack, which was brown or black and had a cooking-pot strapped to it, and a grey blanket-roll wrapped round it, or slung over the left shoulder and round the body. A brass-hilted wavy-bladed sword bayonet carried on the left side in a brass-mounted steel scabbard; the small red fez (tarboosh) had a short black tassel hanging from its top. Officers wore a very dark-blue, single-breasted, short thigh-length tunic, with voluminous skirts and a row of eight yellow metal buttons; with it was worn a white shirt and black stock. On the shoulders were gold-fringed epaulettes, varying to indicate rank. Trousers, the same colour as the tunic, were full and tapered towards the ankles. Headgear was a red tarboosh with long black tassel hanging from the crown. Black leather waistbelt, with square yellow metal buckle bearing star and crescent; swords were either steel, three-bar hilted in plain steel scabbard, or white-hilted Mameluke-type sword in black leather and yellow metal scabbard. Cavalry were dressed as infantry, with black pouchbelt over left shoulder, and black waistbelt and slings carrying a steel, three-bar hilted sword in a steel scabbard. Short

Bedouins firing and running away.

black boots without spurs, instead of gaiters.

Infantry were armed with Remington 11-mm (·433) rolling-block repeater rifle, capable of 17 shots a minute; made in USA under contract, 60,000 had been delivered in 1876. It was also supplied as a carbine for cavalry and a musketoon for artillery; the sword-bayonet was mounted on the right side of the barrel. Because it held sand and led to 'hanging-up' of locks and breech-mechanism, oil was never used on Remington rifles, which were so rubbed by their owners as to look as though made of silver. Their musketry left much to be desired and was always better at long rather than short range; at Tel-el-Kebir, 18 infantry battalions, advantageously posted, poured out hails of fire, but only killed two men! Conscripts were armed with old brass-mounted, muzzle-loading muskets.

Divided equally between the lines of Kafrdowar and Tel-el-Kebir were 80 Krupp guns and two field batteries, with mitrailleuse and rocket batteries at both places; at Tel-el-Kebir were 12,000 infantry, chiefly young soldiers although said to be 'the flower of the army', plus 6,000 irregular Bedouins and a regiment of cavalry. Although Arabi had a basis of well-trained men and many field-guns, rifles and stores, he lacked efficient officers and NCOs, but he did have unlimited numbers of excellent workmen to build military works. The emphasis on fortification at Kafrdowar, Tel-el-Kebir and other places undoubtedly arose from his commonsense disinclination to meet the British in an open and general action; it was thought that if he held out until the Nile was high enough, he could cause infinite trouble. His artillery were Krupp field-pieces of the pattern used by the Prussians in their 1870 war against the French; they were only slightly inferior to the ordinary muzzle-loaders of the British artillery.

Graham's small force brushed aside resistance at Mahuta and entrenched at Kassassin, with Drury Lowe's Cavalry Brigade at Mehsameh, some miles to their rear. On 28th August determined Egyptian attacks across the Canal were repulsed by the Royal Marine Artillery; their infantry showed considerable skill in strengthening their left flank by moving along reverse slopes with only skirmishers on the skyline. Advancing in excellent attacking formation, they halted and dug a line of shelter-trenches about 1,000 yards from the British position, pushing infantry along the Canal to the left to within 90 yards of the

The Battle of Tel-el-Kebir, 1882.

York and Lancaster Regiment. Throughout their guns were extremely active and splendidly served, many shells bursting among the British troops. Fortunately, they were common shell with percussion fuses which, when plumping deep into the soft sand, burst in such a fashion that few splinters flew upward; later, when using shrapnel, the fuses were badly cut causing the fire to be ineffective. Reinforced by 7th Dragoon Guards and three squadrons of Household Cavalry (Lifeguards and Blues) in the evening Graham counter-attacked when the ponderous horsemen, cheering wildly, rode straight into the Egyptian infantry, trampling and sabring them into a disorganised retreat.

Arabi now withdrew behind the entrenched lines of Tel-el-Kebir, and in the next few weeks repeated skirmishes occurred between British and Indian cavalry against Regular Egyptian Horse, aided by Bedouins who fired from the saddle at long range; these brief encounters indicated a boldness and dash creditable to the Egyptian cavalry. Constructed to the most advanced principles of military engineering, on a four-mile-long ridge, the lines of Tel-el-Kebir were garrisoned by about 22,000 men with numerous guns. Wolseley planned to tackle this formidable position at first light, after a 5½ mile night march at one mile per hour by his 17,000 men and 67 guns, beginning at 1.30 a.m. on 13th September. After hours of patient plodding through the dragging soft sand, a paling of the sky showed dawn to be near. Dramatically the darkness was shattered by a torrent of firing from all along the Egyptian entrenchments; British bugles sounded the charge and relieved men filled the air with cheers as they dashed forward, bayonets fixed and without a shot being fired. Only 150 yards of open ground had to be covered, nevertheless nearly 200 men went down before reaching the 6-feet wide, 4-feet deep ditch fronting the 10-feet high parapets. In the darkness, the Highland Brigade on the left of the attack went forward faster than the rest and were first to break into the enemy entrenchments; their bagpipes could be heard screeching above the tumult of the battle as the Highlanders fought grimly with bayonet and rifle-butt. On extreme right the Irish Regiments screamed wildly as they carried the position with the bayonet; while on the far side of the Canal the Indian contingent met with little opposition and turned Arabi's right flank to complete the rout of his broken men. So quickly and successfully had the works been stormed that the Guards, in Wolseley's second line, did not fire a shot. Arabi lost his camp, stores and guns, suffered many casualties and his army was damaged beyond recovery.

The Egyptian infantry at Tel-el-Kebir were said to have borne the unexpected attack out of the darkness with the discipline and desperation of first-class troops; the Highlanders, losing 243 out of the 339 casualties suffered by Wolseley's force, encountered strong resistance from the Egyptian Guard Regiment, who fell back silently and sullenly before them. Commanding the Highland Brigade, Sir Archibald Alison said the following words:

'I must do justice to those much maligned Egyptian soldiers. I never saw men fight more steadily. They were falling back on an inner line of works which we had taken in flank and at every re-entering angle, at every battery and re-doubt, they rallied and renewed the fight. Five or six times we had to close on them with the bayonet and I saw those poor men fighting hard when their officers were flying before us.'

It was mostly the black Nubian infantry who fought well; hitherto stationed at Damietta from whence they came to reinforce Tel-el-Kebir, they were considered by many to be the best troops Arabi had, with finer physiques than the fella-heen and better shots, their eyes unaffected by the chronic ophthalmia of the Egyptians. Tel-el-Kebir showed that while Egyptian soldiers were unable to meet Wolseley's men in open fighting, they were by no means to be despised within such earthworks and had Wolseley waited until daylight to deliver his attack, his losses would undoubtedly have been much heavier. Earlier, after the action at Kassassin, an attack from out of Tel-el-Kebir had impressed the correspondent of the *Standard*, who wrote:

'It was impossible not to give the enemy credit for skilful tactics, and it was not from any fault of their leaders that the attack was unsuccessful. For a quarter of an hour, the position of our force and camp looked exceedingly critical, and our infantry were in eminent danger of being out-flanked, until our cavalry forced the enemy back by moving round their flank.'

On the night of the day following the battle at Tel-el-Kebir, British cavalry made an arduous forced march of about 40 miles, to enter Cairo just in time to save the city from destruction, and to capture Arabi himself. Their leader gone and wearied with a war in which they had no substantial interest, the rebel army dispersed and the campaign was over.

11   The Kaffirs

The vaguely defined frontiers of Cape Colony were racked with insecurity as black and white men competed for grazing land in the 1770s, when colonists met the independent tribes of the Xhosa who were established in the High Veld (Zuurveld). For a while they lived in relative peace, but inevitably incidents and clashes occurred between white settlers, Bantu tribes and Kaffirs in Kaffaria, the native land to the north-east of Cape Colony. From the Arabic word for infidel or unbeliever, Kaffirs was the semi-disparaging name given by Europeans to the Bantus as a whole. There were nine major clashes: in 1781; 1789–93; 1799–1803; 1811–12; 1819; 1834–5; 1846–8; 1850–2 and 1877–9 – these border wars only ending when a considerable part of the British Army had become involved and all tribal areas incorporated into Cape Colony in the late nineteenth century. The sequence of events was invariably the same – white men (often Boers who had settled in the area) had their cattle stolen by black Xhosa tribesmen, who measured wealth in heads of cattle; punitive expeditions were organised against the rustlers, leading to savage and prolonged hostilities.

In early wars the British government's inclination to appease rather than take military action encouraged the Kaffirs in their violence and plundering; the Boers felt hard done by as it seemed the British authorities invariably regarded them as instigators and the Xhosa as being innocent and put upon. Later, frontier-farmers were infuriated when similar situations were excused by letters and reports of Churchmen and other do-gooders, suffering from a misplaced sense of sympathy for the tribesmen.

At the turn of the eighteenth century the country from the Cape to the Limpopo was in a state of flux and thousands of tribesmen were slaughtered in wanton massacres by followers of Mzilikaze (founder of the Matabele in Rhodesia), Matiwani and Mantatisi, who were in turn scourged by Shaka, organiser of the Zulu nation. A population of displaced persons was created by the dis-

ruption of tribal life, bringing into existence the Fingoes, allies of the British in the frontier wars. Also involved in these struggles were the Hottentots, often in uneasy alliance with one or other of the protagonists.

The Xhosas' racial stock and language was similar to that of their cousins, the Zulus; although military they were not in the same class and did not maintain a standing army. In battle, Kaffirs were usually naked and covered with grease, although some wore a reversed-hide cloak wrapped round the left arm and held across the body for protection, both cloak and skin dyed a rich brown with ochre stain. Besides showing a liking for bead-decorations, some affected a head-dress of grey wing-feathers in a headband; chiefs displayed a single crane-feather as an emblem of seniority. Each man carried a bundle of throwing spears although, for the 1846 war, theft and illicit trading had brought them muskets with plenty of ammunition. Oval ox-hide shields about 4 feet high, similar but inferior to those of the Zulus, were used in tribal conflicts but soon abandoned against the white man when their uselessness against bullets was demonstrated. Throughout the wars, the Kaffirs displayed a surprising ability to adapt strategy and tactics to situations, substituting wild rushes into the face of musketry by raids from dense bush where the strong, active and lightly-armed native had a great advantage over the heavily accoutred, cross-belted British soldier. Much of the fighting was in dense forests where thick foliage interwoven with baboon-ropes and creeper made movement difficult, giving the Kaffirs a cloak of invisibility.

The traditional Xhosa battle formation resembled the Zulu 'chest and horns', being an encircling movement of warriors advancing frontally with bodies of men wide on both flanks; veteran warriors remained in the rear acting as the chief's bodyguard. In attack, Kaffirs charged down on the enemy, spear-bundle held in the left hand and throwing with the right when within range; the accuracy and penetrative power of the

Kaffirs lie in wait behind the bush to attack the waggon train.

throwing spears was accentuated by causing them to vibrate in flight. The last spear was retained as a stabbing weapon for fighting at close quarters. Sir Harry Smith, that colourful Peninsular War veteran sent to the Cape as Commander-in-Chief, knew as much about the Kaffir as anyone and wrote of them:

'...these determined barbarians...these treacherous savages, with whom self-will alone is law...although as a UNITED enemy nothing could be more contemptible than the poor athletic barbarians, yet to inflict any punishment on them the most rapid and gigantic marches were requisite and every patrol must be conducted on the most vigilant and scientific principles. Most enterprising men were watching (our) every movement, ready to take advantage of inactivity or error.'

And, on another occasion:

'The world does not produce a more beautiful race of blacks than these Kaffirs, both men and women; their figures and eyes are beautiful beyond conception, and they have the gait of princes. It was one of my great endeavours to make them regard appearing naked as a grievous sin, now that they were British subjects; and no one was ever permitted in my camp, much less in my presence, but dressed in his karosse. This karosse is the skin of a bullock, but beautifully dressed so as to be pliant and soft, and then ornamented by fur, beads, buttons, etc. The head-dresses of the chief's wives are really beautiful.'

In 1846, ten years after the last war and nine years since Queen Victoria had become Queen of England, dispatches from Cape Town told of:

'...the opening scenes of a struggle of life and death to the Colonists of the Cape of Good Hope...the Lieutenant-Governor, Colonel Hare, was actively placing the Eastern Districts in a defensive as well as aggressive position; and the Kaffirs, on their side, prepared for their peculiar style of warfare. Nor were our difficulties inconsiderable; for all who knew the state of Kaffirland, foresaw the certainty that all the chiefs would join whenever a prospect of plunder was opened, and that we should have to cope with 8,000 warriors, provided with firearms, in their own fastnesses, and, at the same time, defend 150 miles of an almost untenable frontier line. Such was the extent of the exposure for the feeling of the T'slambri and Congo tribes was very doubtful, and even the distant Amagaikas leaped for joy when the news of the anticipated forays was announced to them. On the causes of this disastrous train of events, far be it from us to hazard an inference unsupported by the circumstances of the case. We know not how much may fairly be attributed to an unfortunate exercise of the influence of Exeter Hall, grounded on very partial information; we know not what mischief may have been done to the Kaffirs themselves by diplomatic amusements and treaty-making with an uncivilised people, who are, for good purposes, under no sort of Government whatever: but this we do believe, upon the faith of the Governor of the Cape, Sir Peregrine Maitland, a man of humane character and high principle, that in the present affair, the Colonists are not to blame. Annually, for the last ten years, in defiance of the treaties, have murders been committed, and thousands of their cattle swept away, without any means of protection or reprisal.

'We have also the details of an affair in the immediate presence of the Governor, at Post Victoria, on the 19th, in which our troops and the Kaffirs fought with the most determined bravery, through a bushy country; our troops file-firing as cool and steady as if on parade with blank cartridge; the Kaffirs fired 2,000 shots, at least, and is supposed numbered some 15 or 1600: their skirmishing was truly surprising; their firing high must account for the miraculous escape of our troops, who fought their way through a determined horde, with the loss of only one man — a distance of five miles.

'In the general order of the 20th, the Governor remarks that the Kaffirs are not the same foe as formerly, when armed with native weapons; but have become much more formidable from increased numbers, considerable mounted force, and especially through the possession of fire-arms, an acquisition particularly adapted to the entangled country which was the scene of the last operations.

'An Extra Supplement to the Graham's Town Journal, to the date of April 25, states the whole country, from Kaffirland to Bushman's River, to be in the hands of the Kaffirs, who were ravaging it with impunity.

'The whole country south of Graham's Town was lighted up at night by the burning houses and lighted produce of the isolated, defenceless farms. In all, up to April 25, five thousand head of cattle were known to have been swept off the Colony by "the Friendly Tribes", whilst our troops were keeping our undisguised enemies, the Amagaikas, at bay.

'Immense herds of colonial cattle were driven through the Fish River by large bodies of Kaffirs; they passed close under the guns of the post, and suffered much loss from the grape and canister shot thrown in amongst them; the dead and wounded were instantly placed on pack bullocks and carried off.

'The events occurred in the neighbourhood of Graham's Town, from which nearly all the troops had been withdrawn; or in Lower Albany, which was protected in front by a small force at Fort Peddie. The Kaffirs, therefore, avoided the troops; and by intercepting messengers, kept the Governor in ignorance of their movements on his right and in his rear. The Burgher force was only

then beginning to arrive at this scene of danger.' (*Illustrated London News*, 26 July 1846)

The *South African Commercial Advertiser*, of May 6th, gives a picture of the environs of Graham's Town:

'The Kaffirs, in parties of considerable strength, are ravaging Lower Albany, and almost every night attack cattle posts within two or three miles of Graham's Town. To the west of Graham's Town they are also met in sufficient number to arrest ordinary communication along the whole line to Fort Beaufort, and to render it unsafe to move in that direction any but very strong escorts. The Town itself is felt to be in danger, and they have no power to assist such places as Bathurst, or to spare reinforcements to posts on the right, where the Commandants are no longer able to check the bands of marauders entering the Colony and returning with droves of cattle.

'Fort Beaufort and Block Drift Post are in front of Sandilla, Macomo and Botma's Country, whose people are thus kept in check. On the left is the Kat River Settlement, the Kaga, and Baviaan's River, and in the rear, at the distance of 50 or 60 miles, is the village of Somerset. The troops cover this large area against masses of the enemy in front, but detached parties have moved far beyond the camp, and are also ravaging that part of the country.

'Cape papers to the 16th of May have also arrived. Continued skirmishes with the Kaffirs on the frontier furnish the staple of news, and the loss of property to the settlers had been great in consequence. The Governor was waiting reinforcements before he took the field against his adversaries, and this delay is supposed to have given them encouragement in their attacks.'

On 28 July 1846, a correspondent of *The Times*, writing from Fort Beaufort, wrote:

'The Kaffirs are entirely changed since the last war, by the general possession of fire-arms; they now come on boldly, and are most expert in bush fighting, which is the great thing in this horribly tangled country. In fact, they are a nation of tirailleurs and sharpshooters. So the army have found to their cost. They lost half their baggage, and ran the gauntlet through thousands of these savages, banging at them from every bush — that is, from almost every inch of the country, and causing much loss and annoyance. A horrible feature of this warfare is the ferocity of the Kaffirs to the wounded: when one of our men is down,

Rescue of ammunition waggons.

they rush at him in spite of guns, great and small, drag him off, rip him up, and do all sorts of horrors. One unfortunate man they got hold of, they actually roasted on one of the captured waggons. We have found a much more formidable foe than we expected, which promises a long and severe war; we have captured 1,800 head of cattle from them, but I fear they have taken many more, and better ones, from the troops and colony.

'It is thought best to move through this country in the night, as the Kaffirs are less alert than in the day. Martial law has been proclaimed for the whole colony, and the Burgher force has been summoned from every district. Levies of Hottentots are also being made, who will be organised into provisional companies. In the meantime, large parties of Kaffirs are entering the colony above and below us, murdering stragglers and couriers on the roads, driving off cattle, and burning the detached farmhouses. There are constant skirmishes between them and the Burghers.

'The ammunition is the great attraction to them now. The adroitness with which they carry off cattle is almost miraculous; you never know they are near till they suddenly appear in the midst, and then, with a peculiar whistle, they make the beasts follow them with a run. They lie hid, and creep along, so that our sentries can seldom see them; only the Hottentots' eyes can match the Kaffirs, and detect them.'

The *Illustrated London News* for Saturday 8 August 1846 deemed the situation serious enough to devote its leader article to it:

'THE KAFFIR WAR. It is the fortune, or rather the misfortune, of all border districts to become the seats of violence and war, and to continue so, long after the interior parts of a colony or country are settled. This is the case even where nations akin to each other, and equally advanced in civilization, join their boundaries; still more likely is there to be strife where the white man approaches the territory of the savage; there

100

"knowledge is power" in every sense of the term, and the superiority of the civilised man is at once felt, feared and hated. He is submitted to as an inevitable evil; but the submission of the aboriginal inhabitant is only regulated by his weakness. Any cause that gives him a chance of recovering his lost position, revenging his wrongs, or gratifying the love of gain by plunder, which large sections of mankind have often preferred to labour, is sure to be seized. And, in an unsettled country with a wide frontier, and a boundless continent beyond it almost unexplored and unknown, such opportunities are not unfrequent. The population is thinly scattered; all parts are not equally defended: and though a savage race may be quiescent for longer or shorter periods of time, they have a quick instinct in detecting the weak points of a frontier or settlement and, if capable of any organisation among themselves,

are sure to fall upon it. If their numbers increase greatly in proportion to those of the Europeans, similar results ensue. Then the Colony is not always in the same state as to its defence; the Empire of England is wide, and her army comparatively small; if troops are wanted on the Banks of the Indus or the Sutlej, they cannot be at the same time at the Cape of Good Hope. Where the exigency is greatest, there strength is concentrated: other points must shift as they can.

'Such a Border War we are at present engaged in with the Kaffirs; it is the old conflict between the invading white man and the savage, which is for ever being renewed. And it behoves the authorities to act promptly now, and on a better system hereafter; the enemy we have to meet is evidently not to be despised. We do not now come in collision with them for the first time; the race that inhabits the "steppes" of the interior of South Africa is strong and hardy, cunning, ex-

Kaffir chiefs.

ceedingly numerous, and for skill in cattle-stealing and bush-fighting, unrivalled. The names of some of their chiefs have become known in Europe; formerly we were able to gain – and keep – Hinza, one of the ablest of their chiefs, in alliance with us; but, possibly, there may be a "Young Kaffir" party, who, like "Young Ireland", renounces all Saxon connection, and not only talks of physical force, but uses it with considerable effect, as the losses of our colonists prove. The leader of the present movement against us is said to be a young man of a Chief's family. At all events, the crisis must be met boldly and at once, or the dangers of 1826 will be revived.

'Next to knowing ourselves, it is, perhaps, of the most importance that we should know our enemies; we add, therefore, a brief sketch of the general characteristics of the Kaffir race. The Kaffirs, then, are a race with some affinity to the Negro; they are brown-coloured, the darkest among them coming from the north-east. They have their own language, which our missionaries have been able to acquire and use in spreading a knowledge of Christianity among them. That they do not practice its rules, cannot be made a peculiar reproach to them; few Christian nations, in their dealings with savages, have ever set the example. At present, the use they are making of their Bibles and Testaments is for loading their muskets against us: if they knew the history of the last European war, they might reply that men far better taught desecrated holy things quite as unscrupulously. Their great and favourite occupation is breeding cattle; they "glory in their goad and their talk is of bullocks." The employment is held in a sort of honour among them. They hunt extensively, and are not particular as to what the game is; the gazelle and antelope serve when lions, buffaloes, elephants, and such minor prey are scarce; and sometimes, the lions in return hunt them. They know the use of money, build kraals and villages of mud, and wood huts, and are expert in the use of the assagai or dart, which in their hands is a very formidable weapon; but the extent to which they have obtained fire-arms and ammunition by the suicidal avarice of the white-traders, makes them still more dangerous. Their chiefs are hereditary, and exercise despotic power.

'Collect such a people in large numbers on a badly-defended frontier, armed, with farms and cattle all around them, and the havoc and des-truction they can commit can readily be fancied. Their skill in cattle stealing and love of the pursuit is unsurpassable: the ease with which they convey large herds of cattle from place to place, and the way they manage them, are said to partake of the marvellous. They have repeatedly spread consternation through the colony by their inroads; boundary treaties made with them have been always broken: it may be questioned if they understand such obligations. They must be met by force, or the colonists will be ruined.

'To check the progress of these disasters, the whole colony is under arms, and the force that can be brought together numbers 18,000 men. The main difficulty will be, not to check the advance of the Kaffirs, but to prevent their harassing and perpetual attacks. We fear we shall have an Algiers of our own at the Cape, if the Kaffirs ever produce an Abd-el-Kader.'

The war dragged on for two years, being finally settled in 1848 by Sir Harry Smith, fresh from his triumph at Aliwal in the First Sikh War of 1846, who dashingly led an *ad hoc* force to defeat the Xhosas and declared British sovereignty over a large part of the Kaffaria. However, the fruits of victory were dissipated by Lord Glenelg, British Colonial Secretary, who believed these recurring troubles on the Cape frontier were always due to the intransigence of the white settlers and never to the defenceless Xhosa. His remark that 'the original justice was on the side of the conquered, not of the victorious party...' was deeply resented by Sir Harry Smith, who recalled in his autobiography 'Every act of the murderous Kaffirs during the war was regarded as a just retaliation for a previous wrong.' Those who mattered, the white settlers in the area, regarded Smith's expulsion of the Xhosa from the Fish River as the best possible guarantee of future peace on the eastern frontier.

It was only a temporary peace in 1851; because of the influence of good government and spreading civilisation, the Kaffir chiefs found their ancient power and authority melting away. Subsequently Sandilli, the paramount chief, urged them to make a last struggle for independence, and the Umlanjeni (witch-doctors) predicted that now the fortunate time had come. At this stage the Kaffir tribes possessed upwards of 3,000 stand of arms, six million rounds of ball cartridge and half a million assegais, with ample supplies coming in as a trade in arms and ammunition had long been open and unrestricted.

Sir Harry Smith had to carry on an intermittent war over an extent of country twice the size of Great Britain and Ireland, overrun by a most enterprising horde of savages, and to maintain 12 forts. But so long as the insurgents held together and acted in large bodies, they were defeated. Writing of it, he said:

'The peculiarity of the present contest must be borne in mind; it must be remembered that this Kaffir warfare is of the most completely guerrilla and desultory nature, in which neither front, flank nor rear is acknowledged, and where the disciplined few have to contend with the undisciplined but most daring and intrepid many, in the midst of the holds and fastnesses of the latter...The country in which the operations were carried on is far more difficult to ascend and penetrate than even the Amatolas; hence the gallant and enterprising exertions of the troops became the more conspicuous, and called forth that expression of my satisfaction dictated by experience in war which enables a Commander to estimate justly the success he had obtained, and to commend as it deserves the conduct of his officers and soldiers.'

There had been unrest and signs of mutiny among the Kaffir Police and even the Cape Mounted Rifles were disturbed. A report tells how, in December 1851, a patrol of 850 men

'...had been sent to Keiskamma Hoek, where Sandilli was supposed to be concealed. En route they were treated in the most friendly manner by the cunning Kaffirs, till they reached a narrow gorge among the tulip-covered rocks of the Keiskamma, where they could only proceed in single file, and after the Kaffir Police and Cape Rifles (all of whom were natives) had been suffered peacefully to pass, a sudden and destructive fire was opened on our infantry.

'The latter returned it resolutely, but were unable to dislodge their securely-concealed assailants without considerable loss – in all, twenty-one officers and men.

'There was no doubt that our troops were purposely lured into this ambuscade by the Kaffir Police, who were allowed to pass unmolested, and who, next day, deserted to the number of 365 strong, taking with them their women, cattle, arms, and what was more annoying, their knowledge of drill and training. Their desertion was speedily followed by others.'

Soon the country from Graham's Town to the Orange River was almost a desert with homesteads abandoned, flocks and herds driven to safety or captured; attacks were made on British columns and two small forts were besieged by Hottentots and Kaffirs who swarmed across the frontier. A contemporary account reads:

'Christmas day was named as the epoch of a general revolt, so martial law was proclaimed along the whole frontier.

'A party of the 45th Regiment, while quietly escorting wagons to King William's Town, were surprised on the Debe Neck by a large force of Kaffirs, clad in carosses of skin, and with crane's feathers in their hair, and before the unfortunate fellows could form for their own defence the whole were barbarously murdered. Their bodies were found by Colonel Mackinnon's patrol, "with their throats cut from ear to ear" says Captain King of the 74th Highlanders, "and otherwise horribly mutilated, which was afterwards discovered to have been perpetrated before death."

'As this party– a serjeant and fourteen privates – formed a portion of the handful of troops at Fort White, the Kaffirs at once proceeded to attack the weakened garrison; but were gallantly repulsed.

'The inhabitants of all our military villages – discharged soldiers and their families – were now assailed by a concerted attack, and a massacre ensued under circumstances too atrocious and cold-blooded to be detailed in print. The Kaffirs came upon many when in the midst of their Christmas dinner. Johannesberg, Woburn, Auckland, and many other villages were destroyed, and in the last named every man perished.

'Sir Harry Smith himself was hemmed in by the enemy in Fort Cox, but escaped in nondescript garb by a hair-raising solo horse ride across country.'

In the early part of the next year, the Gaikas, on the beautiful range of the Amatola mountains, on being joined by the Tambookies and T'slambies, mustered not less than 15,000 men, and it was confidently expected that Kreli, a most influential chief, could bring 10,000 more into the field.

By 30 January 1852 the Kaffirs had overrun the whole country down even to Graham's Town and the Addo Bush, perpetrating awful outrages; among many others, publicly roasting three men alive at the Kat River.

The war in Kaffirland, and death of Captain Bambrick.

Now followed months of hard fighting in the almost impenetrable forests and mountains of the Kroome Range, the Blinkwater and the Waterkloof and south in the rough country between the Fish and Keishamma Rivers. The Kaffirs were daring and aggressive, making raid after plundering raid from their natural citadels. Throughout all these operations the natives fought naked, only chiefs of rank wearing the caross and headbands of feathers; they fought with muskets and assegais, black woolly heads and musket-muzzles all that could be seen of this invisible enemy, who even fired perched high in the trees. An account of the war (*Campaigning in Kaffirland*) written at the time says:

'The smoke of the enemies' fires curling slowly up from the dark bush, on a steppe, or lower ridge or the elevated range in front, and on the opposite side of a lovely valley which lay at our feet, carpeted with the smoothest and greenest grass, dotted with mimosa, protea, and clumps of tangled bush. On our left towered the lofty peak of the Hog's Back, the highest point of the whole chain, and below it lay a finely-wooded ravine, down the centre of which foamed a milk-white cataract, the dark forest stretching away on either side, and filling the kloof.

'The order was given to "advance in columns of sub-divisions." The valley was now crossed, and as the lofty ridge was neared the dark hordes of Sandilli were seen clustering on its summit, where their arms flashed and glittered in the rays of the morning sun. Their position, from its steepness, appeared absolutely impregnable, save where lay a grassy slope destitute of all cover.'

In later 1852 Sir Harry Smith was succeeded by Major-General George Cathcart who fought and defeated Macomo and Sandilli and their followers, chasing them into the mountains where previously no British troops had ventured, forced them to surrender. In the aftermath of defeat, the Kaffirs unearthed a latter-day Joan of Arc but instead of inspiring them to heroic deeds on the battlefield, her visions told them to destroy all their cattle and crops, causing a self-inflicted national disaster. Not only did thousands die of starvation or abandon their lands, but the Kaffir's will to resist the onward march of the white man was irreparably weakened.

Notwithstanding this, in 1877 Chief Kreli optimistically led his Galekas to unsuccessfully attack a police post; this provoked a surprise attack on his kraal, when flimsy huts were set on fire by shrapnel-shell while independent rifle-fire at 200 yards exacted 1,550 casualties. In a sharp combat at Unzintzani the desperate Galekas, women, children and cattle hidden in a safe place, charged courageously forward to be mowed down by case-shot at 60 yards range and driven behind boulders and anthills. Under a bright African moon, the Galekas again advanced but were beaten off after one and a half hours of incessant rattle of musketry and booming of guns. Five hundred head of cattle or £1,000 was offered for the capture of Chief Kreli but no man could be found to betray his chief, although the Galekas were starving and eating the bark of trees.

Early in 1878, the Galekas and Sandilli's Gaikas attacked two British infantry regiments and a naval battery of 24-pounder rocket-tubes, but were driven back by galling fire and hissing rockets into ravines and a wooded area where they withstood rockets and shells from a 2-pounder gun for over an hour. Later, they were lured into attacking a post at Quintana, heavily defended by three companies of infantry, a 24-pounder naval rocket-tube and a 7-pounder gun, plus some irregular cavalry. About 4,000 strong – Kreli's Galekas from the south and Sandilli's Gaikas from the north-west – the Kaffirs rushed across open ground until, at point-blank range, rockets, case-shot and bullets tore into them. For 20 minutes they stood their ground exchanging fire with their old muskets until a looming mist saved them; when it lifted they had come forward to within 150 yards but were blasted back, leaving 300 dead and many wounded on the ground. This was one of the first occasions when the Martini-Henry rifle was used in action, one Kaffir being killed at 1,800 yards range. Never recovering from these reverses, Kreli surrendered and was permitted to settle in his old kraal; the Gaikas continued the war for a few months until Sandilli was killed.

Probably without knowing anything of each other, the Kaffirs of Cape Colony and the Indians of North America – over the same period, for the same reasons, and in the same way – suffered identical fates. Like numerous other indigenous populations, both ran out of land and had nowhere else to go – the Kaffirs without even a Little Big Horn triumph to ease their passage!

12   The Mahrattas

In the crowded century of conquest which marked the reign of the East Indian Company, the Mahrattas put up the stoutest and most prolonged resistance to the expansion of British rule. Four times within a 65-year period they faced the Company's armies in the field, on each occasion acquitting themselves as staunch and worthy foes. When the Mahratta army was at its best there was nothing else like it until the rise of the Sikhs under Ranjit Singh, but it flowered and withered in a remarkably short space of time; swift in its growth through soon-forgotten fresh principles but reverting to old ways gave rise to decay and degeneracy even while the Mahratta empire was still expanding. Their forward march began in 1639 when the vigorous power of the Mahrattas, personified by the simple hardy peasants of the Deccan and the Western Ghats was nearly forged into a nation by their great eighteenth-century leader Sivaji. Standing midway between Akbar and Ranjit Singh as the outstanding leader produced by the subcontinent in two centuries he tried to unify them by reducing the strength of feudal allegiance and caste. His soldiers were Indians, not invaders, and belonged to the Sudras or manual labourers – cultivators, shepherds, cowmen and the like – the fourth great group in the Hindu caste system. He allowed them to mix freely, but 200 years after him only two classes from the Deccan were accepted into the Mahratta regiments of the British Army. Many of his infantry were tough mountaineers from the Ghats; at first there was not the emphasis on cavalry that marked later armies, when swift-moving horsemen might erupt at any point and could usually defeat a larger but more ponderous army, being able to manoeuvre and move quickly in the face of the enemy and possessing the military virtues of discipline and loyalty.

Sivaji died in 1680 and, although his principles were increasingly neglected, Mahratta power continued to spread – by the end of the eighteenth century their cavalry had 'watered their horses in the Indus'; Calcutta had been forced to construct the 'Mahratta Ditch' as a defence against their raids, they had taken half the Nizam's territory from him, and had won battles in such distant areas as the southern tip of the Indian peninsular. Majestic as these triumphs seemed, they bore a hollow ring, decline setting in with his successors and rapidly increasing. By the mid-eighteenth century, pay was usually in arrears and the cream of the forces – the cavalry paid and mounted by the state – had dropped from two-thirds of the army to less than one in six. There were other cavalry – the silladars, who brought their own men and mounts, the ekadars, each buying his own horse and equipment. There was also a new fourth class called Pendharis, termed by the British Pindaris; of any creed or nation, they were freelance robbers who raided where they chose, giving a sixth of their loot to the state and glad to have a 'home-territory' in which they could recoup and refit.

The Mahrattas won battles because they were disciplined, mobile, tough and united; but over the years lost many of these attributes. Perceiving the success of troops trained on the English and French model, how their disciplined ranks of infantry brought victory and how their small compact bodies of foot were able to repel attacks of lancers and cavalry, who never dared to come to close quarters, they employed foreign instructors. Drilled infantry battalions were formed, mostly of non-Mahratta mercenaries with officers of many nationalities. This system bore the handicap of reducing their greatest asset of swift movement, causing Sir Thomas Munro to comment:

'By coming forward with regular infantry, they gave us every advantage we could desire. They opposed to us men that never could be made so good as our own, from the want of a national spirit among their officers and of the support of European battalions; and they trusted the success of the war to the event of close engagements.'

In the late eighteenth century, they had a Regular Army under De Boigne, a soldier of fortune, who raised and trained armies in the European fashion. At this time, the infantry were a mixture of many creeds and tongues – Sikhs, Rajputs, Sindis, Baluchis, Arabs, Rohillas, Abyssinians and even Portugese. There were few of the old peasant types as it had become unfashionable to be in the infantry, and mercenaries were paid higher wages.

In 1803, eight short years after the great victory over the Nizam, the Battle of Assaye tolled the knell, but it took another war from 1817 to 1819 to bring the Mahratta Empire to its knees. The first of these two great wars included the famous battles of Wellesley and Lake; but its end did not mean prolonged peace for the Indian Army, and in 1817 the Mahratta States, chafing under restrictive treaties and garrisons that prevented them raiding the territories of weaker neighbours, were busily planning fresh resistance. In that year things had come to such a pass that 'if we were to keep India as a land for honest men to live in' (McMunn), the Mahratta Confederacy had to be reduced to a proper status. The combined forces of the Mahratta States and the freelancing Pindaris, bands of lawless horsemen plundering where they wished, amounted to 100,000 horse, 70,000 disciplined foot and over 500 guns.

The enemy in the second war were mainly the Mahratta chiefs who controlled huge bands of mercenary foot and horse, largely trained and officered by Frenchmen. The two wars, particularly the last, confined these chiefs to their rightful provinces and curbed the high pretensions and planned conquests that obsessed them; it was the final conclusion with the Mahrattas, when the country was ridded of the scourge of the Pindari bands.

True so far as it went, but the years that followed were not all peace and bliss; Sir Harry Smith, veteran of the Peninsular Wars, coming to India from South Africa to take command in Sir Hugh Gough's army, wrote: 'It is well known that these Mahrattas have been advocating hostility in every court of the East.' And 1843 dawned as a year full of uneasiness and anxiety to those responsible for British rule in India, with prestige sadly affected by the calamitous happenings in Afghanistan during the previous year, giving rise to highly dangerous thoughts in the minds of the independent princes whose tone became haughty and insolent. More ominous was a noticeably defiant attitude emanating from the

Punjab and the State of Gwalior, causing nightmares that they might consider combining to bring 120,000 men and 500 guns into the field against the East India Company army. Gwalior, ruled by a boy of nine through a powerful minister, was in the throes of internal dissension with the military showing hostility based on the well-grounded conviction that the British sought disbandment of the standing army, a very considerable force still retaining much of the European organisation from past times. Their fears were justified, for large and powerful native armies were inconsistent with East India Company aims; wherever British power reached standing armies were stamped out. Lord Ellenborough, the Governor-General, required that the rulers in Gwalior should attend him in person to discuss the future on a permanent basis; they were prevented from so doing by the military faction who, claiming they were being betrayed, declared their intention of resorting to the test of battle and marched out of Gwalior in the highest spirits, anxious and eager to cross swords with the British.

Displaying a certain lack of military acumen, they divided their forces, sending 14,000 infantry and 3,000 cavalry with 100 guns to oppose Gough 12 miles north of Gwalior; while 12,000 men and 40 guns marched south to meet Grey.

Their reasoning was understandable because the extinction of the army meant personal ruin as they had no other source of employment, no means of livelihood other than that provided by military service. They were the survival of old fighting days when the soldier's calling ranked next to that of the priest's, taking precedence over trader, artisan and agriculturalist; a calling handed down from father to son cherished as honourable, necessary and righteous. At Assaye 40 years before these same fathers and grandfathers had formed a disciplined and trained army that fought with a prowess worthy of a European force, serving guns well, and infantry shoulder to shoulder, firing withering volleys from close-serried ranks, cool and resolute, reserving fire until the word of command. By 1843, they might not have been of the same quality, but undoubtedly they were a force to be taken seriously, as Sir Harry Smith wrote: '...when we reflect that the army of Gwalior consists of at least 22,000 veteran troops, for years disciplined by European officers, and well supplied with artillery'. And later:

'Now if we regard the victories recently obtained over the Mahratta force, 28,000 men whose discipline has gradually been improving under Christian officers since 1803 (the days of Lake and Wellington), well supplied with cannon and every implement of war, animated by a devotion to their cause not to be exceeded – in a military point of view they are achievements in the field which yield alone to Assaye and rank with Dieg, Laswarree, and Mehudpore...'

The Mahratta infantry, formed in regiments, wore varicoloured robes; broad sashes held swords (tulwars); some wore turbans, others a tall, peakless shako broader at the crown than base; armed with matchlocks, some carried round shields. The Mahrattas consistently excelled in the artillery arm on which they greatly prided themselves; Scindia's Grand Park, emplaced at Maharajapore, enjoyed the reputation of being the finest and most powerful artillery park in India. For 60 years the Mahrattas had been casting cannon, the art had been brought to perfection in their arsenals and guns were held by artillerymen as objects of worship and great affection; servicing of them was accomplished almost as an act of religious devotion. During the battle, they fired grape, canister, roundshot and even old horse shoes – in fact, anything that could be crammed down the muzzle.

However, it seemed that neither Lord Ellenborough, the Governor-General, nor Sir Hugh Gough, commander of the army, were impressed with the Mahratta enemy, believing they would not fight; Rait, Gough's biographer, says that Gough did not sufficiently appreciate the strength of the enemy, being misled by political officers. Sir Hugh, his proposals sanctioned by Lord Ellenborough, sent a dispatch to the Duke of Wellington in London:

'Your Grace will not, I trust, consider that I have decided on an injudicious movement by advancing from such opposite points, and leaving to an enemy the option of attacking either Wing, when no support could be afforded it by the other. But I feel perfectly confident that either Wing would be amply sufficient not only to repel, but to overthrow the whole Mahratta force in the field, while, by such a movement, the attacking force would be cut off from the Capital and stronghold of Gwalior, together with what the Mahrattas place so much reliance on, their immoveable park of 300 Guns, by a rapid march of the other Wing. On the other hand, I shall place their Army between two powerful bodies capable of taking in reverse, or of turning the flank of, any position they may take up. It will also enable me, in a great measure, to prevent what I have so long apprehended, the dispersion of their force into bodies of armed men, who would assuredly become bands of Robbers, and make incursions into our territories.'

These sentences may be taken as the key to Sir Hugh Gough's policy in all his Indian wars. One single decisive blow, sufficient to satisfy the enemy that he had much to learn from the European in the art of war, and that, man for man, the British soldier was the superior of even the Mahratta or the Sikh.

So strong was this over-weening self-confidence that when the 12,000-strong army marched out, the Company's heavy guns were left behind at Agra, and officers' ladies were permitted to accompany the army into the field! In fact, the first shots of the war were directed at elephants carrying among others Lady Gough and Sir Harry Smith's wife Juanita, at the head of the columns of march to avoid the dust, almost stumbling upon a large Mahratta force with 28 heavy guns in a strong position around the villages of Maharajapore and Shikapore.

The foe, who at the first glint of British scarlet would, it was confidently assumed, retreat in terror, did no such thing. On the contrary instead of falling back, they advanced during the night and took up a strong position around two villages four miles nearer. These and the intervening space between them, well adapted for defence, they fortified with 28 guns of heavy calibre, supported by several regiments of infantry.

Now followed a 'solider's battle', won by the bayonet without benefit of tactics or manoeuvring; Gough displayed no generalship whatsoever, giving but one laconic order – 'On and at them!' to send his infantry over about four miles of open ground at three formidable lines of defences, with numerous well-served guns and competent infantry behind entrenchments. There were many accounts all concurring in praising the gallantry of the Mahrattas. One observer wrote:

'The enemy deserved the greatest credit for selecting so strong a position and defending it so well. Their numerous and powerful batteries swept the plain from end to end...they behaved with heroic courage, firing round, chain and grape shot supported with withering volleys of musketry, until our gallant fellows drove them

Mahrattas at Maharajapore, 1843.

from the very muzzles of their guns, where the bodies of their artillerymen lay heaped in death.'

Sir Hugh Gough did them equal justice in his dispatch. 'The position of the enemy was particularly well chosen and obstinately defended,' he writes. 'I never witnessed guns better served, nor troops more devoted to their protection. I regret to say our loss has been very severe, infinitely beyond what I calculated. I did not do justice to the gallantry of my opponents.'

In fact Gough lost more than 800 men; the Mahrattas had over 3,000 killed and wounded, and lost 56 guns. In a letter to his son (20 January 1844) Gough described his surprise at the resistance he encountered: 'I thought I should have a mob without a leader, with their heads at variance, I found a well-disciplined, well-organised army, well-led and truly gallant.'

Sir Harry Smith, who fought in the battle, wrote:

'These Mahrattas, nor indeed does any Indian army, know no more than to occupy a strong position and hold it as long as able, sticking to their guns *like men*...the Mahrattas guns were most ably posted, each battery flanking and supporting the other by as heavy a cross-fire of cannon as I ever saw, and grape like hail...the enemy was driven back at every point with great loss, yielding to force, not retiring in haste. A more thorough devotedness to their cause no soldiers could evince, and the annals of their defeat, although an honour to us, can never be recorded as any disgrace to them.'...'In the late conflict no one gave our foe credit for half his daring or his ability...the debris of the army of Sindia now disbanding are as handsome, well-clothed and appointed soldiers, as regular in their engagements as Frenchmen, and inclined to fight in their gallant and vivacious style...'

On the same day, by a strange coincidence almost unique in British military history, some 20 miles away at Punniar, General Grey's force of 4,000 came upon the other Mahratta army in a commanding position on a series of steep hills. Immediately advancing upon them, Grey's force completely outmanoeuvred the enemy and, after a short but spirited struggle, sent them fleeing from the field, leaving over a thousand casualties and more than 20 guns. In sharp contrast to Maharajapore, Grey won his battle by skilful generalship and a striking demonstration of co-ordinated action by his small force, although the Mahrattas did not fight anything like as well as against Gough.

These two victories stamped out the last spark of the Mahratta fire which had so often set India ablaze, and another large and opulent state was annexed to the British Empire. However, it did not end there as the Mahratta resistance in pitched battles against the Company's army led the Sikhs to believe, as they were better soldiers than the Mahrattas, that they could dispute the superiority of British arms in India, and did so two years later. However, it all ended well; during the Indian Mutiny of 1857 there were 8,000 Mahratta soldiers serving with the British, and they stood firm – surprising perhaps, because Nana Sahib claimed to be their traditional ruler and had raised their famous saffron banner.

13   The Maoris

New Zealand was wracked with strife from Captain Cook's arrival in 1769 throughout the nineteenth century, as the Maoris' intricate tribal structure was shattered by drink, disease, fire-arms and the seizure of their lands. Initially, the brutal depredations of rough and tough Europeans – sailors, whalers, traders – caused relations between Maoris and Europeans to degenerate into sporadic warfare. Arming themselves with muskets by trading, the warlike and hard-fighting natives tore their society apart in relentless tribal warfare estimated as causing 65,000 casualties up to 1840. The cause of strife changing into Maori grievances over land turned the 1840s into a decade of war; in 1843 two chiefs, Te Rangihaeata and Te Rauparaha, led their people into a conflict causing the deaths of 22 Europeans, and Hone Heke raised a large war-party in the area of Auckland, sacking a

A Maori war dance.

township and several times in the months of skirmishing that followed, beating British troops. In the biggest action, after artillery had been used against a strongly fortified Maori fort (*pah*), a third of the assaulting party of sailors, soldiers and marines were killed or wounded before retreating. Like a forest fire, strife flickered and died out, to burst into roaring flame. This sporadic warfare, known as 'the fire in the fern' saw again and again an outbreak quelled here while another flared up there. In the late 1850s, the remaining 56,000 Maoris, realising they were rapidly being outnumbered by increasing arrival of European settlers, formed a separatist movement under Wiremu Kingi, that put them on an inevitably divergent path to the newly-granted self-government of the Europeans.

A notorious land-purchase – the Waitara Purchase – triggered off ten years of what the settlers called 'The Maori Wars' and the Maoris 'te riri pakeha – the White Man's Fight'. The

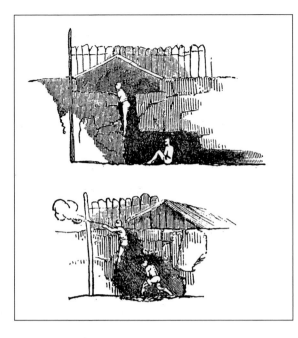

Maori entrenchments.

First Taranaki War was more a campaign spread over 1861/2 in which British and 'Colonial' troops, only 1,000 strong, were outnumbered by hostile local tribes, whom they could rarely pin down to a decisive engagement through their ability to vanish into dense forests, with no lines of communication or towns which could be attacked. Strong, agile and cunning, these first-class fighting men displayed unsurpassed skill and native genius in constructing *pahs* – earthworks held with desperate courage, an aptitude for military engineering sometimes arousing unfounded suspicions that they were directed by Europeans. *Pahs* were never abandoned for fear of adversaries, their principle of warfare lay in the rapidly constructed fort being held long enough to inflict delay and loss on the attackers, then quietly evacuated its garrison retired to an identical *pah* behind it, defended equally stubbornly. Their remarkable ability in defensive warfare was aided by British commanders' preference for direct frontal assaults.

The typical Maori *pah* was about 90 yards by 50 yards, with projecting flanks at each side; surrounded by three rows of palisades, with a 5-ft deep ditch, from which the natives fired, between each. Palisades were made of timbers and tree-trunks 15 ft high and 9–20 in in diameter; flax leaves were stuffed between the timbers, and layers of flax covered the palisade in an elastic and tenacious armour that closed up after a cannon-ball had passed through it. The whole was a series of interconnected trenches and rifle-pits, often in a zigzag trace, one within the other in the manner of a labyrinth; subsidiary trenches flanked approaches to main works and allowed enfilading fire; traverses and banks of earth prevented flanking fire into the defences. The trenches were roofed in with wattle hurdles of branches thatched with ferns over a layer of earth; this roof was supported by timbers that allowed a narrow gap at ground level through which the defenders could sweep the ground before them with their shotguns and rifles. Chambers were hollowed out in the trench sides to shelter the garrison during the preliminary artillery bombardment, who came out when the assault drew near – in the manner of the Germans on the Somme in 1916, 50 years later. In one attack, an Armstrong 110-pounder gun was landed from a naval vessel – the heaviest gun ever used on shore against tribesmen – and fired 100 shells before running out of ammunition, but caused very few casualties; the Maoris crouching in their hollowed-out shelters, were greatly encouraged by the shells making a great noise and doing little damage. A *pah* was fronted by a loosely constructed palisade that impeded the rush of a storming party in the manner of barbed-wire – these primitive fortifications greatly resembled the defensive systems of the Western Front in World War 1.

When attacking a *pah*, it was rare to see even a single enemy figure, all were safely hidden in trenches and pits, poking gun-muzzles through earth-level loopholes and under the foot of the palisades. At the first barrier, attackers tore at timbers and flax-covering, fired through it, thrust bayonets into it and tried to pull it down – it was a hopeless business. At the best known fort *Gate Pah* (Pukehinahina), attacked in 1864, save for the red-and-white Maori fighting flag, marked with three devices of a cross, crescent moon and star, flying above the palisades, nothing could be seen of the enemy although their fire took great effect. At last, the stormers forced their way into the fortification, and seeing no enemy, thought the place abandoned, so downed arms and set about looting. Suddenly from under their very feet from chambers dug in the earth and skilfully

THE MAORIS

camouflaged with branches and turves, completely sheltering them during the eight hours of
artillery bombardment, arose a large number of
Maoris. The fierce volleys they poured into the
astonished white troops caused them to panic
and flee from the *pah*.

There was a brief respite, but by mid-1863 the
province of Auckland was again aflame with insurrection, the Maoris concentrating their forces
at Koheroa in an excellent defensive position on
a narrow, fern-covered mountain ridge, its precipitous sides allowing only direct attack. The
14th Regiment, supported by detachments of the
12th and 70th Regiments, attacking into heavy
fire from unseen opponents, managed to chase
them out of their rifle-pits; momentarily checked
by rattling volleys from a second line of defences
they then drove the Maoris in confusion before
them, some escaping by swimming while others
took off in hidden canoes. Both sides had about
500 men in the two-hour-long fight over an area
of five miles; the British lost 12 killed and a
number of wounded, the Maoris 40 warriors and
many wounded borne from the field. British
troops invaded the Waikato, using gunboats on
the river, and at Rangiriri it cost 100 British
dead to capture 200 Maoris. Three hundred made
a last stand in a *pah* at Orakau, withstanding
three days artillery pounding while short of food
and water; when offered a truce their chief Rewi
Maniapoto replied; 'We will fight on forever,
forever, forever!' Offered sanctuary for women
and children, they said they would fight with
them; late in the afternoon the entire garrison
suddenly rushed out and vanished in nearby
swamps.

The war flamed spasmodically throughout the
1860s as shown by a report in the *Illustrated
London News* of 10 October 1868:

'Recent accounts from New Zealand speak of
an apparently preconcerted outbreak among the
hostile tribes. The notorious Ngatiruanui tribe,
which has become remarkable for its implacable
hatred of the whites, suddenly took the field,
surprised and captured a redoubt erected at
Patea, on the border of Wellington and Taranki
provinces. Since open hostilities ceased, white
men venturing into the neighbourhood have been
repeatedly waylaid and slain. On a portion of the
territory forfeited by the Ngatiruanuis for their
share in the last war a redoubt was lately
erected, but it has failed to hold them in awe.
The Ngatiruanuis can muster several hundred

Chief Wiremu Tamihana, a Maori leader in 1850.

113

Group of Maoris.

warriors of their own and they have the support of the Hauhaus (a fanatical group who believed themselves impervious to bullets, revived cannibalism and attacked with such fanatical ferocity that they unnerved British and New Zealand troops; in battle they continually cried "Hau!" in the belief that it brought immunity). They surprised the redoubt of Turuturumokai on the night of 11th July; of the 25 men who composed the garrison, 10 were killed and five or six wounded, the bodies of the dead being mutilated in a barbarous manner. In expectation of the threatened march of the Ngatiruanuis and the Waikato Hauhaus, all the outlying settlers are fleeing into the towns, and troops of every kind – regulars, constabulary and volunteers – are being collected from all quarters. Immediately after the above-narrated occurrence, a company of natives receiving Government pay, and who were garrisoning another redoubt in the vicinity, deserted to the insurgents carrying with them their breech-loading rifles and revolvers with which they had been provided.'

Like most colonial conflicts of the period the Maori Wars were little more than punitive expeditions, although the punishment seemed to fall as much upon the white troops as on their recalcitrant enemy. The terrain was atrocious – dense forest, bush, swamp, rocky hills, with foot-paths the only lines of communication, and the weather invariably bad. The long and dreary struggle was not popular with the troops who respected the courage and rough chivalry of their native foes, finding much to admire in them when they said: 'It is wrong of the red tribes [the soldiers] to curse us...we are doing no harm...merely fighting them.' Until they had met the Maoris on the ground the British troops invariably underrated their military prowess, but soon found them to be no despicable antagonists, formidable in generalship, energy and courage. Among the noblest of native races, the Maori took readily to Christianity, clinging to old observances so that when a *pah* was taken by surprise on a Sunday morning, they told the stormers they would have been at their posts but for being at Morning Service and felt the soldiers must be strange Christians to fight on a Sunday. However, settlers despised the brown-skinned people who were once cannibals, cared little for land title-deeds, fed on fern-roots and putrid fish, and made their faces hideous by elaborate tattooing.

Sir John Fortescue, famed historian of the British Army, wrote of the Maori:

'He had his own code of war, the essence of

which was a fair fight on a day and place fixed by appointment, when the best and bravest man should win. The British soldier upset his traditions, but could not touch his proud courage nor degrade his proud honour. A Maori was capable of slaughtering wounded and prisoners and perhaps eating them afterwards, but he was known to leap down into the fire of both sides to save the life of a fallen foe. The British soldier therefore held him in the deepest respect, not resenting his own little defeats but recognising the noble side of the Maori and forgetting his savagery.'

Blessed with an innate skill-at-arms and among the most redoubtable fighting men encountered by the Victorian soldier, they were a formidable race, well-armed with skilfully-handled rifles and double-barrelled shotguns; addicted to war their sense of tactics prevented

them being brought to a single decisive encounter. A fiercely independent tribal people, the Maoris enjoyed an organised, natural and highly creative life despite frequent inter-tribal wars. Their daily life was governed by *tapu*, a rigid code of conduct, regulated by a complex set of rules and customs; the chief's authority to maintain peace and order rested on a time-honoured system of taboos; his prestige (*manu*) and the sanctity of their land was paramount. The lands around their strongly fortified villages belonged to the tribe and not to individuals, causing frequent disputes with other tribes over boundaries, when the *manu* of a chief would be affronted, leading to a fierce desire for revenge (*utu*), via an intertribal war. To this military race these wars were an integral part of life, an art-form bounded by its own rituals, courtesies and formal traditions. Faces frighteningly tattooed and in native costume of armless garments with an occasional head-dress of white-over-red feathers, warriors

Tattooed face of a Maori warrior.

A Maori of New Zealand equipped for fighting.

main weapon, the double-barrelled shotgun, was a superior weapon in the thick fern of the bush, more quickly loaded and more effective at short range than the muzzle-loading Enfield, which rapidly fouled and became difficult to load. Maoris held bullets in their mouths, spitting them down the muzzles of the guns, saliva and a tap of the butt on the ground sending the bullet home without the use of a ramrod. Spears could be deadly using a flexible throwing-stick to increase range. At close quarters they used the *meri*, a short, flat, sharp, double-edged stone club; a jade-stone or obsidian *meri* was the weapon of a chief; in the hands of an athletic savage, the wooden club (*patu onewa*) or the *toki poto*, a steel tomahawk on a 5-foot-long handle with pointed butt, was a formidable hand-to-hand weapon.

Throughout the entire war it is believed that the Maori never managed to bring more than 600 men into the field while before hostilities ceased British strength had risen to about 25,000. In most of the set engagements British infantry and their supports outnumbered the Maoris, besides possessing such armaments as heavy artillery, rockets, grenades and other materials of war. The Redcoats also had the support of locally-raised squadrons of cavalry, volunteer militia, and armed Police units; detachments of sailors and marines were landed from warships and gunboats, whose guns pounded the native's defensive positions; and there were detachments of 'friendly Maoris' (*kupapa*).

The main result of the wars, which accounted for perhaps 2,000 Maori deaths, was that their will to resist land sales was broken, and by the end of the century they had sold most of their land to settlers. Many had drunk the proceeds, a tragic outcome as Maoris were among the few people in the world who, when discovered by Europeans, had no alcohol or other stimulants and at first hated 'stinking water' (spirits), but by the late nineteenth century, their insatiable and deadly thirst became a major social problem. It was only when land-hungry British settlers and die-hard Maoris grew weary of war in the 1870s that New Zealand could pursue a peaceful path to nationhood. Then, British soldiers erected in a church a remarkable tablet as a memorial to fallen Maoris. It said: 'I say unto you, love your enemies.'

prepared themselves psychologically by wild gestures, eye-rolling and protruding tongues, establishing a mood of defiance and a contempt for the enemy. Trained from boyhood to use clubs and spears, they showed a fine sense of practicability by restricting fighting to the summer months between planting and harvesting. Being a savage and ferocious people, fighting was invariably very fierce and bloodthirsty, the advent of firearms causing traditional methods of warfare to decline, replaced by close-range slaughter. Sometimes it ended with victors eating vanquished to supplement their meat-deficient diet, but cannibalism was never the sole cause of war. After a victory, savage and noisy ritual dances were performed in exultation; when it was white men they had beaten even wilder dances demonstrated their defiance of the *Pakehas* (white people).

The flintlock muskets, sporting rifles and double-barrelled shotguns traded by European and American smugglers were a great improvement on primitive wood and stone clubs, axes and spears; chiefs increasingly sought *utu* through the use of these new weapons. Their

14   The Persians

A comic opera war, the last fought by the armies of the British East India Company, fortuitously played out against an effete enemy, otherwise farce might well have become tragedy. Leading characters included a septuagenarian admiral who had never sailed, except as a passenger, in Eastern waters, and a general inflicted with ill health and financial problems who shot himself when superseded by one of the two, late-arrival, senior professional soldiers, ambitiously vying with each other. The events leading up to the war began in 1856 when, despite agreements and treaties, the Persians occupied Herat, a town where all routes from the principal countries met, and a buffer between Afghanistan and Persia in an area deemed by the British government to be essentially neutral as a protection for the North-West Frontier. When they refused to relinquish Herat, the British government decided to send a sea-borne force to Bushire as the first target in a projected campaign. Sailing from India, on 1 November 1856, the army of the British East India Company consisted of 5,670 soldiers, of whom 2,270 were Europeans plus 3,750 camp followers, 1,150 horses and 430 bullocks. Coming from the Bombay Presidency, and commanded by Major-General Foster Stalker, the force included HM's 64th Regiment (later the Staffordshire Regiment) and the 2nd Bombay Europeans (subsequently part of the Durham Light Infantry). He was superseded in late January 1857 by Sir James Outram who brought with him Brigadier-General Henry Havelock and another division consisting of the 78th Highlanders; the 23rd and 26th Regiments of Bombay Native Infantry; part of the 14th Light Dragoons; some Horse Artillery and two field batteries; also John Jacob and his irregular cavalry, the Sind Horse.

War was declared on Persia just before the fleet sailed, causing panic in the bazaars of Teheran and the Shah, Nasir-u-Din ordered the priests to proclaim a Jiddah, a holy war against the infidels in the hope of rousing the Moslems of India. A crumbling country with a corrupt Court and timid ministers, the Persian army was said to be in a pitiful state with only 20,000 soldiers considered fit for duty out of a nominal strength of 86,700. There were only 500 regular cavalry, trained by an Austrian officer; but 150,000 irregular horse could take the field, although unlikely to stay in arms for very long.

Describing the army in 1857, the *Illustrated Times* wrote:

'The Persian army, it appears, consists of two distinct forces: the "regular" troops, disciplined after the system of European armies; and the "irregular" troops, who are only called out in case of emergency.

'The regular army of Persia is composed of infantry and artillery. The former consists of a body-guard, mostly in garrison at Teheran, or wherever the Shah happens to be; and of the provincial battalions, who are generally quartered in the principal towns and cities. The infantry are all armed in the same way, but there is a variation in the costume. The body-guard wear white trousers, large and gathered, a red vest, with blue sleeves and collars; while the vests of the provincial troops are of various colours.

'Of the Persian army, the artillery is said to be the best disciplined portion. This force is provided with very fine field-pieces and with ammunition-wagons generally well horsed.

'As for the irregular portion of the Persian army, it is only seen on extraordinary occasions, or when a war renders it necessary to call out all the military forces of the country. Among these irregular troops, which sometimes comprise a considerable though undisciplined number of combatants, there are the Tuffekdjis, or foot fusiliers, and the cavalry. In a country like Persia, where every man is accustomed from infancy to the use of arms and to ride on horseback, it is easy to conceive that these volunteers may become a real force at any given moment. They are moreover brave, clever in the use of their arms; and, although they may be without discipline or military instruction, as it is understood in Europe, their division into families or tribes, fur-

Types of soldiers.

nishes them, nevertheless, with a spirit of cohesion, which compensates, up to a certain point, for what a European commander might regret to find wanting in them.'

Officers and men lived at home, being called out by provincial governors when needed; only regiments stationed in Teheran received any training. In May 1856 19 battalions were in the area of Herat, some were in Teheran and others on the Russian frontier, leaving eight battalions in the province of Fars, in which Bushire lay. When called out for service the Persian soldier was entitled to a year's pay of seven tomans and a penny per day in lieu of rations, but only two tomans actually reached the soldier, the rest being taken by officers or accountants. It was an army burdened with every pernicious fault known to military history – savage discipline; no pensions or allowances to dependants; no medical facilities – sick and wounded men were untreated; and off-duty men 'moonlighted', doing menial jobs to support their families. Their muskets were poor, many unusable through defective locks, and bayonets were broken. Even within regiments different calibres and models of small-arms made ammunition supply difficult and, in the artillery, ammunition often had to be carried by camels or mules through lack of carts. The

guns – 6- and 12-pounders – were generally of good quality. On campaign, the Persian Army suffered from the same handicap as most Eastern armies in that great numbers of camp followers trailed along with it. Groups of soldiers owned an ass or horse to carry their belongings and every officer had a string of horses, mules or camels to carry his excessive amount of baggage – this meant that an army of only 2,000 infantry had 12,000 baggage animals for officers alone! Forage for the animals was always a problem so that through constant foraging soldiers had little time for military duties.

Camels have been used in warfare since the beginnings of military history and there are numerous records of both bactrian and dromedary types being employed. Persia and other countries in the Near and Middle East often used camel-borne soldiers as irregular and regular cavalry; the nomadic Beloutchis, constantly at war with Persia, used camels carrying two men to 'cross the desert and fall upon the provinces ...carrying death and destruction into all the villages through which they pass...' In the

1850s it was the custom to give Persian soldiers a transport allowance that enabled ten men to group together to purchase a camel to transport their baggage. The use of camels to carry light artillery pieces began in 1722, when the Afghans employed dromedaries armed with light cannon against the Persians. Evidently impressed, the Persians incorporated similar light artillery units into their own army by 1729 and used them in battle against both Afghans and Turks.

When Britain came into conflict with Persia in 1856/7, these singular units came to the notice of the war correspondent of the *Illustrated London News*, who wrote of them in the issue for April 1857:

'Persia being a mountainous country, the necessity of having a special corps of artillery capable of moving about easily, and going anywhere, ere long became clear; and this corps, which is not numerous, is provided with small pieces of cannon, of three- or four-inch calibre, placed upon a sort of pivot, and borne by camels. These animals being able to pass through all the bad, mountainous roads, the artillery is enabled to reach any place where its service may be required. It is a corps analogous to that which has been created in the French army for requirements of a similar nature in Algeria, where the artillery is borne on the backs of mules, and where they employ also small howitzers, called mountain howitzers.

'The name Zembourek comes from Zembor meaning wasp, "to indicate by a metaphor common in the East, the constant and incessant annoyance of this light artillery to the troops it is ordered to pursue and attack". The Zemboureks were mounted in companies of 50 and their duty was "to harass, worry, cut off, and attack at a thousand points". When formed with the rest of the army in line of battle the camels would be spaced at 5-ft intervals. Before firing they would kneel, and the gunners would dismount. Reloading was generally done before remounting. When acting apart from the main army the camel artillery would be escorted by irregular cavalry. If this were not possible then a foot soldier would be mounted to ride behind the gunner. In a defensive or static position, and if the ground permitted, the gun would be detached from the saddle and placed on its pivot on the ground. This of course lost mobility, but it permitted a somewhat larger charge to be used. Effective range was said to be about double that of a musket.

Camel artillery of the Persian army, 1853.

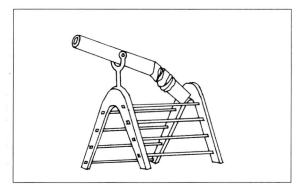

The Zembourek combination saddle and gun-mount – a wooden frame (usually covered with black felt).

'Two ammunition pouches of black leather hung from the saddle sides and a water skin hung under the stomach of the camel. Each ammunition pouch carried 50 ball and grape cartridges and a number of blank cartridges for salutes. Stirrups and harness chains were of iron and the headstall, breaststrap, surcingle, and girth were of leather ornamented with fringes of red, yellow, and blue wool. Behind, and attached to the saddle, was a staff with a red bannerol and a red cloth hanging that covered the rear of the saddle and the ammunition pouches. Total weight, including the soldier, was under 500 lb. and quite easily carried by the camel. In 1853, the Zembourek Corps of the Persian army consisted of 200 men mounted on a like number of dromedaries and armed with a small cannon. The commanding officer was a colonel and was assisted by 2 majors, 4 captains, and 8 lieutenants. There were 20 spare and baggage camels assigned to the corps, and to complete the unit, there were 25 musicians. The band used the Karina which was 8-ft. long and shaped like the Roman tuba, the Koous a large drum with a 2-ft. circumference, the Houl or common drum, the Nagarah or kettledrum, the Nafie or trumpet, the Zourna or oboe, the Zeng or cymbals, and an unidentified instrument called a Balaban. The music produced by the Zembourek Band proved that camels could easily be accustomed to loud noise!

'The soldiers of the Zembourek artillery were paid $19 a year and wore a jacket of blue cloth with red facings. The wide pantaloons were also blue. The high boots were black and at times a grey cloak with long sleeves was worn. Belts were white and a cavalry sabre was carried by the men.'

On the morning of Sunday 7th December the expedition landed on a beach ten miles south of Bushire, with little opposition or answer to the few rounds fired from the ship's guns. They remained in the area until Tuesday when they marched out and, after some difficult going over rough ground and through sandy ravines, came to the last defensible position before Bushire itself, the old Dutch fort at Reshire, where they could see Persian soldiers behind its heaped-up sand walls fronted by a deep ditch. After seeing shells bury themselves in the sand, the three infantry regiments raced forward towards two breaches in the walls, under fairly heavy musketry which took toll of them. A European officer of the 20th Native Infantry won a Victoria Cross by being first onto the parapet and, despite numerous musketry wounds, fighting until his men swarmed over the parapet with him into the fort. After a short and desperate struggle with no quarter asked or given, the rest of the infantry came up; the Persians decided they had had enough and poured out of the fort in retreat; the cavalry were 'too done up' to pursue.

Although it was little more than a skirmish, the Persians suffered heavily and were dispirited by their losses; it was suggested that the Governor of Bushire had purposely sent troops of the tribe of Tungistanis, half Arab and not pure Persian, with little rifle ammunition and only a few bags of dates. The ships shelled the walls of Bushire and were fired upon by guns on the walls; eventually a breach was made in the wall and as the weary British force came up, the Persian flag was lowered and firing ceased at noon,

then the Governor surrendered. Muskets taken from the captured garrison were made in England and stamped with the Tower mark; they had been given to the Persians by the British. The British force settled down in camp outside the town, where the tradesmen welcomed the sudden prosperity they brought; the weather got hotter and every day there were rumours of impending attack by the undefeated force laying out in the hills. The expedition was not aware that the government had decided to extend operations, double the size of the force and send a new commander Sir James Outram and another division under General Henry Havelock.

Outram arrived in Bushire on 27 January 1857 to find a potentially dangerous situation, the encampment ill-defended by a puny earthwork and 3-feet-wide ditch and reports of an impending great Persian attack to drive the infidel into the sea. The threat came from the Commander-in-Chief of the Persian Army, Sooja-ool-Moolk, 46 miles away at Borasjoon, with an army of 7,000 men and 18 guns, plus rumoured reinforcements of 12 regiments and 35 guns. Immediately, Outram marched out at the head of 4,500 men and 18 guns to find the enemy, coming up with them in front of Borasjoon, where the Company's army disgustedly saw the Persians retire without a shot being fired. But on the withdrawal to Bushire, Outram came under a night attack said to resemble a Red Indian raid on a wagon train, made even more confusing by European-trained Persians sounding such conflicting bugle-calls as 'Cease-fire'! When the mists of dawn cleared, they saw before them a 6,000 strong Persian army, under Sooja-ool-Moolk and the Eel-Khanee, chief of the nomadic tribes of the region. With cavalry in flowing green and red robes on either flank, infantry and guns stretched in a long thin line with their right resting on the walled village of Khoosh-ab, the left on a gathering of houses around a small tower.

The cavalry and artillery of the Company's army began engaging the enemy while the infantry, in an almost stately formal fashion, deployed from night-defensive formation into battle order. Immediately, and without orders, the Poona Irregular Horse charged, broke and scattered the 1st Kushkai Regiment of Fars. Seeing this, the 500 men of the 1st Regular Regiment of Fars immediately formed square, a defensive formation against cavalry rarely broken in the history of warfare. Piling into it at speed, the mounts of the leading horsemen fell dead upon the bayonets, causing a gap through which following cavalry poured, to ride through, turn and again attack until the square, a solid mass moments before, broke and scattered. For their part in this almost unprecedented feat, two British officers were awarded the Victoria Cross. By now the infantry had completed their manoeuvring and began marching steadily towards the Persian line, which immediately broke and fled, throwing away arms and equipment; officers, being mounted, got away fastest. Reporting the battle in its issue for April 1857, the *Illustrated Times* wrote:

'The Persian force is estimated to have amounted to between 6,000 and 7,000 men, with a fair proportion of guns. Their infantry was almost entirely composed of regulars, and included one regiment of the Persian Guards, 900 strong. Of cavalry they had perhaps 800; so their force was respectable, both in numbers and composition, and a stout resistance might have been looked for from it. Yet it was routed speedily and utterly.'

Losing 700 men on the battlefield and many more in the pursuit by the exultant cavalry, the Persians were given no quarter as they were known to kill captives and abuse surrender-terms after acceptance. Outram's force lost 19 killed and 64 wounded; they captured hundreds of muskets, two brass 9-pounder guns, and a standard with a silver-hand on its staff. Under appalling conditions, their return march to Bushire became a disorganised nightmare; Outram was not unduly concerned, saying: '...all precautions against an enemy being superfluous, with the certain information I possessed of the flight of the Persians in a contrary direction'. The British commander considered he had won a glorious victory: his enemies painted his withdrawal from Khooshas as a panic-stricken retreat in the face of the enemy. Nevertheless, the Persian Army was badly disheartened, the soldiers complaining their officers had deserted them; later it was told how one Persian infantry regiment of 800 men cornered a single mounted lancer, who charged and scattered them!

The capture of Bushire and the battle of Khoosh-ab having failed to force the Shah's surrender, the invaders moved to attack the town of Mohammerah at the junction of two big rivers, known to be heavily defended. There were two large batteries protected by earthworks 18 feet

thick and 18 to 25 feet high, strengthened with the trunks of date trees; there were also a number of smaller batteries and entrenchments – all garrisoned by an army of 13,000 under Prince Khanler Mirza. The plan was for the Navy to shell the forts and silence their fire, then the army would be landed from their transports above the northern battery to attack the Persian camp and town. The action began at dawn on 26 March 1857, when warships of the Indian Navy began attacking, in broad daylight, heavily defended positions with Persian guns firing all along the line and doing considerable damage to hulls and rigging. The heavy guns of the warships battered the forts and one by one the Persian guns ceased firing until, after three hours of consistent fire, the troop-transports were ordered up-river to the disembarkation area past the forts. Incredibly, these vessels with soldiers crowded on their decks like cattle in pens, sailed *between* the warships and the forts, sometimes being as close as 100 yards to the enemy guns, yet seemed to escape harm.

Taking several hours the landing was unopposed; raised tide made the ground impossible for Horse Artillery and Cavalry so eventually the infantry advanced alone through date groves, creeks and broken ground. Sighting the enemy, they halted to form a line-of-battle, then, outflanked by the far larger Persian army, marched forward. It was too much for the enemy who flitted away as in a dream, leaving only deserted tents to prove to the attackers that it had once been an army camp. Greatly disappointed at lack of fighting, the British were consoled by the vast amounts of plunder, everything having been abandoned by the fleeing enemy including, in the Prince's tent, a half-written despatch announcing: '...the glorious victory over the British, who had been driven into the sea and their ships captured'. The perfunctory pursuit was ended by darkness and next day the British took residence in the former Persian camp at Mohammerah, where it was seen that of 16 guns captured, one was cast at St Petersburg and presented by the Tsar in 1828.

Three river-steamers and 300 men were sent up the Karun after the retreating Persian Army coming up with them at Ahwaz, when a lucky shell from a gunboat landed near the Persian commander, who immediately ordered his 10,000 men to withdraw – they did not stop until reaching Shuster, 100 miles away. That was the last action of this inglorious war that provided what must be some of the easiest battle-honours ever won – through a skirmish at Reshire, a cavalry-only action at Khooshab, no contact at all at Bushire, and the enemy ran away at Mohammerah. In a war of incompetent commanders, the Persians were the worst and were greatly humiliated by their defeat, their armies' reputation at low level and probably not improved when the Shah ordered those officers who had run away at Mohammerah to be publicly disgraced, dragged along the ranks by rings through their noses, beaten and imprisoned. Their general was rewarded for the same battle by a sword and robe of honour, after presenting £8,000 to the Shah's Chief Minister.

15   The Russians

Today, the Crimean War is regarded as the close of one military epoch and the opening of another amidst a miasma of misery, a purposeless war into which Britain drifted in 1854, the only conflict in Victoria's long reign when the foe was an established European power. It started when Russia, in one of her periodic efforts to gain control of the Bosphorus, went to war with Turkey, regarded by Britain as a flank-guard against Russia's steady eastward advance towards the North-West Frontier of India. Fearing threats to trade routes, the European powers determined to foil Russia, their support for Turkey causing a drift towards hostilities; eventually such an atmosphere of warlike enthusiasm was created, that Britain and France (hereditary enemies allied for the first time) could not bring themselves to abandon plans for an unbelievable military operation.

In an armada of 150 warships and transports a force of about 60,000 (25,000 each from Britain and France plus Sardinians and Turks) were to be landed on an open beach of the Crimean Peninsular in the Black Sea, march 30 miles overland without any transport to the fortified Russian naval base of Sebastopol and besiege it, with their rear exposed to attack by all the strength of Russia. Amazingly the operation actually took place, and was one of the most striking examples on record of the strength of an army based on sea-power. Lacking maps and information, once ashore the force blundered about more blindly than any army since the Crusades, as the Russians incredibly managed to surpass their tactical and administrative blunders. As the war progressed, it became increasingly evident that generalship and command lagged far behind all other military aspects and that the most significant feature of the war was the incredible ineptitude, the thorough indifference and incompetence of governments and commanders of both Allied and Russian forces.

The Crimean War reflected little glory on anyone save for the heroism and endurance of the lower ranks of the contending armies standing out as a shining beacon, the soldiers displaying astonishing courage and fortitude under great hardship and terrible conditions. Thousands died of disease through lack of adequate clothing and food, and through poor sanitation – at one stage two-thirds of the British Army were unfit for duty. The Allies lost 250,000 men – 70,000 in combat – and two out of three Russian soldiers, through starvation or disease, failed to even reach the area of operations; their total losses were 256,000, less than half through battle.

After landing, in a parade-ground exercise on a mammoth scale the Allies, weakened by cholera and the heat, marched to the River Alma where

Alexander 11, Emperor of Russia.

Prince Menschikoff, late commander of the Russian forces in the Crimea.

Prince Menschikoff, the Russian Commander, had concentrated 39,000 men and 96 guns on the heights in a position said by old Peninsular War officers to be as intimidating as anything they had seen. Menschikoff, convinced he had created another 'Lines of Torres Vedras', boasted to the Tsar he could hold for three weeks, but three hours was sufficient for the British infantry to storm the heights in the face of heavy fire, taking 3,000 casualties and inflicting 6,000 on the enemy. The Russians were dismayed to see the British line enduring pulverising artillery fire yet continuing to advance, causing Russian guns to limber up and withdraw before the British closed with them. Menschikoff's infantry, trained to resist dense columns similar to their own formation, had no experience of the British line, long and sometimes irregular, stretching beyond their flanks. Captain Hodasevich wrote: 'We did not think it possible for men to be found with such firmness of morale to be able to attack in this apparently weak formation our massive columns.' In line, the 42nd Foot (the Royal Highland Regiment, the Black Watch) routed the 16th

Division, among the elite of the Tsar's troops. It is recorded that second-in-command Gortschakoff gave the Kazan Regiment orders for a supreme effort, and they began to move down on the Fusiliers; the 55th Regiment wheeled, positioning themselves to pour a killing fire into the Russian flank. Then, two guns firing over depressed sights cut what Captain Hume called 'regular lanes' through the packed Russian ranks. It was not possible for the Kazan Regiment to reply as only outer ranks of the column could use their old smoothbore muskets, with little hope of doing much damage; the remainder fired aimlessly into the air. Forced to a halt, they stood wavering momentarily, surviving officers bravely exposing themselves endeavouring to get their men to go forward – shouting, waving swords, pushing, punching, dragging by the collar, and even grasping men by the throat. It was to no avail, they had taken more than any soldiers could be expected to withstand; hopelessly handicapped by their unwieldy formation they turned and began slowly retiring, as more guns galloped up and poured fire into them and other columns. An artillery officer wrote: 'We opened from 18 guns; they stood it for some time...at last they broke, flung away everything and ran like fun.' Another witness said: 'They scattered like sparrows.' Captain Heath, watching through a telescope from the maintop of the *Niger* lying off shore wrote: 'The Russians did not deploy but gave way whilst still in their solid formations and ran off, beginning at the rear of the mass...with a few individuals, but the numbers increased every minute until the formation became exactly like a rocket, or a comet, with a bushy tail.'

Declining a costly assault on the northern defences of Sebastopol, the Allies marched round to take up position on the Chersonese Upland, a plateau before the city's south front, the British based on Balaclava and the French on Kamiesch. The time taken by this manoeuvre and the delay in bringing up the siege artillery allowed Colonel Franz Todleben (a genius in field-engineering and probably the only senior rank on either side to emerge from the war with credit) greatly to strengthen defences, so that the opening Allied bombardment had little effect. Employing 100,000 troops and 10,000 workmen, within a few weeks the Russians had made the town's defences formidable, based on two strong points – the Malakoff and the Redan. The former in a

The siege of Sebastopol – interior of the Redan.

commanding position was the key to the southern fortification, consisting of a semi-circular masonry tower, mounting five heavy guns around which was a circular entrenchment with a short flank at each end armed with a further ten guns. It overlooked the rear of all the defensive works on the eastern side of Sebastopol, including the Redan. Built on a former vineyard 306 feet above sea level it had two faces 70 yards long, meeting at an angle of 65 degrees. At its base was a fortified line of earthworks spanning the ridge. In front of it was a ditch roughly 20 feet wide and 14 feet deep; above this the Redan rose 15 feet, making its escarpment nearly 30 feet from top to bottom. Between it and the nearest parallel constructed by the British was approx-

imately 450 yards of ground, much uphill and all exposed to Russian batteries on right and left. Guns mounted in the Redan itself commanded a wide field of fire; Russian gunners were protected by mantlets, tough rope mats slung across the embrasure with a collar through which the muzzle of the gun protruded. There were secure bombproof shelters for the officers and men. Nearly every magazine was wired and could be exploded electrically if required.

After the Alma, Prince Menschikoff marched his defeated army into Sebastopol, then out again to lay threateningly on the Allied flank, attacking at Balaclava in October and Inkerman in November. Originally, he had left General Moller in command of land forces and Admiral Nachimoff sharing command of the Navy with Admiral Korniloff, and both were greatly re-

Russian guns and bells from Sebastopol just received at Woolwich Arsenal.

lieved when Korniloff took over supreme command of the garrison consisting of 16,000 men, three-quarters of them sailors from the Russian Black Sea Fleet which had been imprisoned in the Sebastopol roadsteads by the sinking of ships to bar the entrance. Along with Todleben, Korniloff was entirely responsible for inspiring the garrison with the will to defend the town so resolutely, although he commanded them for only a fortnight, being killed at the Malakoff on the 18th October.

The Battle of Balaclava on 25 October 1854 began when a large force of Russian infantry, cavalry and guns overwhelmed, after stubborn resistance, small forces of Turks in redoubts on the eastern approaches to the Balaclava Plain. A large cavalry group moved on the British base at Balaclava itself, defended only by the 93rd Highlanders under Colin Campbell, whose repulse of the horsemen is part of the fabric of British military history. The horsemen were reported to have suffered few casualties from three British volleys of musketry, perhaps after 40 years of easy victories over Asiatics they were devastated by the reputation of the Minié rifle in the hands of British infantry. Although Cossacks were the most numerous, there were also cuirassiers, dragoons, hussars and lancers, all resplendent in the

characteristic ornate cavalry uniforms of the day – and none of them showed up very well at Balaclava. Scarlett's eight squadrons of the Heavy Cavalry Brigade, suddenly confronted by Rykoff's 3,000- to 4,000- strong Russian cavalry, charged headlong into the halted mass and forced their way through, in a jostling crowded mêlée where blunt sabres did little damage, the thick overcoats of the Russians causing them to 'bounce off'. The unwieldy formation crumpled and fled the field, having displayed no courage, skill or enterprise, with general cavalry morale so shattered as to affect those contesting the immortal Charge of the Light Cavalry Brigade an hour later: 'If they had any pluck at all,' wrote Lieutenant Robert Portal who rode in the Charge, 'not one of us, if we had been ten times as strong, could ever have come back again.' The Russian cavalry in the North Valley showed aggressive spirit only in hunting down stragglers and lancing to death disabled or dismounted troopers.

For the remainder of the war the Russians were demoralised at the thought of meeting British cavalry; the historian of the war, A. W. Kinglake, wrote: 'It is probable that for a long time afterwards it would have been impracticable to make the Russian cavalry act with anything like confidence in the presence of two English squadrons.' It has been said that if Napoleon was correct in claiming the ratio of moral to physical courage being 3 to 1, then the losses of the Light Brigade were not suffered in vain. (W. Baring Pemberton, *Battles of the Crimean War*). The Russians could not claim Balaclava as a victory, despite taking three redoubts and seven guns, and repulsing the Light Brigade who, as Lord Raglan said were '...attacking a battery in front, contrary to all the usages of warfare and the customs of the service'.

On 5th November, under cover of a thick fog, Menschikoff attacked at Inkerman with nearly 50,000 infantry; caught by surprise and in small groups, 3,000 or so British troops fought a dogged 'soldier's battle', a confused action amid scrub-covered valleys and defiles, lacking coordination and control. From the confusion Russian actions can be sorted out, beginning with a vital tactical error in allowing three huge col-

umns to be defeated separately, instead of sending them in together to overpower the defenders. At times they attacked with a dash and spirit they had not been given credit for possessing, with a fury or fanaticism born of either extra rations of vodka and brandy, religious exhortation by their priests, or confidence in overwhelming numbers. Trained to fight under artillery protection, when it was denied them by fog and battle conditions, they lost confidence, their dense and compact columns broke up so that they were alone and no longer part of the comforting all-enveloping mass in which they had been trained to fight; they began to lose their nerve, hid in bushes or lay down, pretending to be dead. Resembling when Scarlett's small cavalry force pushed their way through the Russian-horsed mass at Balaclava, a huge Russian infantry formation, bewildered by British daring, showed that same hesitancy, the same slow-witted inability to react with any agility, and allowed the Guards to 'scrape past' them, so close to the almost zombie-like ranks that they could smell the peculiarly strong leather-like odour that invariably emanated from them.

The 77th, one of the best trained regiments in

The Russians entering Balaclava to take possession after the Armistice that ended the War.

General Osten-Sacken, commander of a Russian division at Sebastopol.

defeating and demoralising Russian columns, repeatedly stopping them in their tracks when the weight of fire with the penetrating power of the Minie bullets became too much to bear – a Russian officer said that a single Minie bullet could kill or disable as many as six or seven men. At short range the Minie struck like a wall of lead that was unanswerable by the inadequate Russian muskets, whose rate of fire could approach that of the rifle of the Allies but at a much shorter effective range; wounds indicated that Russian soldiers were trained to fire low. On numerous occasions it was noted that the Russians made a brave show of returning fire with their antiquated muskets, the standard equipment of the Russian infantryman for much of the war, although by its end many regiments had been issued with rifles which undoubtedly gave them increased confidence. At Sebastopol on 18 June 1855 Russian riflemen were ranged two-deep along the parapets, when those in the front rank had discharged their muskets they passed them back over the left shoulder, to receive instantly over the right shoulder another loaded and at full cock, thus enabling a constant fire to be maintained.

Artillery was much the same on both sides, although in the field Russian 18- and 24-pounders were too heavy for the light British 9-pounders and, at Inkerman, British fortunes changed when two 18-pounders were dragged up and went into action. Russian artillerymen knew their job, at Inkerman (after in the fog, firing into the backs of their own troops) batteries on Shell Hill judged the range so finely that round shot skimmed the crest of the ridge three-quarters of a mile ahead and screamed down the other side only two or three feet above the ground; at the Alma, ranges were marked out by previously-planted stakes in the ground. In Sebastopol they used brass Coehorn mortars of 4⅖ inch calibre; guns defending the Malakoff were raised *en barbette*, to fire grapeshot down at a steep angle. Russians were obsessed with the disgrace of losing a gun and often withdrew guns prematurely rather than risk them; it was said that this contrasted with the callous abandonment of their own dead and wounded.

In the army for life, the Russian soldier was a 'long-service man' but never a professional. A process of grossly unjust selection allowed landowners to rid themselves of troublesome, lazy, stupid or unfit serfs so that the Army became a

the British Army, were confronted by a Russian column looming up out of the fog less than ten yards away. The order to fire was smartly given and, at five yards range, a volley of Minie bullets tore into the wall of living flesh, each one passing through several bodies to build up a heaving wall of dead and wounded. Delaying only to methodically reload, the 77th tore into the column; despite being badly shaken, they courageously fought back, crossing bayonets for a few moments until beginning to waver, then turning and fleeing, flayed by bullets and bayonets as they were driven headlong down a small ravine. Brave as they were, the Russians never liked the bayonet; the Guards at Inkerman fought with the bayonet held high, best suited for close combat, the Russians were trained to bring the bayonet down, which was less effective.

There can be no doubt that the Minie rifle of the British infantryman played a major part in

vast herd of physical and mental misfits. The stolidity of the Russian temperament, together with pride of regiment and a dog-like devotion to Holy Russia and the Tsar, enabled these peasants to be turned into reasonable soldiers capable of fighting ferociously in the face of heavy losses. But once their ranks broke they were hard to rally and drew off, although frequently they returned or renewed the attack at another point. Usually led by incompetent commanders with little regard for the life of the common soldier, Russian troops of this period manoeuvred in great grey bovine masses, patient and impassive under fire, showing little emotion or enthusiasm and no initiative, having been harshly disciplined into stolid automatons. This may have been because, as the French Revolutionary armies found 60 years before, unwilling and poorly trained soldiers fight best surrounded by friends in tight, controllable but unwieldy columns. The Russian infantry *never* charged, but came on slowly in a lumpish sluggish movement, marked by the 'white-pudding' faces of the innumerable ranks of the stolid formations that presented an almost static target. Onlookers at the Alma said that the Vladimir Regiment, marching ponderously down from the redoubt with lines of skirmishers protruding on either flank, resembled a great beetle. But, as frequently happened, the huge formation halted or faltered to lose momentum when nearing the enemy; the Russians seemed to become immobilised by the elation of success or achievement, losing interest in everything else, they halted to irresolutely gloat over their 'conquest'. Like children singing in the dark, these massive Russian formations came forward singing a dirge-like tuneless hymn, but more often it was 'the regulation howl', said by Wolseley to be a horrible jackal-like rasping screech, a discordant yell which '...with the Russians takes the place of the manly British cheer'.

Their courage could never be doubted, but it was passive rather than the active courage encouraged by the *élan* common to armies of free men; at the Alma, when retreating before the Highlanders and the horse batteries pouring deadly enfilading fire into them, they did not increase their rate of movement beyond a quick step, despite the punishment they were taking. When the Guards swept into the redoubt at the same battle, after an advance resembling an army of giants moving effortlessly forward, the

An incident in the Crimean War.

Russians 'withdrew...in very tolerably good order, firing at us and in no confusion or disorderly haste' despite the awe inspired by the Guards and the heavy casualties they had caused. They had been instilled with the belief that the British were brutal monsters, told that if they fell into British hands they would have their ears cut off. At Inkerman, their wounded pleaded for mercy on bended knees, scowled and muttered at those tending them, and *The Times* correspondent wrote: '...glared out from the bushes...with the ferocity of wild beasts. Reluctant supplicants crying for water turned away to drink as though ashamed at taking it from such evil men.' The Russians were known to have bayoneted British wounded at the Alma and at Inkerman; answering a formal complaint, Prince Menschikoff denied it was generally justified, claiming particular cases were due to the 'outraged piety of an eminently religious people... filled with horror...at hearing French troops had pillaged a Russian Church'.

Surprisingly, Russian troops were not as inured to cold as might have been expected, becoming distressed and little inclined to fight during severe cold weather. Trying to keep warm and exist in the appalling conditions, sentries carried on as their forebears had done in the Peninsula 50 years earlier, ceasing to worry about the presence of the enemy and indeed acknowledging each other's existence and the right to exist, in strange alliance against the force of Nature. Captain Hugh Hibbert of the 7th Foot wrote in a letter: 'We have now come to a

Russian soldiers at the handing over of Balaclava after the War had ended.

kind of understanding with the Russians as the cold has forced us all out of our holes, to walk about without molestation, so we now perambulate within 150 yards, looking daggers at each other through the sleet.'

Charles Elton told his father: 'I was on a covering party and the Russian sentries were lying all night within ten yards of ours but of course it is against the rules of war to annoy sentries unless you intend an attack or something serious.'

Traditionally, the full dress of the Russian Army was spectacular and colourful, but it was not worn in the field and the infantry were described in long drab yellowish-grey overcoats reaching down to the ankles, black leather helmets with tall flame-shaped spike, and brass mountings, or flat 'muffin-topped' linen forage caps; and top-boots. Officers uniforms closely resembled those of other ranks, the only difference being small stars on the coat. Artillerymen wore infantry-style uniforms and a dark green flat cap with black band and red piping. Russian cavalry, apart from the ubiquitous Cossacks, were cuirassiers, dragoons, hussars and lancers, all splendidly arrayed; particularly the Guard, where cuirassiers wore all-white uniforms, black shiny boots and golden helmets surmounted by a crowned eagle. Reports reveal lancers in dark khaki coats; grey-coated, white-trousered dragoons; hussars in light blue and silver; most seemed to wear glazed leather or fur-crested helmets. Cossacks came from many parts of Russia and each displayed regional differences in dress – Black Sea Cossacks wearing stringy long-haired caps and with scarlet lance-pennons; Ural Cossacks with fur caps. Contemporary woodcuts show Cossacks wearing long light-coloured overcoats over soft leather boots, with flat-topped linen forage caps; blue/white lance pennons seemed standard.

In early September 1855 with dignity and honour the Russians evacuated Sebastopol after a universally admired defence for nearly a year, leading the future General Gordon to say: 'What plucky troops they were.' Maybe, but against a numerically inferior enemy, the Russians displayed such incredible incompetence it is hard to conceive that for 50 years British diplomats and politicians believed them capable of the colossal military enterprise required to attack India through Afghanistan – a mistaken belief responsible for the majority of wars and expeditions on the North-West Frontier of India.

16   The Sikhs

The army garrisoning British India, defending it and fighting its wars, consisted of the Queen's troops, the Company's troops, and contingent troops of Native States. The Queen's troops were conducted to India at the Company's expense and paid by them; the Company's own army was formed of British and native troops, brigaded together. Without greatly concerning the home government, the small wars waged by the Company's armies in India gradually produced the nucleus of the forces that were to win the colonial wars of the later Victorian period.

The British Army had traditionally always been deficient in artillery with a low establishment of guns per 1,000 men, invariably of lighter calibre – all most marked during the Sikh Wars when Gough's tactics, particularly at Ferozeshah, were undoubtedly affected by the knowledge that his guns were so inferior in weight of metal to those of the Sikhs that they were little more than musketry of greater calibre and longer range. Nevertheless, the British commander left his heaviest guns – the 18-pounders – behind at Mudki when he marched to Ferozeshah, to face the Sikh 24-, 32- and 48-pounders with only 6- and 9-pounder guns, which could do little harm. After the battle, captured enemy guns showed scarcely any marks of round-shot or shell, whereas almost a third of the British guns were disabled in their carriages or tumbrils. The only horse-drawn guns were the 6-pounders of the Horse Artillery (weighing 27 cwt with carriage and limber); the 9-pounder field batteries were mostly drawn by slow and hard-to-handle bullock teams.

The Sikh Army, the Khalsa, were well-trained, well-equipped and numerous. Dedicated, and stimulated by religious zeal, their manoeuvres and firing had been brought almost to the standard of the Company's British troops and was infinitely superior to the Company's native regiments. Twenty years before, Ranjit Singh – the Old Lion – ruler of the Punjab, had increased the natural fighting ability of the Sikhs by the training and experience of imported foreign instruc-

tors who turned them into a disciplined regular army with a superb artillery arm, backed by massive irregular forces. But after Ranjit's death, the Khalsa were weakened by doubtful loyalty, poor officers and discontent caused by being paid irregularly and much in arrears. In 1822 Allard, a former captain in Napoleon's Hussars and Ventura, a Colonel of French infantry, arrived in Lahore, and were later joined by Frenchman Court, Italian Avitabile and American Gardner. Revolutionising the Sikh infantry army and enlarging it into a disciplined and well-trained force of 40,000 men, forming and improving the cavalry and, above all, providing a practised artillery arm of 400 guns – these foreigners presented the British with opponents incomparably higher

Ranjit Singh from a drawing by an Indian artist.

131

Ghulab Singh from a drawing by an Indian artist.

prime and fire guns first at the walk and then the double, gaining actual firing experience on prepared ranges; they were also given the same tactical training as the infantry.

Sikh guns were of much heavier metal than their British counterparts, their 4-pounders being as heavy as the British 6-pounder; it was said at the time that Sikh guns had less recoil on the carriage and did not heat as quickly as British artillery pieces. The additional weight and thickness of metal in the breech allowed shot and shell to be fired with a greater charge of powder that gave a longer range and more effectiveness.

The Khalsa were well supplied with Zambureks, long matchlocks 1 inch in calibre, that could fire from swivels on walls or from camels' backs, with considerable accuracy up to a mile.

In 1835 Allard brought from France two million detonating-caps and Ranjit endeavoured to re-equip his army with the percussion-cap musket, but this had not been achieved when war broke out. Some ten years before, Ranjit bought from the British 10,000 flintlocks of the old Brown Bess pattern which, used as a design, were reproduced in Lahore by experienced workmen lured from the British by high pay; Sikh infantry went to war in 1845 with a musket resembling the Brown Bess.

The swords carried by both Sikh cavalry and infantry were said to be razor-sharp and inflicted great gaping wounds. At Ramnuggur in the second Sikh War,

'The Sikhs wore voluminous thick puggeries round their heads, which our blunt swords were powerless to cut through, and each horseman had also a buffalo-hide shield slung on his back. They evidently knew that the British swords were blunt and useless, so they kept their horses still and met the British charge by laying flat on their horses' necks, with their heads protected by the thick turban and their backs by the shields; immediately the British soldiers passed through their ranks the Sikhs swooped round on them and struck them back-handed with their sharp, curved swords, in several instances cutting our cavalrymen in two. In one case a British officer was hewn in two by a back-handed stroke which cut right through an ammunition pouch, cleaving the pistol bullets right through the pouch and belt, severing the officer's backbone and cutting his heart in two from behind.'

Sikh infantry wore red or blue turbans, the most popular being blue with one end loose and spread to cover the head, back of neck and shoul-

than any others ever encountered on the Indian continent. From the battle of Mudki on, this was made obvious by the competent manner in which the Sikh army handled their fine heavy guns while their infantry fought stubbornly and efficiently.

Above everything else, the Sikhs appreciated artillery and a marked feature of these 1840s wars was the way in which gunners stood by their beloved guns to the end. Ranjit's European advisers, Court and Avitabile, built and supervised arsenals and foundries, employing craftsmen lured from all over India to produce well-cast guns with three-wheeled carriages of well-seasoned sissoo wood; they were without limbers. The Sikhs had little horse artillery, hauling their guns by bullock with as many as 40 or 50 to a heavy piece. Shot was of brass and iron; shells were fused to burst accurately over a target or on impact at 800/900 yards. Although their gunpowder was not of the highest quality, Sikh gunnery was raised to European levels with gunners trained in the French system, employing words of command in that language, to lay, aim,

(top) The Sikh trophy guns 'forming up' in the Fort of Monghyr.

(bottom) Sikh guns at Windsor Castle.

ders, scarlet tunics with yellow facings, black belts and white cross belts, white linen trousers; others wore black uniforms with yellow facings and white crossbelts, loose linen light blue trous-ers with a yellow stripe, and a loose yellow turban. Some infantry carried a round shield slung across their shoulder; infantry carried great yellow and blue silk standards. On occasions, infantry wore Kurtis – white jackets with white stripes of braid across the chest, made of banat or broadcloth. Those infantry units formed of Gurkhas wore shakos or caps of black banat, and

133

Sikh soldier.

stripe; and crimson silk turbans brought to a peak at the front, ornamented in the centre with a small brass half-moon with a 2-inch glittering sprig rising from it. Saddles were concealed with a crimson cloth edged with a border of blue and white stripes; the horse harness was ornamented with brass studs. Other Sikh cavalry wore white uniforms with yellow turbans, and carried red, gold and green silk banners. The cavalry were armed with long bamboo lances, heavy tulwars, carbines and pistols.

Drawn mostly from the sons of nobility and considered to be the elite of the army, the Irregular Cavalry – the Ghorcharas – supplied their own showy uniforms, often of loose-quilted yellow silk covered by inlaid armour of chain-mail; loose white silk trousers and soft leather riding boots; silk turbans, close-fitting inlaid steel caps or polished helmets surmounted by heron plumes, crowned the array.

Artillerymen wore black felt-cloth coats and white trousers, high black bearskin-like turbans; black leather crossbelt, belt and foodbag (toshadan); and a pouch for powder. There were other artillerymen who wore white tunics, black trousers and yellow turbans.

An unusual and colourful group were the Akalis. There were only 3,000 or so of them, but their strange dress and equipment, together with their fanaticism, made them conspicuous. Said to be identical in character and in the manner of their onslaught as the Ghazis of Afghanistan or the Sudanese 'Fuzzy-Wuzzy', they had to be handled with care by their commanders. They wore little clothing – a turban that was blue and peaked or conical, over it was placed steel quoits made to fit the turban's shape, getting smaller as they reached its top. On the body they wore a long blue shirt and a pair of shorts; around their waist a sword girdle and country-made shoes or sandals.

In spite of their European officers and training, the Khalsa retained many of the glamorous elements of an Eastern army.

THE FIRST SIKH WAR, 1845–6

On 12 December 1845 the Sikh leaders Lal and Tej Singh threw their army across the River Sutlej at Ferozepor. Sir Hugh Gough, Commander-in-Chief, and Sir Henry Hardings, Governor-General (both in their mid-60s) marched their army 120 miles from Ambala in five days to the mud village of Mudki at noon on 18

green jackets faced with red similar to English Rifle Regiments. Regiments were distinguished from each other by different colour facings, in the English manner. In hot weather, the entire Regular army wore white with different colour turbans of green, yellow and red; in the hills and during cold weather leather suits (postins) or quilted and padded uniforms.

Unlike the infantry and artillery, Sikh cavalry were never very effective, yet were perhaps the most colourful troops in the army. In the mid-1820s, the Frenchman Allard had raised a corps of dragoons on the French model, hand-picked horses and men equipped with cuirasses and steel helmets; dull red jackets with broad buff facings crossed by a pair of black belts, one supporting a pouch, the other a bayonet. Over a cummerbund was a sword belt supporting a heavy brass-hilted sabre in a leather scabbard; carbines were either slung across the back with the butt in a small leather bucket attached to the belt, or carried in a bucket attached to the saddle. The Regular cavalry wore light crimson dragoon jackets, dark blue trousers with a red

Captured Sikh gun 'Futteh Jung – the Conqueror'.

December 1845, having covered 21 miles since dawn through ankle-deep sand. Almost at once a Sikh army was upon them, and a desperate conflict was fought in semi-darkness, notable by the courageous and efficient handling of the Sikh artillery, the brave showing of British infantry regiments, the timidity of allied native units, and spirited charges by the 3rd Light Dragoons.

Sikhs – 22,000 infantry and cavalry; 22 guns.
Heavy losses including 15 guns.

British – 10,500 men – 5 cavalry regiments (1 British);
4 British and 9 Native battalions;
5 Horse and 2 Field Batteries of artillery.
872 men killed and wounded.

Two days later on 21 December, the shortest day of the year, Gough's army made an eight-hour march over heavy ground to the entrenched Sikh camp at Ferozeshah. Gough attacked at 3.00 p.m. with only two hours of daylight in which to defeat a confident and disciplined army twice his strength in a strongly fortified position. British infantry cleared the entrenchments and village of Ferozeshah, withdrawing at nightfall, when the Sikhs repossessed their abandoned positions and guns, and maintained a night-long cannonade. At daybreak the British went forward to roll over the entrenchments, carrying battery after battery at the point of the bayonet until the enemy fled.

Sikhs – 35,000 infantry; 88 guns.
Heavy losses including 78 guns.

British – 5,674 Europeans, 12,053 Natives –
6 Battalions H.M. Infantry; 20 Battalions Native Infantry;
6 Regiments Cavalry (1 British); 6 Horse Artillery Batteries of 6-pounders; 4 Field Artillery Batteries of 9-pounders;
1 Battery 8-inch Howitzers.
2,400 men killed and wounded.

Sir Harry Smith caught the Sikhs under Ranjur Singh at Aliwal on 28 January 1846, where he fought the only satisfactory tactical operation of the whole war. The 16th Lancers repeatedly broke Sikh infantry squares in a classic cavalry action.

Sikhs – 20,000 infantry and cavalry with 70 guns.
Completely destroyed and driven from the field, losing 56 guns, camp, baggage and ammunition stores.

British – 12,000 men; 11 Battalions of infantry (including three H.M. Battalions); 2 cavalry brigades and 32 guns (6- and 9-pounders). 257 men killed and wounded.

obraon, a huge semi-circular position connected by a bridge of boats to the far bank of the river, with 16-foot-thick earthworks, bristling with triple rows of guns plus numerous camel swivel guns. Gough's guns opened fire at daylight on 10 February 1846; immediately the Sikh guns responded, and for two hours the thunder of a grand but aimless artillery concert filled the air; it had no effect upon Sikh guns secure behind massive earthworks; the British artillery eventually ran out of ammunition. British and Native infantry battalions advanced courageously to secure a foothold in the fortifications, despite being repulsed more than once. The Sikhs fought valiantly until tightly packed on and around the bridge of boats which broke up, choking the river with guns, men and horses mercilessly flayed with grape and canister by British Horse Artillery. Completely shattered, the remaining Sikhs on the North bank scattered, and the war was over.

Sikhs – 42,626 men, 20,000 in the fortified position and the rest on the far bank of the river. 70 pieces of artillery, and some 200 zambureks (camel swivel-guns).
Casualties 8,000–12,000 men; all guns lost.

British – 15,000 men; 9 H.M. Infantry Battalions and 12 Native Battalions; 2 British and 4 Native Regiments of Cavalry; 9 Horse Artillery batteries, three 9-pounder Field and two 12-pounder batteries, six 18-pounder guns and 18 heavy howitzers and mortars.
320 men killed; 1,963 wounded.

THE SECOND SIKH WAR 1848–9

A valiant and turbulent race, the Sikhs were unlikely to submit after a single disastrous campaign and in spring 1848 there was a rebellion by Mulraj, Governor of Multan. Raja Shere Singh took his army and guns over to the rebels, to lead the rapidly growing Sikh revolt.

Gough's army marched North to Ramnuggur where, on 21 November 1848, cavalry and horse artillery were caught in the deep sand of the bed of the River Chenab, trying valiantly to recapture a gun, losing 85 men.

(top) Charge of the cavalry through the breaches at Sobraon.

(bottom) Sikhs fleeing into the river at Sobraon.

On 13 January 1849, Gough came upon the Sikh Army at Chillianwallah in a formidable, entrenched position fronted by a dense thorn jungle where they outgunned and outnumbered him 4:1. When the British went forward in a 3-mile-long line, inadequate scouting caused them to be overlapped on both flanks. The battle was confused, bloody and uncontrolled as Gough's divisional generals endeavoured to fight a set-piece pitched battle in a dense jungle. Solely through the dogged courage of the men in the ranks, eventually the Sikhs were forced to retire with their army still intact, despite heavy losses. Bringing in his wounded, Gough withdrew to his baggage camp, giving up the ground that had been so hardly won in this wasted battle.

Sikhs – 40,000 men in 15 old and 10 new regiments of infantry; 4 regiments of cavalry; a large force of Irregular cavalry (Ghorcharas); and 62 guns.
Fairly heavy casualties, lost 42 guns.

British – 12,500 infantry (4 British and 11 Indian Battalions); 3,500 cavalry (3 British and 7 Indian regiments); 66 guns – (6 batteries of Horse Artillery, 3 Field batteries, and 2 Heavy batteries).
2,300 men killed, wounded and missing.

Gough, refusing to attack Shere Singh's army in a natural fortress of great strength, forced them through lack of provisions to march to Gujerat, where in a strong position, Sikh infantry battalions and guns were drawn up behind three fortified villages on a 6,000 yard front, cavalry on the flanks. For the first time in either of the Sikh Wars, Gough had the advantage in numbers and weight of artillery-metal and he did not waste it. On 21 February 1849, his artillery batteries fired a two-hour cannonade that crushed the enemy guns. The British infantry, in a long and majestic line, swept up the green corn-covered slopes, taking losses from enemy artillery and musketry as the Sikhs, although under great pressure, remained steady, their cavalry being held off the British flanks by artillery fire and mounted

Citizen of Moultan and Sikh soldier.

counter-charges. Soon Sikhs began to flee the field, and British cavalry transformed the retreat into a rout extending 15 miles past Gujerat.

Sikhs – 40,000–50,000 men plus 1,500 Afghan cavalry; 59 guns. Very heavy casualties, 53 guns captured.

British – 20,000 men with 106 guns – 12 cavalry regiments (3 British); 23 Infantry battalions (8 British); 7 Troops Horse Artillery, 5 Light Field batteries, twelve 18-pounders and ten 8-inch howitzers.
96 men killed and 700 wounded.

A relentless pursuit was carried out until with considerable dignity, the remnants of the Khalsa laid down their arms. Within a few years these same men and their descendants proved themselves among the most loyal and brave of all the Indian soldiers who marched under the banner of the Queen Empress.

17   The Tribesmen of the North-West Frontier

Following the conquest of Sind in 1843 and success in the Sikh Wars of 1845/6 and 1848/9, British India found itself saddled with an ill-defined border on Central Asia, extending in a great sweep from the Mekong River and Siam in the far east, along the vast Himalayan Range to the spurs of the Hindu Kush, the inhospitable Afghan hills, and the deserts of Baluchistan. Throughout the nineteenth century a steadfast watch had to be kept along this immense extent of frontier, on every tribe and clan, each pass and trade route, where every rock could conceal a foe. The British quickly found the most trouble came from a 400-mile long, 100-mile wide strip of wild and mountainous territory known as the North-West Frontier which was to become the sole part of the British Empire never fully conquered. It was a terrible country; harsh, relentless and jagged with rocky and precipitous peaks and serrated ridges, narrow passes that penned up the heat and dry, icy, high ground. This was a perfect natural arena for the wars of ambush and sniping by tribesmen with deadly matchlocks hidden amid the heat of the hillsides, waiting their chance to pick off stragglers or to tumble down in a rush of savage yelling fanatics, sworn to die for the faith of Mahomet. Every tribe – and there were plenty of them – under the generic name of Pathans, had different characteristics and methods of warfare, yet all shared a common militancy along with identical traits of being disdainfully courageous, marvellous natural fighters in their own familiar terrain, and first-class marksmen.

The struggle for existence in such a barren country produced men of great physical endurance, who respected no authority and were extremely truculent. They were, as John Lawrence said: 'men of predatory habits, careless and impatient of control...' and it made no difference to them whose control it was – after 1849 they transferred their belligerence from Sikh to Briton. Of all the many races of fighting men encountered by the British in the Victorian period, none were as consistently hostile nor better fighters than the Pathans of this territory. Tall, hawk-eyed, bedecked with matchlocks and knives, keen as hawks and cruel as leopards, the Pathans were Pushtu-speaking Eastern Afghans of mixed ethnic origin, divided into many tribes, sub-tribes and clans; since the tenth century militant (if not always orthodox) followers of Islam, these hill-dwellers had controlled the rugged mountainous territory astride what is now the Afghan/Pakistan border. Their tribal sections, each with a malik (headman), were composed of blood relatives in a little community of separate dwellings; several of these sections formed a clan (khel) and the various khels constituted the tribe, each with a khan or arbab.

Of the Pathan tribes, the Isazai Yusufzais composed of the Hassanzais, the Akazais and the Mada Khel inhabited the Black Mountains, east

North-West Frontier tribesmen.

of the Indus and British territory north-west of Abbottabad, a 30-mile-long narrow ridge about 8,000 feet above sea level, surmounted by high peaks and thickly wooded country with deep and narrow passes between large spurs. The Ilaszai Yusufzais consisted of the Bunerwals of the Buner Valley, the Chagarzais of the Indus Valley at the northern end of the Black Mountains, and the Malikazais of the Dir and Panjkora Valley. In Chumla and the Indus Valley lived the Mandan Yusufzais, formed of the Utmanzais and the Usmanzais. The Allied Tribes were Swatis of the Swat Valley; Utman Khel of Lower Swat Valley; Mamunds of the tumbling mountains of the Bajaur; Gaduns who ruled between Chumla and the Indus Valleys; and Mohmands of the Kabul Valley, whose frontier was only 20 miles from Peshawar, and who gave more trouble than any other tribe in the district.

About 30,000 strong, the Afridi Tribe with its numerous clans was the largest and most turbulent on the Frontier, and probably the best fighters. Among their most truculent clans were the Kuki Khels of the Rajgal Valley and the Zakka Khels of the Maidan, Bara and Bazar Valleys, the last named said to be: '...the greatest thieves, housebreakers, robbers and raiders among all the Khyber clans, their word or promise never being believed or trusted by their Afridi brethren without a substantial security being taken for its fulfilment' (Warburton). A leading Afridi clan was the Orakzais of Southern Tirah and Samana Ridge, not as well-armed nor warlike, nevertheless numerous British expeditions had to go out against them; after the last in 1891, forts were built in their territory and garrisoned by Sikhs, traditional enemies of the Pathans. Also in the Maidan and Bara Valleys were the Malikdin Khel; Kambar Khel, Kamar Khel, and Sipah Khel; the Aka Khel inhabited Warran and the Bara. The Dam Khel lived between Peshawar and Kohat, and the Zaimukhts north of Thai in Kurram Valley; the Jowaki Afridis in the Kohat Pass, while the Ghilzais exacted toll on numerous all-important mountain passes into India. There were the Turis of the Kurram Valley; the Mullagoris and Shinwaris of the Khyber; and the Khattacks of Kohat.

Lying between Kurram and Zhob, touching the Afghan frontier on the west and north-west, Waziristan is rugged, mountainous and barren, and scored by narrow ravines whose gorges (tangis) form natural defensive positions. Its prin-

Mohammed Din, a North-West Frontier tribesmen.

cipal tribes, the Darwesh Khel and the Mahsuds (known collectively as Wazirs), are perhaps the fiercest of all North-West Frontier tribes, being likened to wolves or panthers and officially recognised as '...the earliest, most inveterate and most incorrigible of all the robbers of the border'. The Mahsuds, it was reported, '...cannot be reformed and induced to relinquish their old ingrained habits of murdering, raiding and thieving by anything short of permanent occupation of their country'. Their rock-citadels were jumping-off points for endless raids on settled districts to the east, whose position was likened to that of early French settlers in Canada 'who always moved about in constant dread of the Iroquois tomahawks'. Other Wazir tribes or clans were the Dawaris of the Tochi Valley; the Bhitannis of the hill country near Bannu and Tank; and the Shiranis of Takht-i-Suliman.

On the west bank of the Indus was Khelat, populated by non-Pathan Baluchi tribes, Brahuis, Bozdars, Bugtis, Gurchanis, Kasranis, Khetrans, Khosas, Lagharis, Marris and Mazaris

– more law-abiding but no less truculent than the Frontier clans. Other occasional opponents of the British were the slant-eyed Mongol-descended Hazara tribesmen from the Bamian Valley; the Ghazis, mounted irregulars and fanatical Moslems who sought glory by dying in battle, wielding curved tulwars and fighting under the green flags of Islam. And the Hindustani fanatics, the only tribesmen who made trouble during the Mutiny of 1857, who lurked on the slopes of the Black Mountains on the northern Yusufzai frontier. They were a colony of Moslem refugees of the Wahabi sect from India originally founded in 1820 by Sayid Ahmad Shah of Bareilly, killed in an unsuccessful jihad (holy war) called to eject the Sikhs from the Punjab before changing their objective to ousting the British. In 1895 a major campaign was fought against the Northern tribes – the Chitralis of Chitral District; the Chilasis of Chilas District; the Kanjutis of the Kanjut Valley and the Kohistanis of Chicharga and Nila Naddi Valleys.

Without exception, internecine warfare and the raiding of Frontier villages formed the major part of the lives of all these tribes and clans; it seemed impossible for the fragmented Pathan nation to act together against the common foe, even the holy men who always fanned the flames of war could not cement this fragile unity. When Pathans went out to battle they did so not as Pathans but as Afridis, Orakzais, Mahsuds, Mohmands or Wazirs. Characteristically, it was the most troublesome and warlike tribes whom the British most admired – the Pathan most of all; the meek subservient tribes were despised.

Their battles were fought in an extraordinary spirit because when Pathan and Britain looked upon each other, both saw men – men aware of death and deprivation, exhaustion and hardship, but above all courage. Over the years the cruel and harsh terrain was softened by a mutual sense of respect arising from each knowing that the other admired and displayed the same qualities – first courage, then loyalty to the side you happened to be fighting for at that moment, and personal honour. The long history of nearly a hundred years of conflict between Britain and Pathan resounds with pious sentiments about one fighting for his religious beliefs and the other for law and order, whereas it might just have been that both found fighting added a little spice to life! Those soldiers, probably officers, sufficiently articulate to ponder on the Pathan did not always see him in the same light: 'Ruthless, cowardly, robbery, cold-blooded, treacherous murder are to him the salt of life', wrote one. 'Brought up from his earliest childhood amid scenes of appalling treachery, nothing can ever change him...a shameless, cruel savage.' Another saw him differently: 'To set against his vices the Pathan is brave, sober, religious according to his lights and, on the whole, clean living; he has a ready sense of humour...is a lover of sport...And, to those who can speak and understand his queer guttural language, he is amazingly good company.' And another: 'There is a sort of charm about him, especially about the leading men, which makes one forget his treacherous nature...For centuries he has been on our frontier at least, subject to no man. He leads a wild, free, active life in the rugged fastness of his mountains; and there is an air of masculine independence about him which is refreshing in a country like India.'

John Ayde said of them: 'They are poor but brave...and although turbulent and difficult to deal with, still have a great love of their country and cherish their independence, possessing qualities that we admire in ourselves, and which deserve consideration and respect.'

In 1855, when Britain's frequent encounters with them were getting under way, the Secretary to the Chief Commissioner of the Punjab wrote a report on the Frontier tribes:

'Now these tribes are savages – noble savages, perhaps – and not without some tincture of virtue and generosity, but still absolutely barbarians nevertheless...They are thievish and predatory to the last degree...They are utterly faithless to public engagements: it would never occur to their minds that an oath on the Koran was binding, if against their interests. It must be added that they are fierce and bloodthirsty ...They are perpetually at war with each other. Every tribe and section of a tribe has its internecine wars, every family its hereditary blood-feuds, and every individual his personal foes ...Reckless of the lives of others they are not sparing of their own...They possess gallantry and courage themselves and admire such qualities in others.'

In their uninviting territory, law in the normal sense of the word could not be administered because no system of maintaining law and order could be imposed; tribes were always feuding with each other and lacked recognised chiefs so

Wild Afridis and Khyberees at Peshawur.

that there was no overall body with which to deal. Every tribesman was armed and skilled in the use of his weapons which he was prepared to use without compunction, so that it required the frequent intervention of British and Indian armies to capture an outlaw, force a tribe to come to terms, or punish (invariably destroy) a village. The little wars which arose from this were the staple diet of the British and Indian armies throughout the Victorian period, and it might well be asked 'Why did Britain persevere with this incredibly harsh country and its fierce lawless and militant peoples?' The simple answer was that the thought of Russian Cossacks pouring through the Khyber Pass was a British statesman's nightmare – during the nineteenth century the area seemed to be the logical route for Russian invasion of India via Afghanistan, thus the Khyber, the Bolan and other trans-Indus passes were as strategically important to the British as was Gibraltar. And, of course, it was an unparalleled training ground in which every British soldier of the Queen's Army sooner or later served. Here in the appalling heat of sum-

mer and cold of winter, in rocky mountains and passes, the nineteenth-century British soldier could prove himself, amid comrades whose respect he cherished, in unrelenting contests against foemen like himself bred for battle, with the same fierce sense of independence, customs and violent way of life, albeit on a more primitive scale.

The Pathan, tall and lean, moved with predatory grace, inner ferocity reflected by an impressive face framing deepset hawk-like eyes, prominent hooked nose, thin cruel mouth half concealed by shaggy scrofulous beard (dyed when whitened by age). Tribesmen living in the north-east wore hair clipped short, south-western warriors had it long, ranging from carefully combed and curled bobs to greasy ringlets. The Afridi was also tall, wiry and muscular, with a long, gaunt face, high nose and cheek bones; long dark hair, but with a fair complexion; he walked with a characteristic springy stride. Beneath a large long and loose white robe (angarka), on the Afridis it was a coarse home-made blue garment, he wore loose tattered ankle-length white cotton trousers, sometimes taken in at the ankle; around a pointed cap (kullah) a turban or lungi – a sash that could be worn over the shoulder as a body covering or round the waist as a cummerbund, when it also served as a repository for a large flintlock pistol, two or three long knives and a razor-sharp curved tulwar (sword); in cold weather a poshteen (sheepskin coat) worn with the hair inside, or a cloak (chadar). On bare and filthy feet he wore leather sandals (chaplis); Afridi sandals were made of grass. Resting lightly on the shoulder or cradled in the crook of the arm was a long-barrelled jezail, always loaded and ready to fire.

Although quite without any uniform characteristics except for always being dirty, dust-covered and never washed so assuming the colours of the rocky slopes on which they lived and fought, Pathan tribes wore clothing of varied colour and cut. Mostly white and dirty, black and dark blue were favoured by the Bunerwals and in the Buner Valley area; Khyber Pass Afridis a coarse grey or blue angarka and white trousers; Wazirs a dark brick-red or dark-blue turban and a dark-red or pink lungi; Orakzais preferred pearl-grey robes; while the Turis of the Kurram Valley (physically different in that they were short and compact) liked ear-rings and wore a dark blue angarka patched with white or vice versa, with a blue or white turban and cummerbund. Shiranis, medium height and thin, tied a black blanket around the waist and another over the shoulders, a sheepskin cloak and a turban made of a length of white cotton cloth. Brooding in appearance and often with a hawk on the wrist, Waziri tribal dress consisted of a natural colour or white angarka of coarse sheep's wool, a dark-red or dark-blue lungi, white cotton trousers and a white chadar. A Wazi malik or headman from Bannu was described as wearing dirty cotton robes set off by a pink lungi over shoulder and breast, with 'a rich dark shawl interwined into locks that had never known a comb' and thick boots laced with thongs and rings. Pathan maliks also wore more ornate clothing – from the Jandol Valley an Utman Khel headman affected a crimson waistcoat encrusted with gold lace over a cotton angarka whose flowing sleeves buttoned at the wrist; his loose cotton trousers buttoned above the ankles above native-style pointed-toed sandals; a richly embroidered skull-cap and ornamented sabre complimented his appearance.

Frontier tribesmen were superb warriors bred to their trade of fighting, perhaps the best marksmen in the world at the time; in the mid-nineteenth century their long-barrelled jezails had a longer range and were more accurate than the smoothbore muskets of British and Indian infantry. At this period Indian units were sometimes armed with Brunswick rifles sighted to only 250 yards, some even had smoothbore muskets issued for use in the Peninsular and at Waterloo. Later, most tribesmen used locally produced rifles effective at 400 yards. The Afridis, made relatively wealthy through the subsidy paid them by the British to keep open the Khyber Pass, could afford to buy modern rifles so that some used Enfields and even breech-loading rifles. The jezail, a flintlock firearm 6 feet long, was sometimes so heavy it had to be fired from a rest which gave it a range of up to half a mile. In later campaigns of 1896–8 many tribesmen had Martini-Henry rifles; Russian agents and unscrupulous traders sold them breech-loading rifles, sometimes condemned weapons from the Frontier stations. North-West Frontier natives have always been known as superlative manufacturers and imitators of firearms and for much of the period the Adam Khel Afridis of the Kohat Pass were the Frontier armourers and provided a local source of weapons, while many came in from Afghanistan. In the Tirah Campaign of 1897, when Afridis and Orakzais combined to form an army of 40,000 to 50,000 men, some tribesmen had Lee-Metford rifles captured in previous affrays, and throughout the Victorian period many of their best marksmen had more than one rifle and used loaders to speed up their rate of fire.

British officers at the head of Indian units, conspicuous by their different headgear (sun-helmets) and their demonstrations of forthright leadership, were perfect targets for concealed marksmen; in days before khaki, infantry in red tunics made shooting easy for tribesmen hidden in perfect natural cover or behind stone sangars on the hillsides, while the troops could see nothing whatsoever to fire at. Fortunately, the tribes had no artillery – an Afridi headman is quoted as saying: 'With the exception of your field and mountain-guns – which we have not got – man to man we are as good as any of you...' In fact, it was common knowledge that it was probably the little mule-borne mountain-gun – Kipling's famous screw-gun – first used in 1852, that won many battles for the British. Perhaps not very accurate, but artillery in the hills had a great moral effect upon the wild tribes of the

Wild tribes of Western India defending a mountain pass.

Frontier, who hated it.

Other native weapons included the tulwar, a curved sword with scimitar-shaped blade, and a chora (heavy knife or mini-sword) with a blade more than 2 feet in length, a 5-inch brass-mounted bone or ivory hilt, carried in a brass-ornamented black leather sheath. Some tribes – the Chagarzis and the non-Pathan Kohistanis – carried iron-bladed spears; shields were circular, made from steel or animal hide, and had metal bosses. Horsemen carried a profusion of arms – one or two short brass-bound carbines, two or three pistols and a knife in the cummerbund with a side-slung sword. Groups or bands of tribesmen carried flags, these might be square or triangular, in a variety of colours (red was a favourite) and devices.

Tribesmen, born hunters and mountaineers, were natural guerrilla-fighters accustomed to utilising all the defensive advantages of their rugged and rock-strewn terrains, aware that the true art of fighting their defensive campaigns consisted of fighting no battle at all if it could be avoided – but remaining ever-present, ever-threatening and ever-active so as to be ready to seize any opportunity presented by fortune or a military blunder by his opponent. Then, from an empty landscape, from behind every rock and boulder, hundreds of tribesmen would appear to threaten flanks and rear, particularly if by coming down too quickly from high ground the British had lost their advantage of 'crowning the heights'. Experienced Frontier-hand Colonel C. J. Younghusband wrote:

'Afridis may be driven all day like mountain sheep but when night begins to fall and their tired pursuers commence of necessity to draw back to lower levels for food and rest, then this redoubtable foe rises in all his strength, and with sword and gun and huge boulder hurls himself like a demon on his retiring enemy.'

His skill lay not in winning battles but in harassing British lines of communication so that a large force had to be kept back to protect it. The tribesmen had no lines of communication to worry about, although they did not like an enemy across their lines of retreat and a show of doing this was often enough to cause a less than stout-hearted tribe to pull out of even the strongest positions. Utterly reckless of life, they could assemble their lashkars (tribal armies) in a few hours and disperse as quickly; carrying personal food, water and ammunition enough for a few days prevented supply problems and they would melt away when nothing was left.

With the exception of the Waziris, most tribes preferred fighting defensively in a prepared position, inviting attack on their almost invisible sangars (stone breastworks made from materials at hand) or their stone or mud forts. Most villages were enclosed by mud walls surmounted by thorn-branch *chevaux-de-frise*, with towers enfilading approaches.

A deadly and effective defensive measure employed by some tribesmen was the stone-shoot, made in a place where a precipitous incline dropped onto the path beneath; ideally at some unexpected and exposed point. On the hill above, boulders and big rocks were collected and, when an enemy appeared, were rained down in a continuous storm of missiles. The men operating it were usually invisible to soldiers on the path below, and the shoot was usually unturnable; in operation it was almost impassable to troops.

The Pathan would fight to the death to prevent his village and territory from invasion, demonstrated in 1863 at the start of the Ambela Expedition, when the British marched through Bunerwal territory to reach the Hindustani Fanatics at Malka, causing all the Pathan tribes to forget their blood-feuds and other differences and pick up guns and ammunition, sling a food-bag over the shoulder, and set off for the Ambela Pass to fight the British.

Repeated demonstrations of Pathan excellence at guerrilla warfare over more than half a century aroused undisguised admiration in the British soldier; General Lockhart told British regiments severely mauled by a small Afridi lashkar: '...you are facing perhaps the best skirmishers and the best natural shots in the world...the country they inhabit is the most difficult on the face of the globe.' A noted war correspondent told his British readers:

'....the Pathans...are mountaineers of the best type. Born and bred amongst steep and rugged hills...inured to extremes of heat and cold, and accustomed from childhood to carry arms and to be on guard against...treacherous kinsmen...it is small wonder that they are hardy, alert, self-reliant, and active, full of resource, keen as hawks, and cruel as leopards.'

To their guerrilla expertise the Afridis added professional knowledge of British field tactics gained during service in the Indian Army and Frontier Militia. They made good and loyal soldiers when in British service, but notoriously restless and homesick, their terms of service were shorter than normal, consequently many trained soldiers were always available to aid their tribes against the British – this was particularly evident during the Tirah Expedition of 1897/8, when British drill manuals and musketry instructions books, translated into Urdu, were found in deserted villages. Colonel H. D. Hutchinson, *The Times* correspondent, did not entirely agree:

'They have absolutely nothing to learn from us, these Afridis. Contrariwise, their dashing and bold attack, the skill with which they take advantage of ground, the patience with which they watch for a favourable moment, and their perfect marksmanship – all these qualities have

Marauders of the Mangal tribe.

again and again won our admiration.' All these things the Army knew well already.

In 1842 Pollock's army became the first ever to force the Khyber Pass, something that not even Tamerlaine and Akbar the Great had managed to do; on his return journey the uncrushed Gilzais sniped at his force all the way. Conversely, the 25 August 1895 was the blackest day in the British history of the North-West Frontier, when the Khyber Pass was lost – such a blow to British prestige that an unparalleled effort had to be made to recover it and punish those responsible – the Afridis and the Orakzais, the biggest threat to British rule on the Frontier. In the extensive campaigns that followed, learning a lesson from the slogging match at Dargai, these tribes resorted to fighting in the way they knew best by attacking supply columns and survey parties, sniping at patrols, foraging parties and even the main body of the army, pressing heavily on their rear, besides cutting and removing miles of telegraph wire. Colonel C. E. Callwell wrote feelingly of these tactics:

'It is in concealing themselves, in conducting fleet movements through difficult ground, in appearing suddenly in threatening force at points where they are least suspected and in dispersing without necessarily losing tactical cohesion when they find themselves worsted, that the masters of this art (partisan warfare) single themselves out and display their warlike qualities. Such methods are bewildering to the commanders of disciplined troops opposed to them.'

However, it was not enough; in 1897, for the first time in history, the Frontier tribes were beaten to their knees. Of course they did not stay there and continued to be a repeated source of trouble until Britain left India in 1948. They were crushed in 1897 by the most calculated policy of destruction ever perpetrated by the British in India, when a great swathe of scorched earth was seared across their lands in a highly effective demonstration of what has always been British policy on the Frontier. A civil administrator put it succinctly: 'In almost all cases, the aggressive tribes behaved badly before, and well after, suffering from an expedition.' It was not, of course, designed to make the tribes love the British.

Over the years not all British leaders had agreed with it but General Sir Neville Chamberlain – no doubt reflecting on his major campaign at Ambela in 1863, said:

'To have to carry destruction, if not desolation into the homes of some hundreds of families is the great drawback to border warfare; but with savage tribes to whom there is no right but might, and no law to govern them in their intercourse with the rest of mankind, save that which appeals to their own interests, the only course, as regards humanity as well as policy, is to make all suffer, and thereby, for their own interests, enlist the great majority on the side of peace and safety.'

The purpose behind these frequent punitive expeditions, this scorched earth policy directed against crops and livestock, was to create maximum inconvenience and abject poverty to the tribe which, as a whole, was being held corporately responsible for an outrage and, not yielding to pressure and paying compensation, had to be punished. Lacking bargaining power and faced with British implacability (it could not really be otherwise, for unpunished raids would simply have led to more raids) the Pathans usually chose to fight and invariably lost. It was an imperfect and harsh policy in a harsh land, where there seemed no alternative to treating the belligerent tribesmen as fierce animals, confined in a game-reserve, to be subsidised if staying there to prey on their fellows, aware that transgression meant punishment.

In eight years from the second Sikh War in 1849 to the Mutiny of 1857, there were no less than 20 expeditions against erring Frontier tribes, many led by ubiquitous Victorian generals, whose names were household words. How many more there were during Queen Victoria's reign as Empress of India can only be discovered by diligent searching through such books as *Frontier and Overseas Expeditions from India*, an Intelligence Branch Army HQ India 1910 publication. The extensive list that follows details what seem to be the major campaigns and certainly those involving British troops:

Octoer 1847	*Swat Valley*	Expedition of newly formed Guides and Sikh infantry under Lawrence and Lumsden.
December 1849	*Sanghao*	About 2,000 men with artillery.
February 1850	*Afridis*	Force under Sir Colin Campbell with General Sir Charles Napier (Cmdr-in-Chief).
March 1852	*Swat Valley*	Sir Colin Campbell's force.
May 1852	*Swat Valley*	Sir Colin Campbell.
May 1852	*Utman Khel Tribe – North of Peshawar*	Sir Colin Campbell.
November 1853	*Bori villages in Jawaki Pass*	22nd Regt; Gurkhas; Guides (under Hodson) and Mountain Artillery.
August 1854	*Mohmands*	22nd and 42nd Foot; Native infantry; guns.
August 1857	*Narinji village (Buner?)*	27th; 70th; 87 Foot, etc. (about 2,000).
April 1858	*Khudu Khel tribe*	General Cotton and 5,000 men.
Autumn 1863	*Ambela Expedition Against Hindustani Fanatics and Bunerwals*	General Sir Neville Chamberlain. Originally intended to be a three weeks military promenade, this turned out to be the largest operation of the period, lasting three months at a cost of nearly 1,000 casualties, half the total losses sustained between 1849 and 1890 in 42 expeditions on the North-West Frontier.
January 1864	*Area Fort Shabkadar*	1,800 incl. 3rd Rifle Brigade and 7th Hussars.
January 1866	*Sanghao*	4,000 Native infantry and cavalry.
Summer 1867	*Black Mountains*	10,000 British and Native troops.
August 1867	*Black Mountains tribes*	9,500 men with artillery.
October 1877	*Jawaki Afridis*	2,000 British and Indian troops.
February 1878	*Utman Khel tribe*	Small force of Guides cavalry and infantry under Battye and Cavagnari, the latter soon to be murdered in Afghanistan. Battye was killed in 1895.
March 1878	*Shakot in the Swat Valley*	Same force.
November 1878	*Khyber Pass Afridis*	2,500 British and Indian troops.
January 1879	*Zakha Khel Afridis of the Bazar Valley*	General Maude with 3,500 British and Indian troops.
March 1879	*Opening route from Kandahar to Quetta*	The Thal–Chotiali Field Force (8,700 British and Indian troops).
April 1879	*Mohmands*	Fighting retreat, with relief columns.
December 1879	*Zaimukht tribe*	General Tytler with 3,000 men.
January 1880	*Mohmands*	Dakka Column (1,000 British and Indian troops, and Landi Kotal Column 2,500 men).
October 1880	*Malik Shari Wazirs*	General Gordon – 1,500 British and Indian infantry and cavalry, with guns.
April 1881	*Mahsud Wazirs*	Two columns under Generals Kennedy and Gordon (say 6,000 British and Indian troops).
November 1881	*Opening up new route into India from Kandahar*	The Bozdar Field Force.
October 1884	*Zhob Valley tribesmen*	General Tanner with 5,000 British and Indian infantry, cavalry and guns.
September 1888	*Black Mountains*	General McQueen with 9,500 British and Indian troops in the Hazara Field Force.

October 1890	*Zhoh Valley Shiranis*	Zhow Field Force under General G. S. White. Finding no enemy, they climbed the highest mountain in the range, to impress the natives.
January 1891	*Ovakzai tribesmen and Afridis in the Khanki Valley*	1st Miranzai Field Force under General Lockhart. 2nd Miranzai Field Force (General Lockhart) 7,400 British and Indian troops. Small expeditions had been sent out previously against the Ovakzais – Chamberlain in 1863; Jones and Cavagnari in 1868; Keyes in 1869.
March 1891	*Black Mountains*	General Elles with 7,300 British and Indian troops and 15 guns.
September 1892	*Isazai tribes in Baio and Chagarzai territory*	General Lockhart with 6,250 British and Indian troops. First use of Maxim guns on the Frontier.
December 1894	*Mahsuds and other tribesmen of Waziristan*	General Lockhart and Waziristan Field Force (three Brigades British and Indian troops).
April 1895	*Chitral tribesmen and tribes of the Malakand*	Fort besieged at Chitral. Relief columns under Kelly and a force under General Low in what was a major campaign.
June 1897	*Madda Khel tribe in the Tochi Valley*	The Tochi Field Force (General Corrie Bird) two Brigades British and Native infantry, cavalry, guns.
August 1897	*Ovakzais and Chamkannis in the Kohat Pass*	General Yeatman-Biggs and about 2,000 British and Indian troops.
July 1897	*Afridis in the Malakand (Swat Valley)*	A major war beginning with attacks on forts in the Malakand, then General Bindon Blood's Malakand Field Force of more than 10,000 had several hot engagements before quelling the trouble.
August 1897	*Mohmands and others attack Shabkadar fort*	Colonel Woon then General Elles and a force from Peshawar.
August 1897	*Mohmands and Koda Khel Baezai tribe*	Mohmand Field force under General Elles, later joined by Malakand Field Force (General Blood).
January 1898	*Bunerwals and Chamlawals in the Tanga Pass*	General Blood's Buner Field Force (two infantry brigades).
October 1897 – June 1900	*Afridi and Orakzai tribes in the Tirah Valley*	Tirah Expeditionary Force under General Lockhart – 44,000 British and Indian troops – in one of the biggest of all Frontier Wars.

Winston Churchill served with the Malakand Field Force and wrote of the Pathans from firsthand knowledge:

'Every influence, every motive, that provokes the spirit of murder among men, impels these mountaineers to deeds of treachery and violence ...to the ferocity of the Zulus are added the craft of the Redskin and the marksmanship of the Boer.'

It is fitting to end discussion on perhaps the greatest irregular warriors in the world by considering those who held them in check for more than a century – young men from the pastoral peace and urban harmony of Great Britain thrust against them on nightmare terrains. It was a point of honour on the Frontier not to leave wounded men behind, as death by inches and hideous mutilation was invariably meted out to those who fell into the hands of Pathan tribesmen and their womenfolk.

18　The Zulus

In 1786 Senzangakona, chief of the Zulus, one of the many small clans sharing the rolling uplands between the Drakensberg and the sea, fathered an illegitimate son Shaka who, after serving in the army of Dingiswayo, chief of a clan owed allegiance by the Zulus, was sent by him with a regiment to reign over the Zulu tribe when Senzangakona died in 1816. The Zulu march to being a powerful nation began with his arrival; then barely 400 strong (with less than 1,500 people calling themselves Zulus) Shaka's systematic defeats and absorption of neighbouring tribes caused them to flourish so that in 1879 more than half a million people lived in Zululand with over 50,000 men under arms. Making military service compulsory in his newly formed regiments, Shaka so changed battle tactics from relatively bloodless encounters between armed mobs that soon he had the most powerful war machine yet seen in southern Africa. Unimpressed with the throwing assegai, a spindly 6-foot shaft with a 6-inch head, he replaced it by the stabbing assegai with a heavy broad blade 18 inches long and a stout shortened haft or handle; similar to the Roman short sword (gladus) it was a thrusting weapon that forced his warriors to close in shock action – he called it iKlwa, from the sucking-sound when withdrawn from the victim's body. He transformed the shield into an offensive weapon that could forcefully put an opponent off balance by a powerful sweeping movement that hooked the shield edge behind the enemy's shield, dragging down across his front to hamper the use of his spear while exposing the left armpit for an assegai thrust.

Shaka did not believe warfare was a show of force designed to convince an enemy resistance was useless; to him it was fought for total annihilation, hand-to-hand and with deadly intensity, and when the enemy inevitably broke, pursuit was relentless and ferocious. The Zulu tactical employment was highly developed and invariably effective against native forces caught in the open but far too inflexible to be successful against disciplined troops – succeeding at Isandlhwana in January 1879 solely because the British commander formed his troops in a long sprawling line instead of a tight mutually supporting formation; even then it stopped 20,000 Zulus in their tracks, until ammunition ran out. The Zulu Impi (all the men present on a particular occasion) was split into four equal wings – centre (or chest) which attacked head-on to pin the enemy; two 'horns' racing out to encircle the enemy, meet and attack his rear driving it into the 'chest'; and the 'loins' or reserve, seated nearby with backs to the battle to curb undue excitement, sent out to reinforce the encirclement and prevent the enemy breaking out. At its peak, the Zulu army was perhaps the most fearsome native

Lord William Beresford's encounter with a Zulu.

149

military force in the world, uniquely mobile and made up of superbly conditioned and immensely brave warriors.

Dingane, Shaka's successor (and murderer) made a treacherous attack on the trek-Boers filtering into Natal, being badly defeated in 1838 at Blood River when his impi attacked a laagered position so sited that it could only be approached on a narrow front. Mpande, his successor, made no use whatsoever of the army which, over four decades, slowly grew in size but not major battle experience. In 1872 he was succeeded by his son Cetshwayo, intelligent and deeply imbued with the traditions and glories of Shaka's reign; his army of 40,000 to 50,000 warriors, plus frequent injudicious and truculent words, gave cause for unease to his European neighbours. So much so that Sir Bartle Frere, Governor of Cape Colony, believing the major obstacle to South African confederation to be the defiant example of Zulu independence, determined to pick a war and break their power. Frere

Zulu warriors.

issued a demand that Cetshwayo disband his army, fully aware that it could not be done without breaking the Zulu Nation. The 30 short days of grace expired, and in the first days of January 1879 Zululand was invaded by a British Army under Lord Chelmsford, consisting of 5,000 infantry, 1,100 mounted riflemen, 20 guns, 9,000 native foot-levies, and 350 mounted native scouts.

In the seven months campaign Britain put 32,000 men in the field, lost 1,100 Europeans killed and 350 wounded plus more than 1,000 native troops; at Isandhlwana the British Army suffered the greatest defeat aborigines ever inflicted on civilised troops.

Rumours of war had been around for months and in early January Cetshwayo, realising hostilities were inevitable, sent runners to all main kraals with the traditional message – 'Mayihlome!' 'To arms!' Collecting at regimental kraals, warriors marched to the royal kraal at Ulundi, a noisy, arrogant, truculent army spoiling for a fight. But none of them, not Cetshwayo nor any of his inDunas had the slightest idea of the power pitted against them, nor how best to combat it; they had no strategy and the 'Chest and Horns' was their sole tactic. A victory of sorts might have been gained by invading Natal, raiding vulnerable supply-trains and dispersing grazing herds of transport-animals so immobilising them – or they could have avoided pitched battles. Instead, the entire army concentrated at Ulundi and was sent out to launch a succession of attacks, reassembling at the royal kraal after each warrior had been back to his home kraal for purification ceremonies necessary after killing. Within hours of victory at Isandlhwana the Zulu Army had simply evaporated and were not recalled for more than a month. Under such circumstances no organised campaigning was possible, the Zulu impi was good for only one blow at a time; raw courage was their sole military asset, employed until dissipated or victorious.

Few armies can have been as well informed on their enemy as was Chelmsford's, having at hand a detailed report by an experienced Zulu-speaking Border Agent, H. Bernard Finney, revealing how Zulu forces were raised, armed, drilled, officered, organised, fed and doctored. To an exact description of their tactics was added all conceivable details of each and every Zulu regiment, including name of commanding in-

Duna, distinctive uniform, plus number and age of warriors. Circulated to all commanders and senior officers the report told them that the army was built up on rigid lines devised by Shaka, formed of all warriors capable of bearing arms who, when approaching 20 years of age, were drafted into a newly formed regiment (iButo) of perhaps a thousand similar youths from the same district; it was an essential part of the Zulu social system and members of a regiment were linked together until death. As regiments progressed so they had other regiments embodied with them to give younger warriors the benefit of the more experienced elders whose place they might take when they died. They lived either in an existing or newly built military kraal (iKanda), some sheltering more than one regiment, 'brigaded' together and giving names to corps of related regiments. In 1879 there were 12 of these Corps, 5 consisting of a single regiment that had absorbed the original affiliated regiments; there were also 2 single regiments.

The young Zulus were ideal military material and would have made any recruiting-serjeant's eyes sparkle; tall, muscular and endurable through living an entire boyhood outdoors tending cattle. Possessing an intimate knowledge of home terrain, they were skilled in weapons-handling through small-game hunting and seeing off more dangerous predators, aggressive and militant through boisterous games with fellow herdboys. Early in life they were formed into age-groups (iNtangas) under an inDuna or leader from an older age-group; iNtangas remained together in the regiments, corresponding to companys (isiGaba). Varying in size as much as from 2,500 to 300 men, Zulu regiments were divided into two wings, right and left, each led by a senior inDuna; each wing was subdivided into companies averaging about 50 men each, led by one senior and three junior inDunas. The whole was commanded by the inDuna of the senior iNtanga, with a second-in-command; when several regiments were brigaded into an informal corps, it was commanded by the senior inDuna of the senior regiment; the king appointed the overall commander. While the courage and performance of inDunas against artillery, Gatling guns and breech-loading rifles was beyond praise, they were a major cause of the downfall of the Zulu nation; although aggressive and intelligent, they had no tactical vision beyond the traditional 'Chest and Horns' and lacked the ability to adapt.

A feature of the Zulu army was the enforcement of celibacy, although this had been relaxed since Shaka's day when marriage was forbidden to serving warriors until well into middle-age and considered too old for active service, although marriage was a coveted status symbol granted *en masse* to regiments which had done well in battle. Roughly half the regiments were 'ringed' or married units, formed of warriors (iKhehla) entitled to wear the married man's isiCoco, a fibre circlet woven into the hair and plastered with beeswax, polished to a glossy black. Such regiments, made up of seasoned mature warriors, were not necessarily of the highest fighting quality as at least seven of them were formed of 60-year-olds and over. There was no recognised 'retiring age', men answering the call to arms as long as physically able to take the field; several regiments of men aged between 60 and 70 fought in the major battles of the 1879 war, being grafted onto younger regiments if their numbers fell below 300 to 400. For practical purposes, at the outbreak of war, of the 26 regiments totalling more than 40,000 men – 22,500 were 20 to 30 years old; 10,000 were 30 to 40; 3,400 were 40 to 50 and 4,500 were 50 to 60.

Training followed prescribed lines, warriors being drilled in forming the 'Chest and Horns' fighting-formation, in quickly forming circles of companies or regiments then breaking back into their original groupings. Marching, or rather jog-trotting, in long columns *en masse*, Zulus could habitually cover 50 miles a day across trackless country, and go straight into action carrying nothing whatsoever except shields and assegais – their mobility has rarely ever been equalled by foot soldiers. A few herdboys (uDibi) trotted on the flanks carrying light grass sleeping mats, but warriors usually slept on bare ground or on their shields; the boys sometimes carried water, maize or millet but food was usually obtained from grain stores at friendly kraals or by slaughtering captured cattle. *En route* to Isandhlwana in 1879, the impi covered nearly 50 miles in three days, without food for the last two; on the day of the battle they advanced at a run for six miles then plunged straight into the attack. A wing of this impi ran another 12 miles to Rorke's Drift and fought without let-up for more than seven hours. Watercourses and rivers were the only natural obstacles to delay them, sometimes fordable at shallow drifts, but when required an impi would

'rush' a river – in a narrow dense column with arms linked, they plunged in, relying on the sheer impetus of those behind carrying the front ranks across when beyond their depth. Zulus could not swim, nor did they build boats, and crocodiles were often encountered, so some men were lost – but the impi always got across.

Warned by scouts of the enemy's nearness, on the run they fanned out into the inevitable 'Chest and Horns', depending upon the size of the impi in ranks 8 to 20 deep with 2 to 3 paces between lines. This would be done instantly and in complete silence; orders for major changes in formations or dispositions were carried to commanders by runners from the overall commander perched on high ground nearby. However, there cannot have been that number of options for although the Zulus, unlike most other tribesmen, were sufficiently disciplined to fight in close order, their sole weapons were suitable only for a hand-to-hand mêlée, there being no concept of any other method of warfare. Thus restricted, their universal tactic had to be attack, the massed charge surging forward buoyed up with sheer raw courage, until it broke through the enemy line, or was halted in its tracks by sheer weight of casualties.

Zulu dress or uniform was basically simple, clothing and decorations bearing a meaning and a protection both physical and spiritual for every tribal occasion. Boys went naked except for a small box folded from wild banana leaves worn on the prepuce; at puberty the common dress for all males was the umuTasha – a thin leather belt or string worn around the waist with a clout of fur strips dangling in front, and the iBeshu, a rectangle of dressed cowhide at the rear. Elite regiments might wear the inSimba, a war-kilt of genet (fur of the civet cat) or green monkey skin, hanging almost to the knees. Everything else worn was simply decoration, each regiment evolving distinctive and elaborate costumes from a variety of feathers and furs, with innumerable styles of hair-dressing. The full regalia worn for ceremonial occasions included fluffed-up cowtails attached to leather thongs round the ankles, knees and wrists, and suspended from a necklace to hang profusely to the waist and backs of the knees. There might be various types of necklace, such as tiger and baboon teeth as charms against death; shoulder-capes were prized. Regimental

A Zulu scout.

Zulu warriors.

uniforms reached their peak in head-dresses, particularly among younger men not wearing the isiCoco, who often formed their hair into bizarre shapes by stiffening it with clay; it was embellished by feathers, furs or dangling lappets over the ears, hanging from a headband of leopard or otter skin. Pierced earlobes were decorated with painted tips cut from maize-cobs, or cowhorn snuff-horns, or horn nose-spoon reamers in lieu of handkerchiefs. Others wore a skull-cap of black or brown fur; hanging down over the ears and back of head to shoulders were amaBheqe, rectangular flaps of leopard or green monkey skin. Feathers were much in vogue ranging from long 18-in glossy green/black tail feathers of the Sakabuli (Kaffir Finch) or Willow bird, pointing out from sides and back of head, to feathers of the inDwa (Bell Crane) worn singly over the forehead by senior regiments; or the short crinkly

153

Zulu warrior.

mony at the start of a campaign; in 1879 they were hide ovals cut from a cowhide and allowed to dry untanned, hair left on the outside. A series of slots were cut on either side of the central axis and a thick strip of hide woven in and out of the slots; where the hide-strip crossed over down the length of the shield a stout wooden shaft was jammed, grasped by the warrior working his hand under it. In action warriors carried one or two throwing assegais in the hand holding the shield. By 1879 shields (known as umBhumbhulozu) were 3 ft 6 in long and 2 ft wide, developed from the huge isiHlangu ('Brush Aside') of Shaka's days, fully 5 ft long and 3 ft wide. They would not stop a bullet, but could deflect both throwing and stabbing assegais; shields were effective offensive weapons at close quarters.

Personal weapons were limited to the iKlwa – the stabbing assegai – throwing spears that could be hurled 70 yards; and some brawny Zulus favoured the knobkerrie, a spindly 2-foot stick with a heavy wooden ball or burled top. The bow was known but never used in warfare, and they carried no knives, nor did they ever develop cavalry, although inDunas sometimes owned horses used for scouting but playing no tactical role. From the 1850s firearms began to appear, smuggled in from Natal or traded with the Portuguese; crude flintlock muskets (Birmingham gas-pipes) made specially for the African trade – they added nothing to Zulu tactics, and it was said that a Zulu with a gun was simply a Zulu without his assegai, for which the enemy was thankful! Zulu marksmanship was notoriously bad as they tended to hold the stock away from the shoulder and point the muzzle in the air; it was believed that the higher the sights were set, the further the gun would fire. Some warriors braced guns under their arms, against the thighs, or on the ground, and most shots went high; others tried to manipulate a shield in one hand and a rifle in the other. Notwithstanding all this, numerous comtemporary accounts of the Zulu War stress the volume of their musketry, using the many rifles taken after the massacre at Isandlhwana, mentioned in a testimony (later printed in the *Royal Engineer Journal*, X, 1880) by Mehlokazulu, a leading Zulu who fought there with the inGobamakhosi regiment.

'We ransacked it [the Camp] and took everything that we could take. We broke open the ammunition boxes and took out all the cartridges. We practised afterwards a good deal at

bright scarlet flecked with green breast-feathers of the Lourie Bird, worn in bunches at the back of the head by inDunas or men of royal rank.

Sandals had been banned by Shaka, to make his warriors fleeter of foot; subsequently the basic head-dress for unmarried warriors was a porcupine quill worn in the hair, used to dig thorns out of the feet!

Not all the fragile fur and feather finery were worn in battle; enough was retained – shield colours, necklaces, headbands, distinctive feathers – so that, when coupled with a warrior's age and whether he wore the isiCoco headband, it was possible to recognise his regiment. The 'uniform' really began with the shield patterned differently for each regiment – in Shaka's day the best regiments carried predominantly white shields and the younger unmarried men black, white spots being added in accordance with seniority. Shields could be all-white or all-black; black with white spot; black with red spot; red with white spot; white with black or red spots – and similar permutations. War-shields were the property of the State and issued with great cere-

our kraals with the rifles and ammunition. Lots of us had got the same rifles as the soldiers used, having bought them in our country, but some did not know how to use them, and had to be shown by those who did. The cannons were drawn away from the field by oxen. Only one man among us knew anything about loading a cannon and he tried, but the shot only fell a few yards off. We left the camp just before sundown.'

Reminiscent of the Ashantis in the War of 1873 is a description of Zulu firepower in a letter written on 24 January 1879 by Colour-Sergeant J. W. Burnett of the 99th Regiment, telling of Pearson's action on the Inyezane:

'The Zulus stood for about four hours, our people firing shells, rockets, Martinis, and the Gatling guns. I never thought niggers would make such a stand. They came on with an utter disregard of danger. The men that fired did not load the guns. They would fire and run into the bush, and have fresh guns loaded for them, and out again. They fire young cannon balls, slugs and even gravel ... our "school" at Chatham, over a hot whisky, used to laugh about these niggers, but I assure you that fighting with them is terribly earnest work and not childs play.'

It was the battle of Kambula on 29 March 1879 which revealed that the Zulus could make effective use of firearms, when they reinforced traditional weapons and tactics with firepower to make it much more of a fire-fight than other actions of the war. Playing a prominent part there was Captain Edward Woodgate of the 4th Foot (later as Major-General Sir Edward Woodgate, killed on Spion Kop 24 January 1900). He wrote of the British position:

'On the right ran a deep valley with steep, rocky sides in which the enemy massed under cover, the greater portion of the force consisting of the Undi, uNodwengu, and inGobamakhosi regiments, so advancing unseen to within a hundred yards of the laager. But although individuals showed great bravery, no large or formed body could apparently be induced to leave the cover for an assault. Still, creeping up to the crests and surrounding the camp on three sides, skilfully availing themselves of existing cover, the Zulus were able to maintain a heavy cross-fire, many being armed with Martini-Henry rifles captured at Isandhlwana and Luneberg [Intombi] which caused considerable loss.'

So effective was this rifle-fire that it forced two British infantry companies to withdraw from their positions, with many killed and wounded; for the first and only time in the war the Zulus had gained the initiative by their employment of firearms. After the battle, Woodgate listed captured weapons:

'325 firearms, besides large numbers of assegais, were taken, including fourteen Martini-Henry rifles and one Snider Carbine (Royal Artillery). All the Martinis were marked 24th or 80th; they appear to have been distributed among regiments. The other firearms were of various patterns, a large number being Tower muskets and Enfield rifles. No other breech-loaders were found but the fourteen Martinis and one Snider, nor any other kind of cartridge case, except a few Metford.'

The Zulus won three battles in 1879 – the startling victory at Isandhlwana; minor and unimportant successes when catching detachments in the open at Luneberg (Intombi River) and Hlobane, intervalled by harrowing defeats at Rorke's Drift and the entrenched camps of Gingindhlovu and Kambula. In most cases the British got what they wanted – a battle where Zulu offensive power immolated itself on British firepower – even their victory at Isandhlwana, where they killed about 1,445 British and native soldiers, cost them at least 2,000 killed and perhaps as many more wounded. On hearing of these losses, Cetshwayo is reported to have said: 'An assegai has been thrust into the belly of the nation...there are not enough tears to mourn the dead.' And when it was all over, he could ponder on his lack of firm control, how he had directed his army to lash out at concentrations of well-armed troops, to be mown down by disciplined fire from breech-loading rifles, Gatling guns and artillery. There would certainly not be enough tears to mourn the 8,000 Zulu dead and twice as many wounded caused by Cetshwayo's poor leadership.

Incidents from major actions of the war clearly demonstrate the Zulu way of making war – at Isandhlwana the oncoming Zulu horde, not intending to attack until the following day, squatted silently in a ravine until detected, when they surged out shaking themselves into battle order on the run, heading at an earthshaking trot for the British position. The Zulus attacked the camp in a half-circle with another force pushing round the English left to cut the wagon road and line of retreat to Rorke's Drift. The defenders were firing steadily and to good effect while the guns, which had been firing shell, now poured in

Repulse of the Zulus at Ginghilovo, 1879.

case-shot at close quarters forcing the Zulus to waver; they threw themselves down, humming in anger like a gigantic swarm of bees. The wide-swept horns of the Zulu army worked their way round the flanks to show themselves in the rear of the English position just at the moment when the Native contingent broke and fled in disorder, laying open the right and rear of the 24th. The firing began to slacken, because reserve ammunition boxes were screwed down and could not be opened, allowing the Zulus to pour through the fatal gap in the line. The English soldiers were lost in the middle of a fierce hand-to-hand conflict as horse and foot, English and Zulu in confused groups struggled slowly through the camp towards the road to Rorke's Drift. Surrounded by bodies, the 24th stood their ground and fought to the last man while fleet-footed Zulus chased fugitives trying to reach the river. After the orgy of destruction had spent itself, the Zulus ritually disembowelled the dead and dispatched desperately wounded comrades with a merciful assegai thrust under the left armpit. Then carrying off bodies of their dead and dragging away the guns,

they streamed away to their kraals, believing their reputation and fighting tradition to be upheld.

A wing of the Impi, perhaps 4,000 men, held in reserve and thirsting for blood, were sent to destroy Rorke's Drift; they trotted the 12 miles and forded the fast-flowing Buffalo River by 'charging' the current and straightway attacked just before sunset. The battle raged all night as again and again waves of yelling Zulus 'as black as hell and as thick as grass' swept up to the flimsy, hastily erected breastworks, trying to hack and stab their way in. With some 400 Zulu dead lying around the tattered mealie-bag fortress, at dawn they departed exhausted, on the move since leaving Ulundi six days before with little or no food for four days and a great deal of marching and running.

The rest of the war was an anti-climax as a greatly reinforced Chelmsford slowly and methodically worked his way towards Ulundi, where on 4 July 1879 a huge hollow square of troops, blazing fire at all points, smashed the 50-years-old Zulu Empire out of existence. In a great crescent 20,000 Zulus ran towards the square; the Gatlings opened fire at 1,000 yards and although frequently jamming, took their toll but failed to stop the onrush. But when the leading warriors got to within 300 yards of the waiting lines of troops, a terrifying sheet of flame burst out to scythe them down in waves – not a single warrior came closer than 30 yards. A marvelling war correspondent wrote: 'Their noblest ardour could not endure in the face of the appliances of civilised warfare.'

From the cover of long grass, the Zulus kept up a heavy but erratic rifle fire with weapons captured at Isandhlwana while attack after attack was made with despairing courage. None got to close quarters, being blasted out of existence by withering and steady volleys until Zulus were scattered in confusion all over the plain. Then the 17th Lancers were loosed from the square, to ride down the now fleeing Zulus and impale them on lances as though pig-sticking. When it was all over, more than 1,000 dead littered the field. On the exact site of Chelmsford's square can be seen the only memorial erected to honour the Zulu nation – in the form of a small archway bearing a plaque which says:

IN MEMORY OF THE BRAVE WARRIORS
WHO FELL HERE IN DEFENCE
OF THE OLD ZULU ORDER.

General and Specific Sources

GENERAL SOURCES

Battles of the 19th Century
  Described by Archibald Forbes; G. A. Henty; Major
  Arthur Griffiths and Others (1902)
British Empire
  Part Publication BBC TV TIME-LIFE BOOKS (1972)
Colonial Small Wars
  Donald Featherstone (1973)
Illustrated London News 1845–1901
Queen Victoria's Little Wars
  Byron Farwell (1973)
Savage and Soldier Magazine (USA)
Soldiers of the Queen –
  Journal of the Victorian Military Society
Victorian Military Campaigns
  Edited Brian Bond (1967)
The Wars of the 90s
  A. Hilliard Atteridge (1899)

SPECIFIC SOURCES

ABYSSINIANS
  The March to Magdala – Frederick Myatt (1970)
  Handbook for Colonial Wargamers; Victorian Military
  Society Special Publication No. 1 – Ted Herbert
  (1976)
AFGHANS
  Khyber – The Story of the North West Frontier –
  Charles Miller (1977)
  The Afghan Campaign of 1878–1880 – S. H. Shadbolt
  (1972 reprint)
  Tradition Magazine
ASHANTIS
  The Drums of Kumasi – Alan Lloyd (1964)
  By Sheer Pluck – G. A. Henty (1884)
  The March to Coomassie – G. A. Henty (1874)
BALUCHIS
  A Matter of Honour – Philip Mason (1974)
  Handbook for Colonial Wargamers – Ted Herbert
  (1976)
BOERS
  With the Flag to Pretoria – H. W. Wilson (1900)
  After Pretoria, the Guerrilla War – H. W. Wilson (1901/
  2)
CANADIANS
  The Life of John Colbourne, Field Marshal Lord Seaton
  – G. C. Moore-Smith (1903)
CHINESE
  The Boxer Rebellion – Lynn. E. Bodin and Chris War-
  ner (1979)
  Britain's Sea Soldiers – A History of the Royal Marines
  – Col. C. Field RMLI (1924)
  The Life and Campaigns of Hugh, 1st Viscount Gough
  – Robert S. Rait (1903)

DERVISHES
  The Colonial Society Bulletin – Official Magazine of
  the Colonial Wargames Society USA, Jan. 1965.
  Military Modelling Magazine – 'The Camel Corps and
  The Gordon Relief Expedition 1884/5' – R. J. Marrion
  and D. S. Fosten (1976)
  Courier Magazine (USA)
EGYPTIANS
  Britain's Sea Soldiers – Col. C. Field (1924)
  The War in Egypt and the Sudan – Thomas Archer
  (1885)
KAFFIRS
  The Autobiography of Lieut. General Sir Harry Smith –
  Edited by G. C. Moore-Smith (1902)
  The Great Trek – Oliver Ransford (1974)
  The Red Soldier – Frank Emery (1977)
  The Washing of the Spears – Donald R. Morris (1966)
MAHRATTAS
  The Autobiography of Lieut. General Sir Harry Smith –
  Edited by G. C. Moore-Smith (1902)
  Life and Campaigns of Hugh, 1st Viscount Gough –
  Robert S. Rait (1903)
  A Matter of Honour – Philip Mason (1974)
MAORIS
  The Strangest War – E. Holt (1962)
  To Face the Daring Maoris – Michael Barthorp (1979)
PERSIANS
  John Company's Last War – Barbara English (1971)
  Handbook for Colonial Wargamers – Ted Herbert
  (1976)
  Tradition Magazine
RUSSIANS
  Battles of the Crimean War – W. Baring Pemberton
  (1962)
  The Destruction of Lord Raglan – Christopher Hibbert
  (1961)
  The Invasion of the Crimea – A. W. Kinglake (1877)
  MacDonald of the 42nd – Donald Featherstone (1971)
SIKHS
  All for a Shilling a Day – Donald Featherstone (1966)
  At them with the Bayonet – Donald Featherstone
  (1968)
  Khyber – Charles Miller (1977)
  A Matter of Honour – Philip Mason (1974)
TRIBESMEN OF THE NORTH-WEST FRONTIER
  Indian Frontier Warfare – G. J. Younghusband (1898)
  The History of the Mountain Artillery – C. A. L.
  Graham (1957)
  Khyber – Charles Miller (1977)
  A Matter of Honour – Philip Mason (1974)
ZULUS
  The Great Trek – Oliver Ransford (1972)
  The Red Soldier – Frank Emery (1977)
  Shaka Zulu – E. Ritter (1955)
  Tradition Magazine
  The Washing of the Spears – Donald R. Morris (1966)

Index